MEDIA IN CHINA

MEDIA IN CHINA

CONSUMPTION, CONTENT AND CRISIS

Edited by

Stephanie Hemelryk Donald, Michael Keane and Yin Hong

First Published in 2002
by RoutledgeCurzon
2 Park Square, Milton Park, Abingdon, Oxon, OX14 4RN

Simultaneously published in the USA and Canada
by RoutledgeCurzon
270 Madison Ave, New York NY 10016

RoutledgeCurzon is an imprint of the Taylor & Francis Group

Transferred to Digital Printing 2006

Typeset in Sabon by Mews Photosetting, Beckenham, Kent

British Library Cataloguing in Publication Data
A catalogue record for this book is available from the British Library

Library of Congress Cataloguing in Publication Data
A catalogue record for this book has been requested

ISBN10: 0–7007–1614–9 (hbk)
ISBN10: 0–415–40627–7 (pbk)

ISBN13: 978–0–7007–1614–2 (hbk)
ISBN13: 978–0–415–40627–7 (pbk)

CONTENTS

LIST OF TABLES AND FIGURES

Tables

Figures

ACKNOWLEDGEMENTS

The editors would like to thank the following people and institutions for their help: all the contributors for working fast and generously, Cao Shule, Cui Baoguo (Qinghua), Laurie Smith (News Corp) – for dinner and guidance, John Greig (editorial assistance), Kruss (computer assistance), Gerry Groot, Nancy Wood and the University of Sussex, Murdoch University Asia Research Centre, Asialink-Melbourne, Sheng Anfeng and Zhang Li. We also have various sources of inspiration, they include Tony Bennett, James Donald, Tom O'Regan, Krishna Sen, Mary Farquhar, Harriet Evans, Robert Benewick, and the children at Qinghua Linked School.

PREFACE

Yin Hong

This book was inspired by the editors' mutual interest in Chinese media, and in the need to find appropriate research positions and categories through which to understand them. It was also made possible through the imagination of our editor, Peter Sowden, who has rightfully recognized that media systems in Asia are enormously important to scholars and students of media studies worldwide. Our concern in this volume is with China, but we hope that the collection here suggests ways in which students of other zones of media production and use might look to China as a key player in the future of global consumption and content. As editors, we have tried, collectively, to draw on expertise from a wide range of places and disciplines, including myself, a professor of media in a Chinese University, Qinghua. I would like to open the discussion in the book with some questions and insights that are fundamental to my daily engagement with my work and the media in the PRC.

Are there any insights that we can gain from media research published in China? Western research has been largely dismissive of Mainland Chinese critique, arguing that it is part of the ideological machination of the state. Over the past two decades, however, communications research in China has emerged from its doctrinal straitjacket to absorb elements of European and American research. This change is due in part to the numbers of communications scholars either studying abroad, or visiting research institutions outside the Mainland. It also points to disenchantment with a Marxist view of culture that insists on an historical materialist understanding of social change.

In November 1982 the Journalism Institute of the Chinese Academy of Social Sciences conducted the first national communications research symposium in Beijing, an important event that demonstrated that communications research had acquired legitimacy as a mainstream discipline. Western theory and methodology provided a reference point for Chinese scholars seeking to understand the rapid transformations taking place in the media. The principal reason for the attraction to Western scholarship was that it provided analytical tools that explained media change.

By contrast, Chinese research was founded on the less flexible analytic principle that news guides public opinion. This concept was linked to principles of public ownership and modes of management of cultural industries. It was less than helpful in the critique of change such as that brought about by the rapid development of television in China, the interplay and competition among various media, the complex administrative and management requirements resulting from the transition to a market economy, and the penetration and control of the advertising industry. Many important theories have subsequently been translated into Chinese, and have made an impact on scholarship. Daniel Bell, Alvin Töffler and subsequently the Frankfurt School thinkers were especially influential in the formulation of a theory of popular culture (Brugger and Kelly, Chan 1995, Tao 1996). As contemporary communication theory became available to Mainland scholars it was used to analyse local content, media consumption, as well as crises and prospects confronting the Chinese media in the face of globalization and the information age (Yin Hong, this volume). Although few scholars were involved in communication research, at least in the 1980s and early 1990s, many theoretical approaches were adopted and adapted from the European and US communication research traditions. Aside from the official tradition of news and public opinion research, two important trends became evident: a critical humanities tradition and a social science approach based on quantitative methods.

The critical humanities tradition was informed by translations of the European and American scholarship: the Frankfurt School, British Cultural Studies, McLuhan's philosophies of the electronic media, and American post-colonialism. Contemporary communication and cultural studies theory, incorporating (post) Marxist perspectives on ideology, as well as insights from structuralism, semiotics, psychoanalysis, and post-modernism, has also provided a means to re-invigorate media theory in China. Studies have emerged recently that investigate media consumption, media systems (Cui, 1999) the relations between mediated culture and popular culture (Chen Gang 1996), marketization of entertainment, media globalization and localization (Zhong et al., 1998), and the impact of the Internet and the Information Society (Ming, 1999).

China's second main communications research trend uses a social science-based quantitative approach, utilizing methodology from economics, sociology, psychology, such as case studies, surveys, audience analysis and measurement techniques. Chinese journalism's first quantitative audience survey, conducted from January to August 1982 by the Beijing Journalism Institute, was based on random sampling and statistical probability methodology. Following this, the Chinese People's University in Beijing, the Chinese Academy of Social Sciences, and Shanghai Fudan University adopted quantitative methods to research communication and media. This type of methodology has also spread to the informal research sector. The

NGO 'Friends of Nature' (*Ziran zhi you*), uses media sampling and content analysis to inform their work on environmental education. Research has also focused on investigating media management and administration, the social influence and effects of the media, media industry change, both from the perspectives of theory and practice.

There are also initiatives in the field of new media impact. With the development of the Internet, the rapid expansion of media industries, and China's imminent accession to the WTO, a number of real and theoretical questions have received attention. These include globalization and the future of China's media, issues related to the structure of media industries, the evolution of the media in the Internet age, and ethical questions related to media commercialization. Unfortunately, although certain institutions (notably Qinghua University and Beijing University) are working hard to promote excellence in nationally focussed media research and debate, there is still much to do. The crises confronting China's media in the new century lack a substantial research foundation, and therefore appropriate strategic responses. The current era is an exploratory phase of synthesizing Western methodology with Chinese media, qualitative and quantitative research, and humanities and social science research traditions.

This book then is our intervention into this huge but to some extent unmapped territory of enquiry. We would like to thank our contributors for their swift and committed responses to our call for contribution. Without their transnational and generous dedication to knowledge, we could not have produced this book.

SECTION 1

BACKGROUND, HISTORY AND THEORY

1

MEDIA IN CHINA: NEW CONVERGENCES, NEW APPROACHES

Stephanie Hemelryk Donald and Michael Keane

This book concerns a new kind of revolution in China – a revolution in which rapidly commercializing media industries confront slow-changing power relations between the political, social and economic spheres. In conceiving and planning this book we have endeavoured to include a range of disciplinary perspectives. Drawing on the expertise of industry professionals, academic experts and cultural critics, *Media in China: consumption, content and crisis* offers a variety of 'takes' on audiovisual industries in 'the world's largest media market'. In particular, we look at television, film, music, commercial and political advertising, as well as new developments in communications such as the Internet and multimedia resources. We explore evolving audience demographics, new patterns of media reception in regional centres, and the gradual internationalization of media content and foreign investment in China's broadcasting industries.

There is much more that could be written on any one of these issues, and we hope that this book will inspire students and colleagues to work further along these research paths. There are many other topics that we have not had space to consider: new documentary, radio and online broadcasting, offshore broadcasts, e-commerce, digital education practices, and minority programming are important areas of research. We have not been able to tackle them here but we trust they will be addressed in future projects. For these omissions we apologize, but we trust that the argument of this book can be usefully extended in future studies to other platforms and other media.

Issues

The questions raised in the title of this book are purposefully wide ranging. They introduce the key topics of consumption, content, and crisis, which refer not only to the future of media in one of the world's most populous nation-states, but also to the future of the state of China itself. We suggest in this introductory chapter, and throughout the book, that the project of media research must involve the study of economic, social, and creative practices within a geopolitical framework. This may be both a national regulatory framework and a space where the national agenda is contested within its regions. Access is a prime issue in any such study, and media access is key to the contestations over national priorities and habits of consumption. Access to goods, exclusion from goods through poverty, or regional availability issues are aspects of consumption which reconfigure social groupings, collective behaviour (Tse 2001), and, possibly, antisocial reactions. These reconfigurations tend to be embedded in existing cultural formations and social habitus. Nevertheless they represent profound change in the lives and expectations of many millions of people. In this book, we contend that a particular focus on content and a more dispassionate view of media internationalization are required for the analysis of a media system in the prolonged throes of transition.

Our operative concept for Chinese politics and society in the 1990s and 2000 is 'change'. Much of this change has taken place at breakneck speed in accordance with the realization of the 'four modernizations'[1] policy, first articulated by Hua Guofeng in 1975 and officially spelled out at the Third Plenum of the 11th Central Committee of the Chinese Communist Party (CCP) in 1978. The speed of change, coupled with the social and political contradictions that it has engendered, has produced a sense of crisis in the experience of late twentieth-century modernity in the People's Republic. Crisis is not necessarily negative, however. In the case studies of media industries investigated in this volume, the fear of crisis elicits distinctive responses to commercial imperatives, some of these challenging the logic of market rationality, others testing the patience of policy-makers. A number of academic accounts have tackled these issues by emphasizing institutional constraints on media autonomy. We seek to balance these with our emphasis on issues of content and consumption practices. As many of the contributors to this book point out, the consumption practices and aspirations of Chinese citizens have altered greatly during the past twenty years (Fung and Ma, this volume). New economic interest groups, social layers, and generational peer patterns have developed (Donald, this volume). Indeed, the media industries' recognition of audience fragmentation is also an acknowledgment of new, or previously ignored, groups of viewers. The popularity of the dating show (*zhenghun jiemu*) is a case in point (Keane, this volume).

Change or crisis: characteristic socialist media OR media with socialist characteristics?

The question of crisis has been a trope in the history of modern China. The twentieth century was plagued and glorified by huge ideological shifts, revolutionary endeavour and economic and social experiment. Crisis is also emblematic of the media industries as they shift into new financial and policy structures and engage with international partners and trading alliances, but also as they continue to work as fundamental props for government policy and state ideology. However, crisis is too fraught a term to encourage useful comment on the business practices of the media and the consumption choices of their audiences. Within crisis there is change, and this may be charted through traumatic shifts or across relatively small, discrete happenings in the industry. The case studies in this book subscribe to the importance of detail in descriptions of massive transition.

We offer the following preliminary sketch of the past, present and future, as a guide to the contextual structures which frame the case studies elaborated throughout the book (Table 1). The time frames are adequate rather than exact, as we would insist that change happens on a continuum and that without due regard for the past, we have little hope of comprehending the present. The policy changes in the late 1970s did not spring from a vacuum. The architects of reform and the prophets of modernity had been in government before the Cultural Revolution. Their ideas and economic aspirations were not suddenly conceived, nor suddenly understood, by the people. That is evidenced by the alacrity of some Chinese to take on the attributes and self-propulsion of capitalist economics and consumption, and the resistance of others to an impossible – and financially painful – change in lifestyle (Fung and Ma, this volume).

From the time China's economic reforms began in 1978, Western political commentators have attempted to characterize China's transition from planned economy to market economy under various formulations: post-socialism, state capitalism, even social capitalism (Dirlik 1989: 362–84, see Keane and Donald, this volume). The regime, in attempting to differentiate its social and economic reforms from those of post-Communist regimes in Central Europe, has settled on 'the socialist commodity economy', along with the one-size-fits-all epithet, 'socialism with Chinese characteristics'. As Dirlik (op. cit.: 374) argues, the role that 'socialism' plays in these perlocutions is that of 'ideological guardian' to counter the tendency towards taking the high capitalist road. Certain guiding principles of socialism remain as a reminder that, while the road travelled is a capitalist one, the final destination is socialism.

In addition, the Chinese leadership increasingly looks towards Asian states such as Singapore and Malaysia for policy leadership in the management of media systems. The favoured model is a hybrid form of governance that has been termed 'authoritarian liberalism' – a combination of economic liberalism and political illiberalism (Jayasuriya 2001; Birch 1998a, 1998b, 1999, 2000; Lee and Birch 2001; Rodan 1998a, 1998b) This approach 'combines the rational calculation demanded by the operation of the capitalist economy within the authoritarian shell of the state'

Table 1.1 Change and development in China's media

	Pre-reform	*1980–99*	*2000–*
Economic system	Command economy	Market reform: gradual decentralization of management	State capitalism/ authoritarian liberalism
Media regulation	Engineer state model	Deregulation and gradual diminution of subvention for media industries	Architect state model (state facilitates regulatory guidelines for investment in infrastructure)
Social stratification	Egalitarian/iron rice bowl	New middle classes with economic capital; social capital residing in bureaucrats	Emerging digital divide; increasing economic stratification
Function of media	Propaganda/ mobilization of masses	Pedagogic/reform of attitudes and conduct (spiritual civilization)	Informational; provi-ision of repertoire of cultural choices
Types of media	Print, posters, radio loudspeaker networks, film, terrestrial TV	On-line news; chat rooms; pay and satellite platforms; DVD; VCD; cellular telephones	Broadband cable; digital TV, WAPs; iMODE; new media technologies
Media characteristic	Mass line; cultural despotism	Diversification; shift to entertainment function and entrepreneurial self-sufficiency	Convergence; internationalization of content
Crisis	Establishing control and controlling factions within the the press. Making the media into the 'mouthpiece'	Coming to terms with the costs of maintaining a public media infrastructure. Increasing tensions among media workers and problems of maintaining the traditional role of the media	The high cost of upgrading technological infrastructure. The threats of foreign content and the impact of WTO accession. Controlling the technology of the Internet.

(Jayasuriya 2001). The authoritarian liberalism model has increasing leverage in China, which has long operated a pragmatic politics of communication. We might say that a model of governmentality has emerged whereby Chinese people have been allowed an increasing freedom to choose, to consume, and to be self-regulating, but where the authoritarian spectre of the disciplinary state remains as a fallback strategy of governance should civic freedom lead to anti-government uprisings. At the same time the media are called upon to play a positive role. Since the economic reforms began, media such as television have been regarded as technologies by which the 'backward sectors' of society, the undereducated masses, can be instructed in the modern ideology of the socialist market already adopted by the new urban middle classes.

The portrayal of China's media as technologies of power dominates the literature published in the Western hemisphere, particularly in relation to the print media. Accounts emanating from the 'free world' have usually viewed the terms 'propaganda' and 'ideology' in a negative light – as the central problem of authoritarian media systems. From Cold War accounts of the propaganda state of the 1960s (Schurmann 1968; Yu [F.T.C.] 1964; Howkins 1982) through to recent analyses of the Chinese media in transition (Lynch 1999; Lam 2000; Zhao [Yuezhi] 1998), an opposition has been staked out between undemocratic authoritarian media systems and plural, market-oriented public spheres – typified by liberal democratic governance.

Inherent in this opposition is the assumption that the Western liberal tradition represents global best practice for the media. The well-known 'four theories of the press' model (Siebert et al. 1956), which placed the 'libertarian' model at one end of the freedom spectrum and the authoritarian and communist model at the other, is a prime example of this ranking system. As Sparks (1997, 2000) has noted, the assumption was that the characteristics of media systems were entirely dependent on the philosophical and political systems in which they operated. Hence, as it must be a 'Communist' system, China' s media system was the opposite of the 'free enterprise' libertarian model. This model has wrongly implied that Western media systems are unencumbered by government regulation and interference – in contrast to China's media, which are characterized as highly regulated. For instance, an American thinktank, Freedom House, places China third after North Korea and Myanmar in terms of government control of the media (Gunaratne 2000)[2]. While this typology produces a relative rankings of global press freedoms, it tends to mask the fact that centralized control of the media does not necessarily translate into compliance by producers with chapter and verse of the regulatory canon. The media in China are heavily regulated in theory but, due to the sheer size of the media sector, guidelines and policies are difficult to implement and enforce (Keane 2001a; Chan 1997: 103).

Consumption

The practice of media consumption is now widely considered a negotiation on the part of active audiences and readers. This is tempered, however, by the recognition that consumption is framed by economic and sociopolitical conditions. Negotiations around the use of media technology and its products in the public and commercial sectors are also finely tuned in China, when the political will of the state is scrutinized and tested by producers and consumers in their decisions on the practical possibilities of media use.

These conditions also necessitate negotiation between consumers' needs, desires, and reasonable expectations. Such negotiation is an enactment of publicness (a translation of Habermas's term *Öffentlichkeit*), or the sharing and invention of the collective self through mediated experience (Donald and Donald 2000: 115). To a degree, the concept of publicness supports optimism expressed about causal links between market economics, cultural diversity, and public spheres. China's business sector increasingly models management policy and strategy introduced from capitalist economics. In response, Western scholars and media industry spokespeople associate the commercial momentum in the Chinese media sector with the irresistible dynamism of liberalism. This leap of faith rests on deracinated assumptions, which in fact cut against the liberal ideal of a local (or nationally imagined) political public sphere. One such assumption is that the assimilation of global brand name products such as Sony, Coca-Cola and KFC into the Chinese mediascape indicates a shift towards a global consumer consciousness. It is secondly assumed that this consciousness will provide the basis for a consumer revolution. Brand awareness and rising disposable income will consummate a liberating experience to rank with the momentous events that transpired in 1949 ('Liberation', the year in which the People's Republic of China was founded).

All these 'givens' of commercial practice need to be understood, however, within the historical context of the People's Republic of China. In China, the term 'mass media' resonates with the cognate concepts of the masses (the great public or the core of society), the mass line (the purported link between the leadership and the masses) and mass movements (the principal strategy of mass mobilization) (Tang [Tsou] 1986). From the pamphlets and posters of the heady days of revolution and class struggle through to the broadcast media of television and radio, the imagined media audience has always been a mass audience. The media as a (collective) technology of mass persuasion reminds us of the historical importance of Marxism–Leninism in debates about the role of the media from the 1930s onwards. Although a foreign ideology, Marxism appealed to revolutionary intellectuals and prevailed over competing doctrines of liberalism because it offered a theory of total transformation within a systematic and modern epistemology in the form of dialectics (Tang [Tsou] 1986: 263). At the founding of the CCP in 1921, however, Marxism had little to offer as a theory of culture. The distillation of Marxism into Chinese culture would eventually be provided via Soviet Leninism in the 1930s and 1940s.

The shift that necessitates a theory of culture now is the foregrounding of consumption in everyday politics and social policy. The trope of consumption has therefore been prominent in the literature on China's economic reform. It has been argued that consumption is a good thing in that it generates wealth and helps people to aspire to be productive. Consumption of material goods is also seen as an activity that is disproportionately located in the emerging middle classes (Goodman and Hooper 1994; Goodman 1996). Chinese people's consumption has been conceptualized in terms of a 'consumption ladder', that is, as incomes rise so people's aspirations increase and they seek to own different categories of durable goods (Fan 2000). In terms of cultural consumption the picture is less clear. The consumption of cultural and media products is fundamentally a social act and occurs primarily in people's free time. In the Maoist period, free time was meant to be gainfully employed for the purposes of building a disciplined and healthy population (Wang [Shaoguang] 1995). Today, cultural consumption is largely a matter of choice.

The idea of consumer sovereignty has become a recurring feature of media debates in China. An important article entitled 'Who is the God of Television?' identified television's cultural stratification (He [Xiaobing] 1994). The author, He Xiaobing, maintained that, prior to the commercialization of China's media under Deng Xiaoping, the ruling élite, 'leading cadres' (*lingdao ganbu*) who made up 2 per cent of the total population, had assumed a hegemonic mandate to decide what was appropriate culture for the other 98 per cent. Through the workings of state ownership and control of cultural institutions they, and television itself, had avoided being accountable to the audience. In this account, the classical masses were the receivers of messages from the leadership according to a linear model of communication. With the increase in social stratification, the mass audience has begun to fragment into many subcultures (*ya wenhua*) or potential publics, differentiated by income as well as by geographical factors (urban or rural), educational levels (university or high school), and political status. Citing television, He Xiaobing claims that the control of culture is passing into the hands of entrepreneurs and market forces. While the administrative stratum, the 'leading cadres', still controls the political agenda, the urban middle class, especially those working in finance and insurance, real estate, post and telecommunications, broadcasting, television and film industries, now constitute the sector which has the highest income and consumption levels.[3] This social stratum also spends the most money on recreational and cultural commodities. The argument here is familiar and leads into models of market research. It is not just the size of the audience – if that were the case the peasant stratum would control the shape of culture – but also the needs and access capabilities of the audience that require response.

Another interesting description of changing relations of dependency is the need to 'please the *three olds*', namely the old cadres (*laoganbu*), the bosses (*laoban*) and the consumers (*lao baixing*). As in He Xiaobing's categorization of a power shift away from the leading cadres, the new upstart is the *laoban* – represented not simply by the bosses of media institutions but also by the components of the value chain who are stakeholders in policy-making. However, the relationship remains co-dependent in that policy determines the boundaries of expression and thereby decisions relating to investment in production – investors will not directly support content that incurs the displeasure of censors or, for that matter, a lack of interest on the part of audiences.

Content

The term 'cultural industries' is central to our examination of the transitional nature of media content in China. The plural term 'cultural industries' contrasts with the Frankfurt School's demonization of the singular and manipulative 'culture industry' that was said to have emerged in liberal democracies during the 1940s and 1950s. The latter was blamed for the rise of vulgarly commercial mass culture (a threat to which many intellectual élites of the day considered themselves immune). The more recently coined appellation eschews the intellectual pretensions of exclusivity. By virtue of this, it has the capacity to engage with empirical understandings of the production and circulation of cultural products (Sinclair 1996) while critically evaluating the symbolic power of media and their constitutive formations in society. British media theorist Nicholas Garnham has done much to rehabilitate the status of cultural industries. In the early 1990s he wrote that the cultural industries 'employ the characteristic modes of production and organization of industrial corporations to produce and disseminate symbols in the forms of cultural goods and services, although not exclusively as commodities' (Garnham 1990: 155–6). That cogent statement demonstrates how the vocabularies of economic analysis and cultural theory may coexist to good effect.

Garnham revisited the cultural industries thesis in 2000, this time placing emphasis on the imperative to distinguish the inductive power of the symbolic from other forms of control, or social communication. Although concentrating its focus on Europe, Garnham's synthesis allows us to approach the emergent Chinese cultural industries in ways that incorporate the disciplines of political economics and social communications, while acknowledging the public negotiations of meaning that routinely occur in processes of symbolic exchange. As he notes:

> No study of the media can bypass the complex and difficult questions posed by their content, by the symbolic forms they create and circulate. Their effects, whether of agency or structure, are worked, unavoidably, through the symbolic. This is one of the things that makes the mode of persuasion distinct from those of either production or coercion. Here the inducements and sanctions through which power works are and can only be symbolic.
>
> (Garnham 2000: 138)

Of course, the symbolic component is easily set aside – at least for the purposes of description – when we attempt to define the cultural industries in action. In an even more commercial and legalistic sense, cultural industries are represented as 'copyright industries'. Product is increasingly designed for reproduction in multiple and identical copies while being amenable to re-purposing for 'on sale' in different formats (television, CD-ROM, online) and across different platforms (terrestrial, cable, and pay-TV services). The idea of content is thus configured within the industrial idea of durability by which means producers can continue to extract economic rents (e.g. copyright payments) (Caves 2000: 1).

With this in mind another useful term is 'content industries'. The viability of media industries is contingent on the creation and distribution of film, video, music, and information services, delivered through multiple platforms and formats. In this context viability is contingent on the producers creating a relationship with the consumer of content – the audience or public (Garnham 1990: 187). The understanding of content as 'a new growth industry' has gained currency within the developing world following the inscription of the term 'cultural industries' within national cultural policy and cultural development programmes (OECD 1998).[4] This has moved the debate about culture along by identifying it as an important activity requiring government support, not for its inherent aesthetic worth but for its contribution to national economic development. In industry parlance, however, content is the fundamental basis of economic exchange.

The dominant content industries are the audio-visual industries: television broadcasting, cable television, movies, music, video and video games. These industries are producers of economic value, whether this is accrued directly through box-office receipts, broadcasting rights, or the on sale of media product in different formats. They are also incubators of ideas and training sites for creative personnel. The value chain of a television series consists, in the first instance, of writers who develop the intellectual property of the screenplay. Subsequent links brings in editors, producers, managers, suppliers of equipment and post-production technicians; this is followed by the work of agents, promoters and middlemen. The content accrues value through the physical infrastructure of television channels (terrestrial, pay-per-view), as well as through the merchandizing of product (fashion accessories, T-shirts, CDs, etc.) and auxiliary platforms (Web sites). The success or failure of this content is contingent on the work of critics, publicists and marketing agencies. The value chain both boasts (style) and obscures (generic conservatism) its dependence on the exchange of symbolic value, which is encoded and recoded in the work of creative personnel and in the values and expectations that they share with their potential audience (Zhao Bin 1997).

In China, the television value chain has been subject to the administration of officials in the Ministry of Film, Radio and Television (now the State Administration of Radio, Film and Television, or SARFT). Based less on exchange value and more on the perceived social and/or political benefit of the content, the administrative value chain stymied industry development. Until recently, the distribution and broadcasting rights of television drama were tied to the originating television channel. That meant that the drama production unit of Beijing Television (BTV) would be obliged to offer initial broadcast rights to BTV. This presumably impeded innovation, a central feature of viable cultural industries. However, like the Chinese economy in general, the television industry is prone to 'duplicate construction' (*chongfu jianshe*) whereby producers target markets within a particular locality with a product that has been successful in other markets. Formats are thus appropriated or 'cloned' (*kelong*) (Keane, this volume; on formats more generally see Moran 1998). This structural isomorphism – along with miniaturization (the small scale of many stations) – produces a barter system, with undercapitalized television stations 'swapping' programmes (particularly television dramas).

Politics and institutions

Institutional bodies (state ministries and state and local bureaux) play an important role in the management of China's media industries (Redl and Simons, this volume). There is increasing complexity in institutional policy-making as the global momentum of technological innovation, convergence, and market liberalization reshapes the benefits of participation in the global trade arena. In the many accounts of China's media it is therefore politics that occupies centre stage. The political currency of debate about media control has been captured in the term 'cultural despotism', referring to the monopolization of the means of production and distribution of information by the party-state (Su Shaozhi, 1994). In this account, limits on people's capacity to express non-orthodox views in the media, or to register complaints against the paramount leadership of the CCP, illustrate the path dependency of China's leaders, their allegiance to a Leninist media model, and their deep misgivings about democratic pluralism.

Notwithstanding the heuristic potency of the cultural despotism model, debates about media in contemporary China are increasingly organized around the notion of the 'transitional' state.[5] Tensions emerge under this serviceable paradigm as top-down models of public information dissemination give way to more autonomous and plural forms of production and to distribution mechanisms sustained by market relations. The tension that is evident in policy backflips and ambiguous guidelines are easily attributable to a transitional phase – 'from plan to market'. This model can be stretched to explain everything: 'irregularities' such as policy paralysis, crackdown on content, neglect of copyright law, and widespread competition within telecommunication and broadcasting bureaux can all be attributed to the unsteadiness of the bridge that spans the 'plan to market' chasm. The paradigmatic explanation does not provide answers, but rather produces a 'wait and see' perspective on the economics of Chinese media development.

When discussing the shift towards new forms of commercial content and associated arguments about consumer sovereignty, it is imperative to bear in mind the ideological and therefore institutionalized underpinnings of the content. The technological development of China's media during the mid-twentieth century was driven by the necessity to generate effective propaganda – what is referred to within CCP ranks as conducting ideological work (*zhengzhi sixiang gongzuo*). A mass audience even for propaganda is not, however, entirely a creature of its creator. Publics grow from autonomous organization and political activity, as in liberal democratic theory (Donald 2000: 14–16; Evans and Donald 1999a: 18–21). They also emerge through mediated processes, through cultural exchange and in the context of shared events.

> Public memory is created to replace historical knowledge, ... while history is written in order to construct public memory. Thus a seemingly endless cycle of reproduction and reinforcement is always already in train.
>
> Donald and Donald 2000: 126

Cinema was the major mass medium, and mass spectacle, of the 1930s, 1940s and 1950s. Using a version of Soviet socialist realism, revisioned as revolutionary romanticism from 1959, stories could be told and distributed to large numbers of people relatively easily (Chu, this volume). Revolutionary cinema developed from the social improvement tendencies of the 4th May activism of the 1920s and 1930s. After Liberation (1949), cinema grasped the revolutionary wars and the founding years of the People's Republic of China and made history out of them. The heroics of *The Whitehaired Girl* (*Baimao nü* 1950), *Daughter of the Party* (*Dang de nüer* 1958), and *Little Soldier* (*Xiaobing zhangga* 1963), were part of the formulation and consolidation of new cultural memories for a new Chinese tradition of socialism in action. They were also exciting films. The cinema only succeeded as a public visualization of the new China when the films it offered were worth watching, and when the generic features of revolutionary romanticism were made attractive, were emotionally affecting and moved at a pace that fitted the cinematic expectations of the audience. Content was more than propaganda; it was also narrative cohesion, the characterization of heroic (and anti-heroic) types, which appealed to the audience and which made identification with revolutionary history possible and worthwhile. Current cinematic practice has to fulfil the same function in its broad appeal for entertainment within systematic confines (Chu this volume; Pang this volume).

With the development of television in 1958 the potential of the mass media as a national propaganda tool appeared obvious. Paradoxically, however, the intrusion of propaganda into the homes of television viewers was not as successful as the government had envisaged. Due in part to the opening of society in the 1980s, and in part to the residual memory of the Cultural Revolution (which broadly refers to 'ten years of chaos' – 1966 to 1976), televised propaganda failed to hit its target. An increase in the number of channels, along with the technology of the remote control, meant that people could simply switch off. The response to indifference has been pragmatic and locally specific (Shoesmith and Wang this volume; Harrison this volume). Rather than broadcasting doctrinal propaganda about the truth of socialism and the decadence of capitalism as in the past, the Chinese media now inculcate lessons about what it means to live in a changing world where competitiveness drives national economic productivity.

Research literature

Communication research in the Western tradition attempts to mark out distinctions between institutions, texts and audiences. It brings those three perspectives together without losing the differentiating features necessary to clear understandings of media processes in the world (Garnham 2000: 61–2). The pioneering work on Chinese television remains James Lull's *China Turned On: Television, Reform and Resistance* (Lull 1991). This work managed to capture a moment in time – the disenchantment with official television leading up to the heady events that occurred in June 1989 in Tiananmen Square. More recently, Zhao Yuezhi (1998) has produced a political economy of China's transitional media with particular emphasis on print media and radio. Her subtitle, 'from the Party-line to the bottom-line', sums up the widespread momentum within China's media institutions towards a profit-making ethic while yet conscious of ideological responsibilities. Daniel Lynch (1999) uses a literal sense of ideological work (*sixiang gongzuo*) as 'thought work'. He argues that the control of 'thought work' is no longer monopolized by the central leadership due to the impacts of globalization and commercialization. He also argues that fragmentation of authority has created regulatory indecision. His study is subject to an antithesis between liberal and authoritarian systems, but still provides valuable insights into transformations within China's broadcasting and new media industries. Similarly, studies on media internationalization are valuable, but maintain an 'us and them' version of media globalization, which casts the international back into the role of 'The West' and the local as the staunch (or recalcitrant) nationalism of China (Hong 1998, Chan 1994, Yu [Xu] 1995).

This is countered to some degree by work on diasporic consumption, which demonstrates that media flows are regional as much as global and challenges the essentialism of Chinese cultural politics and of audience choices (Sun [Wanning], 1998, 2000; Donald 2000; Yue and Hawkins 2000; Sinclair and Cunningham 2000).

The binary approach to China and 'The West' is indebted to the popular 'effects' trend in media research. There is still a political desire to delineate good and bad actors on the stage of media content. In the Western domestic sphere, children as citizen-consumers are undervalued; in the international arena, media effects are cited to infantilize entire (foreign) populations as unthinking consumers of propaganda. In the pristine frameworks of small media and new media, a move away from an uncritical rehearsal of both the 'effects' and the 'us and them' traditions would be timely. The impact of interactivity brought about by the convergence of broadcasting, the Internet and telephony challenges assumptions about top-down flows of information. The shift from broadcasting to 'narrow-casting', the advent of broadband technologies and digital broadcasting, and the fact that Chinese people – like people elsewhere – can programme their own media rather than be captive audiences, disrupts the control metaphor. So while this volume respects the field as it exists, we seek to map out other ways of thinking through media research in the Chinese context.

We have organized this volume around five media research areas. This is done to provide a gradual entry into the arguments we are canvassing in this volume. Section 1 provides background about media industries in China. In Chapter 2, Anke Redl and Rowan Simons from China Media Monitor Intelligence (CMMI) – a media industry information organization based in Beijing – provide a concise summary of the Chinese media environment, key players and interests, new trends and strategies. Many of these issues are explored in greater detail in Section 4. In Chapter 3, Yin Hong from Beijing's Qinghua University discusses the neglected topic of Chinese television drama and its development within the constraints of politics, profit, and pedagogy.

Section 2 examines the popular consumption and market strategies of film and television industries in China and SAR Hong Kong, as well as tracing regional flows of content. In Chapter 4, Yingchi Chu discusses the relations between film policy reform and industry development in the People's Republic, drawing attention to how the CCP defines mainstream films. This chapter touches on global and national interests and foreign investment in China's film industry, points that are taken up in more detail by Laikwan Pang in Chapter 5, who demonstrates the reciprocal benefits that now accrue between Mainland and SAR Hong Kong film industries. In Chapter 6, Anthony Fung and Eric Ma continue the SAR Hong Kong discussion. Fung and Ma base their discussion on fieldwork in Guangzhou to suggest that Hong Kong television provides a 'demonstration effect', contributing to four distinctive and disjunctive modes of televisual imagination in the minds of Guangzhou viewers. In Chapter 7, Michael Keane takes a look at travelling formats. His argument is that formats are a form of cultural technology transfer that can add value to television systems as long as format cloning does not become the main game. He demonstrates the extent of 'cloning' (*kelong*) in China by examining in some detail the popular 'dating shows' (*zhenghun jiemu*).

Section 3 takes us on a journey through youth- and leisure-related mediaspheres. Jeroen de Kloet (Chapter 8) and Huang Yingfen and Tain-dow Lee (Chapter 9) discuss the flows of transnational influence across the music scene in Greater China, with de Kloet arguing that the local is key to understanding the prospects and future of the rock scene in metropolitan China. Huang and Lee, however, argue from a Taiwanese perspective that the Chinese music scene is global in some respects, if not international in character. In Chapter 10, Wanning Sun looks at how the Sydney 2000 Olympic Games functioned as a form of national spectatorship and as a 'media event' in China. Sun calls the kind of reporting of the games semiotic over-determination or 'indoctritainment'. In Chapter 11, Stephanie Hemelryk Donald argues that children, always important in the Chinese mediasphere, are now emerging as a formidable marketing target group, but that the child audience is also invested with the future of the public good and national belonging. The advertising industry is then put under scrutiny in two chapters: Steve Lewis's Chapter 12 is focused on the domestic advertising industry and its collusion with governmental rhetoric such as 'spiritual civilization', while in Chapter 13, Kenneth Lim from ICL Marketing provides an optimistic account of how advertising can be empowering rather than simply a tool of transnational media interests; Lim uses the story of the marketing of professional soccer in China, including that of 'Team China' and the Chinese women's soccer team, to make his case.

The final section looks in more detail at media infrastructure, new media, and policy directions. Mark Harrison provides a detailed account of China's satellite and cable industries in Chapter 14. This is followed in Chapter 15 by Brian Shoesmith and Wang Handong's discussion of industrial community television (ICT). In Chapter 16, Hu Xin takes up the discussion of new media with a case study of Sina.com and Netease.com. The last chapter in the book, by Keane and Donald, looks at new media technologies and possible futures for China's media industries in the light of World Trade Organization (WTO) accession, digitization, and media convergence.[6]

Notes

1 The four modernizations are 'modernization of agriculture, industry, science and technology, and defence'.
2 The Freedom House argument that freedom helps economic growth is its headline news on the FH homepage: see http://www.freedomhouse.org/media/pressrel/121900.htm accessed 10 January 2001
3 See also China Economic News, No. 36, 22 September 1997, p. 5.
4 See for example the Unesco UK Library and Information Policy Budget http://www.lic.gov.uk/publications/policyreports/unesco.html

5 This notion has already been employed to some effect in the Eastern European experience of post-Communism (Sparks, 1997), a point worth noting as the Party leadership in China is concerned not to mimic the disintegration of that region, and all areas of policy will be cognizant of that caveat.

6 While the spectre of WTO is frequently cited in discussions of China's audio-visual future, it is important to note that the key issue concerns the GATS (General Agreement of Trade in Services) ratified in the Uruguay Round of the WTO in 1995 which broadened the scope of world trade rules to include trade in services. Audiovisual 'services' is now grouped together with banking transportation, travel, and telecommunications. The key to the GATS is in the terms market access (Article XVI) and national treatment (Article XVII). In short this means that signatory countries provide transparent regulations and open access to markets and that members are bound to provide the reciprocal treatment in relation to cross border transactions. The most pertinent aspects of the GATS for China are thus 'cross-border supply' of goods and services and 'commercial presence', the latter having particular importance for foreign direct investment, joint ventures and co-productions (Sauvé and Stern 2000).

2

CHINESE MEDIA – ONE CHANNEL, TWO SYSTEMS

Anke Redl and Rowan Simons

The development of the media, the most political and commercial of modern industries, provides a unique insight into the reality of 'socialism with Chinese characteristics' and the challenges facing China as it emerges as a major world economy and cultural force. In no other sectors are the powerful forces of politics and commerce so graphically and publicly joined together and presented to the people as a single product.

Since the founding of the People's Republic of China in 1949, the Chinese media have been in a perpetual state of change. The industry has always been required to act quickly and sensitively to even the slightest fluctuations in political direction, while maintaining the central Party line. Since 1978, it has faced the added challenges of adapting to new economic and technical imperatives, though not yet direct foreign competition. The Chinese media are still undergoing fundamental changes and are likely to continue to do so for decades to come. As this collection goes to press, significant further policy decisions are expected to change the landscape again as World Trade Organization preparations begin in earnest.

The last major policy and organizational overhaul came three years ago when the State Council announced plans to downsize ministries and commissions. In March 1998, at the First Session of the Ninth People's Congress, the Ministry of Post and Telecommunications (MPT), the Ministry of the Electronics Industry (MEI) and parts of the Ministry of Radio, Film and Television (MRFT) merged to form the Ministry of Information Industry (MII) (see Harrison, this volume). This 'superministry' headed by Wu Jichuan has been given the task of overseeing the management of Chinese information networks into the twenty-first century. The MII also coordinates state policy on construction and management of electronic media as voice, video and data technologies converge. The restructuring also saw the downgrading of the MRFT to become the General State Administration of Radio, Film and Television (SARFT). This body has continued to censor content and to manage the country's existing broadcast infrastructure. Meanwhile, the

Ministry of Culture and the State Press and Publications Administration retain an interest in editorial matters, as do propaganda departments at all levels.

In this environment, SARFT has been struggling to reorganize a chaotic and fragmented industry. There has been talk of 'separation of production and broadcast' and 'merger of terrestrial and cable' followed by a public reversal of the first and the delay of the second after the appointment of the new and more 'hardline' SARFT director Xu Guangchun. In the meantime, the MII and SARFT, jointly responsible for leading the television industry into the twenty-first century as part of China's information highway, are battling out a turf war. SARFT is anxious not to cede any further power to the superministry, while the MII is aiming at controlling all information networks including those of the broadcast industry with its cable holdings.

Terrestrial – cable – satellite

The role of television as a mass medium and propaganda tool did not develop until the late 1970s. Although terrestrial broadcasting started with the establishment of Peking TV in 1958, now BTV (Beijing TV), it only broadcast an hour a day to a handful of leaders. The Cultural Revolution brought an abrupt end to further development (although several regional TV stations were founded in this period) to be restarted only after Deng Xiaoping's rise to power. By the time Tibet TV was established in 1985, all provinces and major cities had established their own broadcasting systems with China Central Television (CCTV) the only national broadcaster. Since then, only China Education TV under the Ministry of Education has received permission to broadcast a national channel. Today, 89 per cent of China's mainly rural population of 1.3 billion people can receive TV signals via terrestrial, cable or satellite delivery, an impressive feat given the economic conditions in remote regions.

As a central mouthpiece of the CCP, extending television services to reach the estimated 150 million citizens still without access to television services remains a top political priority. This drive to extend penetration has contributed to television becoming China's dominant information medium. Sixty-one per cent of people interviewed by Gallup in 2000 reported that watching television with their family members was their favourite weeknight pastime.

China now has more than 980 terrestrial and over 1,300 cable stations at provincial, city and (still) county level as well as over 30 provincial satellite channels. The actual number of broadcasters varies from source to source as stations are consolidated, merged, separated or even reopened following closure. The numbers have been falling in recent years and could start falling faster in coming months as the government finally deals with core issues.

The side effects of the industry's hyperdevelopment under one-party rule are many fundamental contradictions and critical structural and production inefficiencies. Laws and regulations have lagged so far behind actual market developments that the state-owned industry is now facing crippling competition from itself. Expansion of terrestrial services at provincial and city levels in the 1980s and the near-parallel introduction of commercial advertising created the first boom period for television. During this period, the Party successfully exploited new technology to extend its propaganda machine, but local services also weakened central controls over ideological content and provided CCTV with stiff competition for audiences in the major centres.

Responding to the Chinese aerospace industry's ability to launch communications satellites from the early 1990s, central and provincial broadcasters found themselves with a new delivery weapon that could help them regain their political importance and generate additional revenues.

As satellite TV could also provide relatively low-cost solutions to satisfy the long-term Party objective of bringing television services to all citizens, central and provincial governments moved fast to establish analogue satellite feeds and install subsidized reception equipment in China's isolated areas. Guizhou TV and Yunnan TV (using a shared transponder on Asiasat 1) were just the first of many provincial-level stations that found themselves with a 'footprint' covering half of Asia and central funds to speed up installation of satellite reception facilities in the most remote locations. Today, all provincial broadcasters' lead channels are carried on satellite for this reason, although their commercial focus is clearly in reaching affluent urban audiences in the east of the country.

For the first few provincial players on satellite, this was the second period of dynamic growth. Like the terrestrial boom, it was made possible only through political will, but soon resulted in real commercial expansion fuelled by advertising. But, even as satellite was gaining a foothold among broadcasters and manufacturers, the central authorities changed direction again. A combination of fears about foreign channels carried on the same satellites and the opportunities offered by alternative technologies led to the development of new policies, partly designed to stop proliferation of satellite dishes in non-remote regions.

The new drive was towards investment into new communications infrastructure – cable. The process was already in full swing when satellite was unceremoniously dumped with the 1994 ban on private urban ownership of dishes. Relatively cheap MMDS systems allowed cable operators to establish significant penetration in key cities even faster than the original terrestrials. Unlike operators in many other markets, Chinese cable operators were established as traditional TV stations with responsibilities to produce local programming and with censorship responsibilities for all channels carried. By mid-decade, cable television infrastructures were widespread in all cities and many townships. In advanced cities, some consumers are now adding broadband to the list of technologies that deliver content to their homes.

While all these developments might be considered beneficial to audiences, the reality is that government restrictions, poor planning, lack of transparency and inadequate ratings have conspired to produce not healthy multichannel fare, but a basic tier comprising very similar channels broadcasting shows with low production values. Provincial satellite channels (originally conceived as a way of reaching remote audiences) have lobbied hard to be allowed to 'land' in major cities and many have succeeded through reciprocal agreements between cable-TV stations. Indeed, reserving channels for such agreements is one of the clearly political restrictions placed on cable-TV stations. Increasing competition in an increasingly complex media market is putting great pressure not only on cable operators, but also on the terrestrial and satellite channels, all facing their own restrictions, all fighting for the 'adspend' of more sophisticated marketers and for the attention of impatient viewers with clear niche interests (Lim, this volume).

After forty-three years of exploiting every TV technology that has become available to further political and (since 1979) commercial objectives, Chinese television has evolved into a highly competitive and cutthroat industry in which every player is still controlled by the government and still justifies itself primarily as a propaganda tool. For this reason, international channels (many carried on the same satellites as Chinese national and regional channels) are banned from being relayed on cable networks. Foreign broadcasters trying to get a foot in the door have been restricted to selling to hotels (with three or more stars), designated foreign compounds and other relevant institutions for an annual licence fee.[1]

Advertising: driving media forward

Over the last two decades, the Chinese television industry has increasingly relied on the phenomenal growth of the advertising industry to maintain its own expansion. Originally funded through state subsidies, the vast majority of TV stations in urban centres are now relying totally on advertising revenue and third-party investment to fund their development. Nonetheless, even the most profitable of TV stations such as Beijing TV, still receive an annual government subsidy. The subsidy may be dwarfed by the tax levied on BTV's commercial operations, but it stands as a symbol of the never-changing core relationship between mouthpiece and Party.

Television stations first refused, and then demanded complete control over, advertising messages. Beijing TV, for example, controlled all aspects of TV commercial production from 1984 (the year of its first commercial) until 1987, when it gave up strict control and allowed agencies to provide TVC (television commercial) productions of their own. As for the main political arguments against commercialism, these evaporated fairly quickly after the airing of China's first TV commercial in Shanghai in 1979. Since those early days, commercial advertising has literally changed the face of state media in China without ever challenging the political status quo. In 1999, China's advertising industry totaled US$7.4 billion according to (conservative) official figures from the State Administration of Industry and Commerce (SAIC), which regulates the industry. This was up from US$6.4 billion in 1998 and just US$300 million in 1990, a 15 per cent increase for the last recorded year and a 2,300 per cent increase over the last decade.

During the heyday of economic growth in China in the early and mid-1990s, the industry averaged a growth rate of 50 per cent with an average 15 per cent growth rate over the last two years. In 1999, the TV industry had earnings of US$1.8 billion (26 per cent of the total) while the newspaper sector made US$1.3billion (18 per cent of the total). However the increasing number of TV channels and consequent media fragmentation has increased competition for advertising dollars. Broadcasters are becoming increasingly aware of their audience, spurring the relatively new phenomenon of accountable audience measurement tools.

For many years information such as the number of TV sets was regarded as a state secret. Now people-meters are finding their way into sample TV homes in major cities as ACNielsen and CSM (a joint venture between CVSC, a CCTV subsidiary and French Sofres Group) both invest in the roll-out of expensive systems. Even though station directors are now eager to install ratings software, their understanding of the industry often lags behind their enthusiasm. The result is that only a few genuinely open-minded broadcasters such as Hunan Satellite TV have revamped their general schedules and now produce consistently popular programming that delivers advertising dollars.

Competition may force TV stations to gain audience share through popular changes to schedules, but they must always balance their moves in accordance with the wishes of the Party. It is in this environment of intense commercial pressures and highly charged political responsibilities that broadcasters deliver political and commercial messages without apparent contradiction. While foreign media companies wait on the sidelines for investment opportunities, advertisers are funding the state media's production of new programming, in effect working closely with the government to jointly improve production quality through practical and politically safe initiatives.

Information technology – new growth industry

While advertising has for a long time been one of the major sources of financing for the television industry, the cable sector has profited greatly from the global boom in information technology. The Chinese government attaches high priority to the construction of its own information infrastructure in order to sustain economic growth as an active player in the global economy. Not only China's telecommunication industry but also its TV operators, known as secondary infrastructure networks, have been attracting investment from new sources due to their potential for offering combined telecommunications, Internet and TV services through one network.

Vast economic disparities, dispersed populations and geographical obstacles between regions all contribute to the uneven development to date while vested interest in local networks will make consolidation a difficult terrain to navigate. But now, increasing domestic (and looming international) interest from communications sectors and China's expected accession to the World Trade Organization have increased the pressure on the state-owned media to make far more serious investments. This has encouraged the cable sector, in particular, to find ways to accept direct investment from private and even foreign sources. Like satellite players before them, cash-strapped networks all over China are attracting investment from various sources to upgrade their outdated technology. In an attempt to consolidate the sprawling cable industry – and in anticipation of cashing in on the sector – the SARFT has established an Information Network Centre to handle cable consolidation. The ambitious plan involves 3,000 cable operators being regrouped into 32 province-based operators, creating one national China Cable TV network.

The development of a national cable network faces serious problems, however. This was most violently demonstrated by death, serious injury and damage to property that resulted from local wars between cable TV networks and telecommunications operators in 1999. The result was Document No. 82 issued by the State Council, which halted all further network construction and prohibited the overlap of telecommunications and cable services. By continuing to define the industries separately as 'the radio and television system and the telecommunications system', the central government merely delayed essential decisions it must make in regard to convergence. It is expected that the ban will be ended in the near future and indeed, by the end of 2000, reports to this effect were carried in the Chinese press. Once again, as this book goes to press, there are strong indications of real changes, but no substantive policy announcements.

Most analysts agree that to prevent duplication and wastage of resources, SARFT will move to merge terrestrial and cable TV stations at municipal level. Like the ban on cable networks engaging in telecommunications business, the merger policy has not met with much enthusiasm within the cable industry, as operators have been upgrading in order to offer added-value services through their networks. At the terrestrials, however, the mood is much more positive as ultimate control of a merged entity is more likely to rest with them, due to their earlier establishment and superior political relationships. To further confuse issues, many cities have strong telecommunications factions also interested in picking up new assets as part of any restructuring operation.

Implementing the order is posing formidable problems for SARFT, as different cities also have different administrative arrangements, different management structures and different political relationships. After several months of little movement on the issue, merger remedies most recently under consideration include the closure of terrestrial and cable TV stations at the city district and county levels. Under this plan the most local of operators will no longer be allowed to engage in production or broadcast of their own programmes but will instead become relay stations only. While in principle such a move would consolidate control at the more manageable city level, SARFT faces the extremely difficult task of actually closing down the operations in thousands of districts and of keeping them closed.

Programming

The concept of an independent production industry has not been part of the Chinese media industry until recently. Restrictions on establishment of production companies and political controls over content have resulted in China's production industry developing within state structures. The result is that broadcasters remain combined broadcast and production centres, producing predominantly in-house. This has created huge overheads with substandard production exacerbated by the lack of a market-driven distribution system.

To date, only the TV drama production sector has seen significant devolution from state broadcasters and other cultural departments into independently operated companies. With a critical need for 20,000 hours of high-quality TV drama series and films each year, currently only 10,000 hours are produced in total. Of this production slate, CMM-I estimates only 20 per cent are profitable. Although the same trend is now becoming obvious in other genres, duplication of efforts across the country's numerous TV stations, inadequate distribution networks and a failure to exploit economies of scale all compound the crisis. Even after the rationalization of the last three years, there are still more than 2,000 TV stations on the mainland and wide recognition that programme and information resources have not developed with the increase in channels.

The 1998 initiative to make state enterprises answerable to market forces makes no theoretical exception for television production. The response of SARFT has been to call for reforms that 'separate TV production and broadcast' functions. Under the plan, production resources will be released into the market while the state will retain control over broadcast (a commissioning system with Chinese characteristics). The separation policy is not to include the news genre in general or news stories related to society, culture and life, but will include areas still mainly within the stations' current sphere of influence, including sports and animation. Some broadcasters have responded more swiftly than others. National Network CCTV started implementing its separation plans in April 1999 with satellite-delivered cable channels CCTV-5 (sports) and CCTV-8 (movies) acting as trial cases. The relaunch of CCTV's leading channels with a semi-niche remit is designed to facilitate a commissioning-based system.

Beijing TV, which has built up one of China's largest in-house production operations, has also announced plans to create commission-driven programming centres. Production talent is to be spun off into private production companies, which will ultimately run on a market-driven model producing for BTV and other TV stations. BTV plans to buy more programming from outside sources while broadcast schedules will be directed by ratings performance. Whatever the specific interpretation of separation in different places, the release of state production resources into the market is designed to contribute to the growth of professional TV programme production companies. But for this policy to succeed, state TV needs to overcome a large number of fundamental problems including methods of transferring state assets including studios, production equipment, edit suites and personnel into the private sector before assets can be declared independent. The biggest problem, however, is that these new independent production forces must develop their businesses according to strict business conditions in a market where extraordinary relationships with regulators and broadcasters are the key factor in securing licences, scheduled positions and advertisers.

The result is a series of half measures, companies that seem to be independent but are in fact directly or indirectly controlled by the state media. There is still far to go before a truly independent production industry develops in China and time slots for its programmes need to be created. In another sign of changing direction, before the news of 'separation' had reached smaller cities in China, newly appointed SARFT director Xu Guangchun announced his reservations about the policy. He told media leaders that separation is not what it might seem to be and cannot be considered a general policy. Xu has also re-emphasized that radio and television are mouthpieces of the Party, the government and the people, and that they are important ideological and cultural fronts. His comments reflect President Jiang Zemin's increasing pressure on propaganda chiefs that has been widely interpreted as a call to reclaim control over primary media organs.

With established subsidiaries and affiliates (particularly in the TV drama sector), a handful of major broadcasters have already advanced to the next stage and entered the stock market through subsidiary ventures that are not adequately covered by current legislation. Listing can raise much-needed capital, but also raises the question of ownership of media assets. In 1997

CCTV floated part of the capital of Wuxi Production Base in a domestic offering on the Shanghai Stock Exchange. Shanghai also leads the way in new investment structures with Oriental Pearl having listed part of its shares on the Shanghai Stock Exchange and Shanghai Paradise having established one of the first cultural stock companies. Hunan province has also listed the advertising subsidiary of its broadcast units in one of the most successful (and controversial) examples.

Moves to attract outside investment were put on hold by the State Council's Document No. 82, the same document that put a temporary halt to convergence. The document stipulated that radio and television broadcast companies as well as companies related to radio and television business are not allowed to list on the stock exchange. Even the quasi-independent industry that is currently developing should have a positive effect on creative and editorial direction, as new companies are formed and old alliances redefined. It seems likely that privatization and listings will both be employed as means to secure investment for future expansions. But the ultimate decision as to whether programming from these private companies will be broadcast will remain with the state, raising several conflicts for publicly listed companies responsible by law to their shareholders and duty-bound to maximize commercial returns.

Summary

The changing political and economic pressures under which the Chinese media system has evolved over the last forty years have resulted in a unique media model that both defines and contorts the principles behind China's socialist market economy experiment. Its successes may all be attributed to the synergies that exist between politics and commerce, and its failures to the lack of them. The effects of the lack of long-term planning at the highest levels have been compounded by the vibrant state of the Chinese economy and the strong business ethic – fast economic growth has demanded (and funded) developments in the media at a pace too fast for the political centre to control.

Continued government control over essentially commercial media operations ensures that each executive branch fights for its own corner when debate turns to ownership of its assets. Short-term considerations and jealous guarding of hard-won possessions hinders cooperation horizontally between ministries and vertically throughout the SARFT system.

In many ways, therefore, the development of the media, as with all new industries in China, has progressed in a circular manner. Each full revolution (spurred on by a combination of political and commercial factors) results in a larger and more advanced circle, but one that still inherits the imperfections of the previous one. In this way, China has built terrestrial, cable and satellite circles that do reach the people but that are poorly structured for the future and without depth.

There is still no answer to questions about private and foreign investment. These are issues that could, if suitably addressed, result in the most dynamic media boom of all time. Without answers, the Chinese media are in danger of missing out on the opportunity to tap fast-rising advertiser and consumer demand that will be further fuelled by entry into the World Trade Organization. Key production questions also remain to be solved. Will the proposed information infrastructures offer hundreds of poor-quality channels or genuine creative alternatives? Will producers be allowed to operate as independent specialist companies and will their programmes be purchased on their merits? Despite all these obstacles (and thanks to commercial funding), those responsible for producing and scheduling media content do deliver products (in the absence of independent competition) that have a real impact on the lives of their audiences.

Note

1 Hong Kong-based broadcasters, including Asia TV, CETV, Phoenix and TVB, have received local agreement for re-broadcasts on cable in some southern provinces.

3

MEANING, PRODUCTION, CONSUMPTION: THE HISTORY AND REALITY OF TELEVISION DRAMA IN CHINA[1]

Yin Hong

Politics was always destined to be the most important theme in China during the twentieth century. The radical social changes brought about by confrontations between classes, national interest, and interest groups meant that the impact of politics has been felt in almost every aspect of Chinese society, including culture. In this context, television drama emerged as a genuinely popular cultural artifact during the 1980s. Over the past forty-two years (from 1958 to 2000), television drama in China has witnessed three phases of development: the experimental period (1958–1978), the transitional period (1978–1987), and the commercial period (1987 to the present). Television was not a mass medium during the period from 1958 to 1978; neither was television drama a form of popular culture. Even as a propaganda tool, television drama was not as important as the media of press, radio and film. At that time, China had only one television station with a limited broadcast range, and a few hundred television receivers, so the only people with regular access were a very small number of government officials and senior intellectuals. As I describe below, this situation has changed greatly over the second and third phases of development.

The experimental period (1958–1978)

From 1958 – the time of the first television drama, *A Mouthful of Vegetable Pancakes* (*Yikou caibingzi*) – to 1966, approximately 180 television dramas were produced in China. Due to a lack of production facilities and technological support, these were all produced *in situ* and televised live simultaneously. They are more accurately described as televised stage drama. Most of these early dramas sought to explain the political, economic and cultural policies promulgated by the Chinese Central Party Committee and the

Chinese government. *A Mouthful of Vegetable Pancakes* used character flashbacks to relate how bitter and painful life was in the 'old society' (that is, before the founding of the People's Republic of China). In this single-episode drama a sister persuades her younger brother not to waste food by giving it to a dog. The narrative flashes back to difficult times when food was scarce and dogs belonged to the landlord class. This drama was made to promote the ideological position of the Chinese Communist Party (CCP) of 'contrasting past misery with present happiness', and in order to educate people to be frugal with their grain.

When the Cultural Revolution broke out some ten years after the first television drama was broadcast, production slumped to a virtual stop, save for propaganda purposes. Beijing Television Station did however produce *The Struggle at the Examination Centre* (*Kaochangshang de douzheng*) in 1967. This was the first television drama to use black-and-white video-recording equipment instead of direct broadcasting. In 1975, two years after the trial broadcast of colour television programmes, the first colour television drama, *The Sacred Obligation* (*Shensheng de zhize*) was broadcast, also by the Beijing Television Station. Technological developments such as this made it possible for the rapid development of television drama in China.

The transitional period (1978–1987)

When the Cultural Revolution ended, the CCP shifted its emphasis to building up the economy, instigating reform, and opening up to the outside world, as well as to speeding up the modernization drive in China. The frail economy gradually revived, providing a foundation for the development of the television industry. By the end of 1976, television programmes made by Beijing Television (BTV) could reach all the capital cities of 26 provinces, municipalities and autonomous regions, and eight stations in provincial capitals could retransmit their broadcasting signals back to Beijing. On 1 May 1978, BTV was renamed China Central Television Station (CCTV). Soon more provincial stations were established. However, the most rapid increase occurred following the 'four-level administrative' guidelines (*si ji ban*) that were instigated in 1983 in order to develop radio and television broadcasting at four levels (central, provincial, prefecture and county) and encourage local investment.[2] With the rapidly increasing demand for drama programmes and increasing access to funds other than those allocated through government channels, the Central Broadcasting Administration chose the First Annual National Television Programming Conference in 1979 to announce that television stations might produce television drama provided they had the capability. During the thirtieth anniversary year of the founding of the People's Republic (also in 1979) there was a national exhibition of television drama. This is considered to be the first major spur to domestic drama production. In 1980, 131 television dramas were produced, six times more than the previous year. In 1983, CCTV set up its China Television Drama Production Centre. Following this initiative, television drama production again doubled its output (see Table 1).

Table 3.1 Television drama production 1978–1987

Year	*(No of dramas)*
1978	8
1979	20
1980	131
1981	128
1982	227
1983	428
1984	740
1985	1300
1986	1400
1987	1500

The total output of television drama during the decade from 1978 to 1987 was thirty times that of the previous two decades from 1958 to 1978. Audiences also increased constantly, a fact that was reflected in a fall in cinema audiences after 1979. Television drama has gradually taken the place of cinema and become the most popular audio-visual narrative form.

On 5 February 1980, CCTV launched a nine-episode drama series – *Eighteen Years in the Enemy Camp* (*Diying shiba nian*), a landmark in the development of domestic television drama production in China. This was China's first television drama serial, and also its first popular serial. In comparison with previous dramas, which paid more attention to political criticism and artistic expression than to characterization, *Eighteen Years in the Enemy Camp* appealed to audiences because of its dramatic tension and excitement – sheer entertainment value!

The production of domestic drama series was influenced by productions from abroad. In late 1970, cultural products from abroad, including popular television drama series imported from the United States, Japan and Hong Kong as well as from other countries and regions, served as reference points for the transformation of the domestic product from a mere expression of political and cultural tendencies into popular entertainment. At the end of 1979, *Iron-armed Atongmu*, a children's television drama series from Japan, was broadcast by CCTV, and was soon followed by science fiction series from America. These 'entertaining dramas' were criticized – *Eighteen Years in the Enemy Camp* was even considered as an good example of 'capitalist spiritual pollution' and an American 26-episode drama, *The Garrison*, was banned half-way because of pressures imposed by political opinions. Nevertheless, their presence changed the concept of television drama; political connotations have since been removed to a great extent and more attention is paid to popular taste. On 6 May 1984, CCTV launched *Huo Yuanjia*, a martial arts (*gongfu*) series produced by Hong Kong's Asian TV Station. *Huo Yuanjia* was immediately successful, paving the way for a many more martial arts series. Later on, melodramas such as *Doubtful Blood Type* (*Xueyi*) from Japan, *Woman Slave* (*Nünu*) from Brazil, and *Slander* (*Feibang*) from Mexico, were broadcast. These too had a profound influence on family situation drama.

By the 1980s, the first decade of the reforms, the impact of television drama could not be denied. Caught in the transition from an era of 'class struggle' to a new era of economic construction, people were experiencing social turmoil as well as personal tribulations. The television dramas that had most appeal during this time were those described as 'dramas of pains' (*shanghenju*) or 'retrospective dramas' (*fansiju*), recounting the adversities of past political turmoil. The appeal of these dramas was subsequently displaced by 'reform dramas' (*gaigeju*), narratives about political and personal conflicts that were occurring during the reform period. Among these were *Times Wasted* (*Cuotuo cuiyue*) in 1982, *Snow Storm Tonight* (*Jinye you baofengxue*) in 1984, *News Revelation* (*Xinwen qishi lu*) in 1985 and *New Star* (*Xin xing*) in 1986. As well as such critical portrayals of social reality, dramas adapted from classical and modern literary works were produced: *Four Generations under the Same Roof* (*Sishi tongchang*) in 1985 (based on the novel by Lao She); *The Dream of the Red Chamber* (*Honglou meng*) in 1986 (the Qing Dynasty classic tale of decadence); *Nuerhachi* in 1986;, and *Journey to the West* (*Xiyouji*) in 1987. These opened up new topic areas for drama production.

The commercial period (1987 to the present)

The Thirteenth National Plenary Session of the Chinese Party Central Committee held in Beijing in 1987 stated that 'the Socialist economy is a kind of planned commercial economy' and the 'state should have 'macro-control' over the market, with the market guiding the production of enterprises'. Though not all of these economic policies could be applied in the media and communications industries, the impact of commercial forces began to be felt. In 1987, CCTV's revenue from its advertising operation amounted to 27 million yuan (US$3,375,000), more than twice its state allocation of funds. In 1994, its income from its advertising operations had reached 1.2 billion yuan (US$150 million), and by 1998, the figure was 13.36 billion yuan (US$1,670 million). However, the precedent had been set much earlier. In late 1980, CCTV had begun the pilot operation of its second channel, the Economic Information Channel, by means of advertising and the 'leasing' of programme time. The Shanghai Television Station also set up its Shanghai TV 2 in this manner, a model followed by many cable-television stations. The production and broadcasting of television programmes were increasingly sponsored by both domestic and foreign companies.

In 1990 the production and broadcasting of the television drama serial *Yearnings* (*Kewang*) broke new ground. The first multi-episode in-room serial ever made in China, it drew on 'television narratives' and television drama models from Hong Kong, Taiwan, Japan, and Brazil. *Yearning* was a story of the pains and joys of ordinary families. Produced by the Beijing Television Arts Centre, it was a genuine industrial product: it was made with financial support from non-state sources, and shot in a studio, utilizing artificial indoor scenes, multicamera shots, simultaneous voice recording and post-production techniques.

In 1991, the Beijing Television Art Centre also produced the series *Stories from an Editorial Office* (*Bianjibu de gushi*). Also sponsored by business enterprises, it was broadcast together with sponsors' advertisements – the first time ever for a Chinese television serial. Even more significant was the insertion of sponsors' advertising within the storyline (soft advertising). Such models opened new opportunities for the commercialization of television drama production.[3]

Forms and genres: the significance of ideology

The Chinese government has always noted the political significance and impact of television drama. The kind of drama that is promoted by the CCP and the government is that which embodies the 'socialist mainstream melody' (*shehui zhuyi zhuxuanlü*), and that, in the words of one official, seeks to

> put an end to the trend to regard the economic profit (of television drama) as more important than its social benefits, to regard enjoyment as superior to orientation, to promote historical themes over realism, farce over serious drama, long form over short form, epic themes over ordinary themes, and productions that use foreign actors to those that use locals.

The official view clearly criticizes:

> realist dramas that don't describe the courageous spirit of 'workers–peasants–soldiers' and intellectuals during the reform period in a rich and colourful manner, but instead pander to, and express, unhealthy male–female love, and use an uncritical, even licentious approach to extramarital love and 'ménages à trois' ... some television dramas pursue bizarre narratives, chase ratings, and seriously contravene history and common knowledge, thereby passing on confused values and wrong thinking to teenagers.

The Chinese government seeks to impress upon television drama workers that

> they are not only art workers. They should understand that they are Chinese Communist Party information workers first, and second television media art workers.
>
> (Ji Bingxuan 2000: 3)

In view of the emphasis paid to television drama, the General State Administration of Radio, Film and Television (SARFT) has adopted various measures to ensure that during prime time (*huangjin shijian*) CCTV and provincial level stations broadcast 'mainstream melody' dramas and reduce the amount of popular entertainment-oriented 'Royal Court' costume plays and kung fu stories. Understandably there is a conflict between governmental calls for more mainstream melody works and the commercialization and popularization of television drama. Commercialization has challenged the centrality of official ideology while the trend towards hedonist and individualist values found in entertainment fare has eroded the moral standards cherished by state ideology. Official ideology is therefore legislated into culture.

During the transitional period the vitality of television content was subject not only to governmental control and the disbursement of capital within the television industry itself, but also to the needs and preferences of the public and the critique of intellectuals. Chinese television drama expressed power relations and conflicts within these cultural formations. While emerging market forces and the state were the two primary elements that governed television drama, intellectuals involved in production acted as representatives of political power and the market. They were often the gatekeepers (*kanmenren*) of televised information, endeavouring to draw support from both to express their intellectual critique of society reality and everyday life.

Élite (*jingying*) intellectuals with a predisposition towards the elevated values of the Enlightenment tradition regularly project a miserable tirade at Chinese television drama, often focusing on the ideological substance of television drama and its aesthetic quality. They denigrate the social function of commercial television drama and its sense of mission. They criticize its lack of social responsibility, its audiences, its social function, the problem of cultural globalization, and its tendencies towards vulgarity. This kind of cultural conservatism represents a negative, even militant 'anti-marketization' stance that has represented the concerns of a section of the intellectual community towards popular television drama. There are also, however, intellectuals who embrace the common values and popularization of culture brought about by commercialization. They argue that this kind of change has allowed television drama to break away from its pedagogic and propagandist tradition, and also from its élitist aristocratic tradition. And while people ought to be vigilant about vulgarity, commercialization is indeed a revolution of some significance, one that has brought an affective element to drama.

The appearance of many historical dramas in recent years is an inevitable result of the conflicts within television culture. Officialdom, the business sector and intellectuals share a standpoint in choosing historical themes as a strategy through which to maintain and spread their influence. After all, 'History' is distanced from all the sensitive conflicts and power struggles of contemporary China. It provides a rich selection of resources and a more open narrative space. Moreover, the process of historical rewriting allows the respective social forces to construct a contemporary history that obviates the uncertainties and doubts associated with the past. History thus operates as a kind of political strategy for acquiring advantage. All kinds of ideological formations can draw upon history to kick-start a political venture.

In the majority of historical television dramas, the revolutionary history theme has been the most evident and most important phenomenon of the expression of state ideology. Each significant historical event since the establishment of the CCP has been turned into a television adaptation. Influential characters in modern Chinese history, especially those involved in the building of the CCP, are prime subject matter for historical dramas (Chu, this volume).

By the end of the 1990s market forces resulted in many comedic recreations of historical themes (*xishuo lishi*). The themes of these dramas had no direct relationship with current Chinese political reality. *Xishuo Qianlong* and *Huanzhu gege* were representative of this genre. *Princess Huanzhu* attracted a 42 per cent plus rating in Shanghai.[4] This drama not only earned sizeable broadcast rights revenue per episode, but many stations also inserted advertisements, some of the advertising time exceeding the actual broadcast time of the serial. This popularity demonstrated that *xishuo lishi* serials had a definite consumer market in China. In these serials history is invented and played around with. The concept is a kind of game, but one that is an outlet for people's feelings and emotions. Moreover, *xishuo lishi* serials have not only proved popular in China, but were also well received in Taiwan, Hong Kong, Singapore and other places where Chinese culture is well established.

Historical dramas provided intellectuals with a means of expression and certain rhetorical strategies. Recent examples are *Prime Minister Liu Luoguo* (*Zaixiang Liu Luoguo*) in 1996; *Yongzheng Dynasty* (*Yongzheng wangchao*) in 1998; and *The Eloquent Ji Shaolan* (*Tongzui tieya Ji Shaolan*) in 2001. Even though they made use of popular narrative and comedy genre formats, the substance of these works was historical characterization and historical events. They not only recalled history, they also simulated history.

For example, the forty-four-episode serial *Yongzheng Dynasty*, produced by Beijing Tongdao Cultural Development Co., used more than a hundred characters in over more than 600 scenes to narrate the political struggles in the Qing Dynasty from the period of Kangxi to Yongzheng. It drew upon historical allegories and historical rewritings to explore the history and power relations of contemporary Chinese society. Using the past to mirror the present, and drawing upon the past to satirize the present are complementary historiographical traditions in China. These television dramas clearly inherit this intellectual tradition: they are not a rewriting of existing historical accounts as such, but their significance lies in the fact that we can shed light on the present by reviewing the past.

If we can conclude that historical dramas embody the strategies of various social forces, then the appearance of genres can be viewed as the result of drama's commercialization. The trend towards genres began with *Yearnings* (*Kewang*) in 1990. The ethical concerns of the family were represented by this groundbreaking production as well as in *At the Foot of the City Walls* (*Huangcheng gen*) in 1992; *Chronicles of the Capital* (*Jingdu jishi*) in 1993; and *The Love of Family Life* (*Ernü qingchang*) in 1997. Romantic dramas were represented by *I Love You Absolutely* (*Ai ni mei shangliang*) in 1993; *Live It to the Limit* (*Guo ba yin*) in 1994; *The Sun Rises in the East – in the West it Rains* (*Dongbian richu xibian yu*) in 1995; and *Holding hands* (*Qianshou*) in 1999. The popular genre of urban business dramas began with *Miss PR* (*Gongguan xiaojie*) in [1990].

Miss PR is a story about the professional and romantic adventures of a Hong Kong girl returning to discover her cultural roots in the Guangdong hinterland. It attracted ratings of 52.76, and in some regions attracted a high-watermark of 90.78 (Cai Xiang 1993: 2–7). Using a standard conflict-resolution formula, these popular dramas describe social contradictions and power struggles, and the strategies that people use to survive and learn through experience. The outcome is generally that good people come up trumps and the 'bad guys' get their due.[5]

China's first situation comedy *I Love My Family* (1995) drew upon the success of *Stories From an Editorial Office* some four years earlier. Although the popular sitcom format was an imported model, its narrative strategy was localized. This is evident in its use of traditional forms of comedy, and localized comic talk, its use of actors and stars familiar to people, and the insertion of comedy skit routines (*xiaopin*). In re-creating and making fun of people's fantasies and embarrassing situations, and by using comic behaviour to make light of people's frustrations, expectations, and antagonisms, these everyday secular comedies became very popular. However, given the tendency of many of these comedies to become vulgar in the pursuit of commercial acceptance, they also received their share of critical condemnation.

Production, exchange and broadcast: the production system

Since the 1980s funding for television drama has increasingly come from non-government sources, from enterprises and businesses, and even from overseas and Hong Kong. There are now more non-television production companies (companies not principally engaged in television production) and the government has reduced its direct control over production. This does not mean that television drama production is an autonomous enterprise. Television drama production still proceeds under government macro-control.

The Chinese government has always maintained that television drama is an ideological enterprise for which it must provide guidance, management and supervision. Four aspects of the government's recent 'strengthening of management' initiative are pertinent here

The first is that a television drama production permit system was instituted on 1 June 1986. Any organization wanting to produce drama had to gain a permit from the Ministry of Film Radio and Television (later SARFT). There were two classifications of these permits: long-term and temporary permits. Production units that receive such permits are effectively regulated. There are approximately 150 of the first category and 400 of the second category of permit-holder. The second area of strengthening management concerns lies in the actual policing of regulations. Before production can begin, the production unit must report the topic to the Chinese Television Arts Committee for clearance. These regulatory bureaux decide what may proceed at any given time according to the current political terrain and certain approved drama topics. The third area is distribution supervision; television stations in China are all state-run official organizations and foreign investment is not allowed. Private commercial stations are also not allowed. So the distribution and broadcast of television drama has to navigate the supervision of local CCP propaganda departments. Fourth, broadcasting itself is monitored. Today SARFT, CCTV and provincial-level stations have television inspection procedures. When programmes exhibit 'political problems' they can be officially terminated. These measures ensure that production and circulation of programming accords with the political interests of the state.

Television drama production still exhibits a greater degree of freedom and flexibility than cinema, which is subject to the administrative centralization of state power. The regulation of television drama is itself continually adapting to the needs of market development. For example, non-television companies can produce television drama, accept non-state funding, accept investment from foreign and overseas enterprises as well as joint funding arrangements, and allow regional executive branches to monitor without incurring centralized censorship inspection. These relatively relaxed administrative controls make the production of television drama appear a more pluralistic undertaking.

The regulation of television drama production includes the main central and regional drama production organizations – television stations and television drama production centres – which are directly administered by the SARFT. This also includes all state-run cultural industries, Beijing Cultural Audiovisual Publishing Co., Central North Television Arts Company and the like. It also includes drama production units within movie production studios. In addition, there are now many quasi-government television drama production enterprises, such as the Beijing Tongdao Cultural Development Company, which produced *Yongzheng wangchao*.

Funding comes from both public and private sources. Central and local governments have always needed propaganda and have funds available for designated topics. The mainstream melody dramas, however, have no real market clout. By the end of the 1990s the number of purely state-funded dramas had diminished, replaced by a model whereby government and non-government sources contribute to production. A second source of finance is provided by enterprises wanting to raise their exposure and produce an indirect advertising effect by either fully supporting or partially supporting production. The name of the enterprise is of course noted in the production credits. This was the main source of revenue during the early 1990s. As advertising began to gain credibility and competition intensified, this form of backing diminished. A third avenue of investment is the inflow of direct capital in the form of loans from banks or from business. Repayment is made after the drama is broadcast and advertising revenue is secured. By the end of the 1990s this had become the main source of funding. We can distinguish a shift from government funding to enterprise funding, and finally to direct commercialization.

Within this change in funding models there was a corresponding shift in how dramas were distributed. In the early period, television stations would produce their own dramas through their associated production unit and subsequently exchange this with the product of other stations. In February 1992 CCTV paid 3.5 million RMB (yuan) (US$437,500) to buy the rights to the forty-episode melodrama *I Love you Absolutely*, creating a precedent in the use of hard currency as an exchange mechanism. At the same time, regional stations were utilizing another exchange mechanism: money from advertising was used to support production and even to garner profit. Production companies would work together with advertising companies to provide a package of drama and pre-allotted advertising space, which they would then on-sell to the stations. A designated amount of advertising revenue would thus return to the production unit rather than go directly to the broadcaster. This became the dominant mode of distribution during the 1990s, best illustrated by the Northern China Television Arts Centre's *Chronicles of the City* (*Jingdu jishi*). Every episode of this long-running serial included a 90-second space of advertising that was on-sold as it was broadcast to 137 television stations. From 1996 the Beijing Television

Drama Arts Centre produced more than 300 episodes of television drama in a special time slot (Yang Jun 1999). The popularity of this special time slot brings in advertising revenue. By the end of the decade this practice was diminishing as stations began to come to terms with market principles and directly purchase broadcast rights. Television drama can be seen here as a forerunner in promoting market practices within the industry, even at a time when most television production was still produced and broadcast in-house.

When television drama began to separate broadcasting and production, it was still not operating on a level playing field, due to certain monopolies with the sellers having the advantage. Drama production departments were basically losing money. Later on, following the increase in numbers of television stations and the increase in channels and the competition for advertising, television stations needed quality drama to ensure advertising profits and they were forced into buying dramas according to market principles. From 1986 there were television festivals held at Shanghai and Sichuan and later there was a special television week in Beijing. In September 1996 the then Ministry of Film Radio and Television (MRFT) formally instituted the National Domestic Television Programme Exhibition Trade Symposium, in which television drama became the principal form of programme traded.

Due to this commercialization the number of television dramas has gradually increased during the 1990s with the number topping 10,000 episodes annually by 2000. But this scenario is far from satisfactory. Television programming is subdivided across four levels (central, provincial, local, and prefecture) and these four levels each have terrestrial and cable delivers, with one station often broadcasting on more than one channel. China is therefore the biggest country market for the consumption of television drama. If an average channel broadcasts an average of seven hours every day there are estimated to be more than 20,000 hours of programming per year. Every year there is a demand for more than 7,300,000 hours of programming, and even if some programmes are broadcast twice, there is still a huge demand for content. However, in 1994, China only had the capacity to produce 280,000 hours of programming. This meant that the daily production of programming for each station was less than 2.6 hours. The duplication of television programming is a clear consequence of the scarcity of production resources (China Broadcasting Year Book 1996: 319) There has, unsurprisingly in this situation, been a trend to buy outside programmes. China imports somewhere between 10, 000 and 20,000 hours of programming annually (World Radio and TV 1995: 2).

From 1984 local and regional stations started importing programming from outside China with the result that a restriction of 15 per cent was imposed on the amount of foreign content that could be broadcast in prime time (6–10 p.m.). Foreign programming was not allowed to constitute more than a third of content on cable stations. There is also a restriction of sixty on the number of foreign television dramas that can be imported, with each foreign drama being limited to thirty hours (although this has now been reduced to twenty) with a total number of hours per year between 1,200 and 1,800. In fact, the total number of foreign content series is 3,000; more than half of those offered on viewer schedules.

The consumption of television drama has increased rapidly due to the increase in channels. Market research has indicated that television drama rates second only to news in overall popularity, and its influence far exceeds that of cinema, novels, drama and other narrative forms. In contrast to Western models, television drama in China is not merely soap opera, or situation comedy. It is *the* essential purveyor of 'narratives of events' and 'stories of consumption'. Television drama has produced a complex relationship across the practices of cultural consumption and family lifestyles. It also carries a high level of public service function, which echoes its early beginnings but also moves it forward into the media markets of the twenty-first century.

Notes

1 Translated by Michael Keane and Bao Jiannü. This paper is part of a much longer manuscript. We regret that for reasons of space we have not been able to include discussions of well-known serials such as *Beijingers in New York* (*Beijingren zai NiuYue*) and *The Water Margin* (*Shuihuzhuan*).

2 By 1985 there were 172 television stations at city and county levels, and the number of television broadcasting and transmission station also increased rapidly up to more than 12,000. Meanwhile, the number of television receivers had grown quickly. By 1979 there had been 4.85 million television sets all across the country. In 1982, the number soared to 27.61 million, and by 1987 there were 120 million with 47.8 per cent of Chinese families owning their own television sets. By July 1987, the audience was reckoned to be 600 million or 56 per cent of the country's population, up from 80 million in 1978.

3 For a detailed discussion of *Stories from an Editorial Office* and other serials mentioned in this chapter see Keane 2001d.

4 This is a prince-and-the-pauper scenario with an extremely pretty and rambunctious princess!

5 For a analysis of some of these genre television serials see Keane (2001a).

SECTION 2
CINEMA AND TELEVISION

Marketing Strategies, Hybridity, and Survival

4

THE CONSUMPTION OF CINEMA IN CONTEMPORARY CHINA

Yingchi Chu

Introduction

With China's entry into the World Trade Organization (WTO) imminent, fears for the film industry are intensifying. At the June 1999 Film and Literature Conference in Chengdu in Sichuan Province, film director Chen Kaige declared that China's film industry is at the crossroads between survival and collapse (Lu [Shaoyang] 2000: 1). Since 1995, ten imported Hollywood films have taken 60 per cent of China's annual box-office revenue. With China's entry into the WTO, the number of Hollywood 'blockbusters' will double. As a consequence, Chen fears the domestic industry will be destroyed within one or two decades.

Chen's concern is widely shared in China. Between 1999 and 2000 a group of young Shanghai film-makers proposed a production strategy to assist the industry in overcoming its crisis (Ma [Ning] 2000: 4–15). They suggested that the industry should develop a 'new mainstream cinema' (*xin zhuliu dianying*) – a cinema with strong local content, targeting specific markets to seek a quick return. Desperately seeking film consumers, Ermei Film Corporation in Central China reduced its movie ticket prices by two-thirds from November 2000. Cinema theatres in central, southern and northern China have followed the trend to boost the number of movie-goers.

Low consumption of domestic cinema has been a major concern for the Chinese industry since the mid-1980s. Within two decades movie attendances decreased from 34 billion spectators in 1980 to 4.5 billion in 1999 (*Yangcheng wanbao*, 17 December 2000). The anxiety for the future of the industry has resulted in a number of policies to prevent the film market from further decline. In 1993 the MRFT proposed to modify the structure of the industry from the central controlled model to one with more local input. As a result, the centralized China Film Distribution and Exhibition Company (later China Film Corporation) relinquished control over domestic film distribution. Distributors at province and city level were invited to trade directly with the state's sixteen feature film studios. The change in film distribution opened up competition in the market. For the first time in four decades, China's film studios faced market challenge. In 1995 it was decided to import ten Hollywood films annually in a revenue-sharing arrangement to stir up the market[1] and in 1997 production companies, other than the state-owned studios, were allowed to produce feature films.

The key events behind the evolution of the Chinese film industry during the past two decades were the 'open door policy' and the economic reforms. The consequent liberalizations allowed access to more foreign culture, including Hollywood and Hong Kong blockbusters, which were mainly consumed in video and video compact disk format. Throughout the 1980s and 1990s, movie-goers have been encouraged by the relatively easy access to video and VCD to demand cheaper cinema entry prices and more diverse screenings. More generally, the economic reforms contributed to improved living standards, enabling people to participate in a variety of types of entertainment: karaoke, cable and satellite television, computer games and the Internet. Meanwhile, in addition to these competitors, film piracy has proved an incurable headache for the industry.

The Chinese film industry has faced serious market competition and crisis since the late 1980s. Yet, by the end of 2000, the industry was still not operating as a fully commercial enterprise. The factor that hinders the industry from seeking maximum profits in the audiovisual marketplace is the traditional Communist conception of the role of cinema. The Chinese Communist Party (CCP) inherited Lenin's conviction that cinema is the most important art form. Since 1950, cinema has been used mainly as a propaganda tool for the CCP's one-party state. Economic reform in the film industry has therefore progressed more slowly than reforms in most agricultural and industrial areas. On the eve of China's entry to the WTO, the film industry continues to confront the complex issue of how to resolve the relationship between the inherited Leninist view of cinema and the increasingly competitive international and domestic film markets.

Film policy

> Why is it that the more we reform, the fewer film audiences we have? We know what our leaders want from a film, but we don't know what the market wants.
>
> Film director Zhang Jianya, 27 December 2000

Any attempt to understand Chinese cinema must start from film policy. In China, policy documents include statements and regulations issued by the CCP's Central Committee, the State Council, the Ministry of Propaganda, the Ministry of Culture, the Film Bureau, the General State Administration of Radio, Film and Television (SARFT), specially constituted 'leading groups', as well as speeches and talks from Party leaders. Policies are formulated within the remit of political influence rather than through economic concern for the industry. During the 1980s and 1990s, despite political influence remaining strong, the formulation of policy has demonstrated a significant shift towards market economics.

During the first three decades after the establishment of the People's Republic of China in 1949, film policy was developed from the substance of Mao Zedong's *Talks at the Yan'an Forum* (1942) – the guiding principle for works in art and literature. The creation of worker–peasant–soldier (*gong–nong–bing*) images, *targeted at* workers, peasants and soldiers was the aim of artistic practice. The film industry was ideologically influenced by CCP dogma and economically funded by the government. In accordance with the CCP's guidelines (administered through the Propaganda Department), the Film Bureau under the Ministry of Culture made policies relating to all areas of production, from script development and production management to aesthetic values and technical competence. The Bureau was also responsible for developing an annual plan to regulate choice of narrative subject, the cost of production, the areas of distribution and exhibition schedules. Moreover, each film studio, distribution agency and cinema theatre had its own Party Secretary who exercised ideological control, ranging from the implementation of policy to the proper distribution of a film in the market.

During the Maoist period the Chinese film industry had existed primarily to leverage the maximum use of film as a tool of mass education, with scarce priority given to profit. The open-door policy and economic reforms instituted under Deng Xiaoping during the early 1980s brought change. In 1984 the government withdrew its financial backing from the state-owned film studios, but the CCP, through the Propaganda Department, retained its control over script selection, production quantity and censorship. Film studios were required to balance their own budgets and assume responsibility for profits and loss. Consequently, a contract system centred on producer and director was developed in a few studios to encourage the contractor to seek financial investment outside the studio. These initiatives did not stave off the increasing competition from other media markets, in particular television, and the escalating cost of production.

By the early 1990s, the film industry was facing a financial crisis. In 1992, box-office receipts totalled 1.99 billion RMB (yuan) (0.25 billion $US) a decrease of 470 million RMB (58.75 $US) from the previous year. Audience attendances decreased from 14.39 billion in 1991 to 10.55 billion in 1992.

Six of the sixteen feature film studios went bankrupt (Ni 1994: 2). In accordance with Deng Xiaoping's success in formally establishing a 'socialist market economy' in 1992, the government decided to push the industry a further step into the market economy. In 1993, the Ministry of Radio, Film and Television (MRFT, now SARFT) issued the first proposal for change in the state monopoly system (MRFT policy document No. 3, 1993) The document encouraged studios to sell their products individually to distribution agencies at province or city level. It also devolved the regulation of ticket prices to local government.

Although the MRFT document had the undesired effect of creating regional monopolies in film distribution, it was nonetheless a first significant step towards a workable film market model since the reforms were launched in the industry in 1984. In 1995, ten big-budget Hollywood films were imported through the revenue-sharing arrangement. The Mainland Chinese market opened up for competition, and provincial and city film corporations were encouraged to adopt a similar profit-sharing system. In the same year, the Film Bureau introduced another regulation (MRFT No. 1, 1995) to allow thirteen film studios at province and city level other than the original sixteen feature film studios to produce feature films. It also invited individuals and non-state enterprises to participate in investment. If their investment was over 70 per cent, investors then had rights to be co-producer after gaining permission from the Film Bureau. In 1996 this was modified to 30 per cent (MRFT No. 735, 1996) in order to attract more investors. In 1997 another invitation was issued when the Government agreed to grant feature film production licences to television stations and film studios at district level.

These competition initiatives did not mean that the CCP's attitude towards cinema as an ideological apparatus had changed. After the withdrawal of financial backing to studios in 1984, the 'self-responsibility' system in production brought a massive increase in genre films, which in turn contributed to a decrease in the number of didactic films. The genre films, mainly martial arts movies and thrillers, caused official concern for the 'imbalance' between state promotions and commercial entertainments. In 1987, the guiding principle of 'developing the mainstream melody, promoting diversity' (*hongyang zhuxuan lü, tichang duoyang hua*) was formulated at the National Conference for Cinematic Production in relation to audiovisual production (*Dianying tongxu* 1989; Keane 1999: 254) But it was not until 1989, after the student democracy movement clash with government troops in Tiananmen Square, that this principle became the official mandate. In effect the principle refers to a dialectic relationship being established between the 'mainstream melody' – the works that reflect an approved version of events, and the CCP's promise of a more open cultural sphere. In 1990, at an annual art creation meeting, Li Ruihuan, member of the Standing Committee of the Politburo, suggested that a

National Film Development Fund be established to guarantee the correct political ideology in Chinese films,

> ... if we cannot solve the problem of film being led by profit, then we will not be able to regard film's social impacts as our first priority. The result will definitely be to reduce the educational function of film.
>
> (Lin 1993: 37)

Following Li's speech, the National Film Development Special Fund was established in 1991. The number of ' mainstream melody' films (*zhuxuan lü dianying*) increased from eight in 1991 to nineteen in 1992 and 1994 (Lin 1993: 37). Throughout the 1990s the Government heavily promoted the 'political orientation: art for socialism and for the people' (*wei shehui zhuyi fuwu, wei renmin fuwu*) policy and the 'double hundred' policy ('Let a hundred flowers blossom and a hundred schools of thought contend') policy. Thirty of the annual quota of 150 domestic film productions must be 'mainstream melody' film productions (MRFT No. 3, 1993). In 1994 the committee of the National Film Development Special Funds introduced three ways for accessing money: borrowing loans, receiving rewards and gaining financial assistance. In 1995, MRFT stipulated that no less than 15 per cent of total film distribution and screen time should be reserved for 'mainstream melody' films. In 1996, at the Changsha meeting, MRFT proposed a '9550 project' (*9550 gongcheng*) – aiming at producing ten 'high quality' films (*jingpin*) between 1996 and 2000. To assist the industry in this task, MRFT set up five subsidy regulations, including a requirement that no less than 3 per cent of the revenue from television advertising should be contributed to 'mainstream melody' productions (MRFT No. 125, 1996). According to a recent estimate, the government now invests more than one hundred million RMB per annum in 'mainstream melody' productions, one-third of the total public investment in China's film production (Wang [Gengnian] 2000: 7) In 2001 the Government's input will further increase. However, despite the guarantees set up for the 'mainstream melody' films, no policies have yet managed to halt the decline of the film industry as a whole.

In the transition from a planned economy model towards a market economy model, China's film policy has continued to prioritize cinema as an ideological apparatus more than as a commercial enterprise. Minimal state intervention in the industry is still a long way off. Although the market has opened up, sound market models have yet to be established. In several areas the model of a centralized planned economy remains. The Film Bureau continues to formulate annual plans for production quantity and film subject, and involves itself with script selection and supervision. A sustainable film industry can not survive, however, within the tensions between official designs and movie-goers' preferences.

Film industry

> I don't want to make films any more. Half of our financial investments can not be returned. Our job is to make films, and yet our major source of income is not from films.
>
> (Managing director Zhang Zhaotong, Fujian Film Studio, 27 December 2000)

Economic reform has delivered a series of changes in the ways that cinema is produced and consumed. Prior to 1984 the Chinese film industry operated under monopoly state control. The government bore all costs: expenditure in production and distribution, exhibition maintenance and salaries. Each studio was assigned an annual production target by the Film Bureau, and each was expected to complete the task accordingly. China Film (Distribution and Exhibition) purchased product from the studios at a fixed price, which was passed to province distributors who in turn passed it on to the lower levels of city, district or county. These distribution and exhibition policies ensured that even remote areas could expect at least some exposure to cinema. Meanwhile, the importation of foreign movies and other domestic cultural products was restricted to allow domestic cinema free rein as the main popular entertainment for China.

The state's partial withdrawal has forced the industry to struggle in the unknown territory of a commodity economy. The SARFT and the Propaganda Department maintain a level of control over production quotas and subject selection, and intervene in distribution and exhibition. Meanwhile, studios have been left with investment shortages, outdated equipment and overemployment. The market is indeed more 'open' than during the period when China Film Distribution and Exhibition was the sole distributor prior to 1993. However, regional and provincial monopolies have been quickly established and therefore problems of a single or limited distribution channel(s) remain. Box office receipts are manipulated against the interests of the studios. Cinemas obey Government directives to screen the 'mainstream melody films' and exhibitors rely on foreign films for profit. The remaining domestic films are either screened in the 'leftover' time slots or stored for later, if at all. Outside the cinema, a copy of the pirated film on VCD is cheaper than a ticket for the movie screened inside.

Chinese film production now relies on three major financial sources: national film development funds, investment from enterprises and individuals, and overseas investment. Currently about 20 to 30 per cent of films are annually funded by national film development funds. They tend to be high-budget productions. In 1999, the government invested a total of 87.05 million RMB in the film industry, of which 54.51 million RMB was in production (Li [Shi] 2000: 1). As a publicly funded film is privileged in publicity, distribution and exhibition; the return profit from the film is usually higher than that of an average entertainment film (*yule pian*); for an average 'mainstream melody' film 190 copies are sold in contrast to 130 copies for an entertainment movie (Ni 1994: 140). The more successful mainstream melody films such as *Zhou Enlai* (1991), *Kaiguo dadian* (*Founding Ceremony of the People's Republic*) (1989), and *Jiao Yulu* (1990) have all sold more than 500 copies.

Between 70 and 80 per cent of Mainland China films rely on investment by state and non-state enterprises, and by individuals. These investors are the major producers of genre films. It was not until the early 1990s that this form of 'sponsorship' was acknowledged and encouraged as a major force in film production (Lin 1993: 40). Investors therefore have to work within the studio system and annual production quotas (*canbiao*). Film studios receive 40 per cent of a movie's gross profits, while the investors and major film-makers share the remaining 60 per cent (Ni 1994: 82).

Hong Kong, Taiwan and other foreign interests are not major backers of Mainland Chinese films. However, these investments do add up to more than a third of China's total investment in domestic film (Lin 1993: 39). Their impact is also felt in the international arena. This can mean that films financed by overseas investors can 'represent' Chinese cinema outside China, even though they may be banned, poorly distributed, or unpopular in China itself. In 1979 the Government established the China Film Co-production Company. By the early 1990s the number of co-productions increased to one-third of total domestic output. In 1994 (after an incident when a co-produced film, *The Blue Kite*, was screened in Japan without the Chinese Government's clearance) tough regulations were introduced. Post-production was to be completed in China and, apart from the director, scriptwriter, and cinematographer, 50 per cent of the major actors should be residents of Mainland China (MRFT documents 1994, 1996). The number of co-productions has subsequently decreased.

Although Government policy allows for a number of distribution mechanisms, a system of local monopoly (*maiduan*) remains popular. Film distribution across administrative regions is still rare. Developed in the planned economy, distribution systems suffer from outmoded management, excessive numbers of employees and too many overlapping levels of organization. In 1998, Liaoning Film Distribution reduced employees from 1300 to 180. This is regarded as the most significant recent event in the distribution sector. Lack of distribution channels poses yet another problem. Most cities have a single state-run distribution channel, providing a limited selection of films. Moreover, the majority of China's 5,000 cinema theatres are one-screen houses equipped with the old screen projectors. In a country with a population of more than 1.2 billion, fewer than two hundred films are distributed each year. In the Hong Kong Special Administrative Region (SAR) the population is only six million but twice this number of the films are distributed (Mao 2000: 3).

Table 4.1 China Film Productions 1980–1999

1980	83	1990	134
1981	105	1991	130
1982	114	1992	167
1983	127	1993	151
1984	143	1994	148
1985	127	1995	146
1986	125	1996	107
1987	146	1997	88
1988	158	1998	82
1989	136	1999	102

Note: This table has been put together from several sources: the 1980–86 figures are from David Clark (1987: 186); the 1987–91 figures are from Ni Zhen (1994: 165); and the 1992–99 figures are from *Film Biweekly*, Vol. 552 (2000), p. 60.

Changes in distribution and exhibition during the 1990s have actually accelerated the decline of the whole system. In recent years the industry has moved towards vertical integration; between production, distribution and exhibition. Film distribution agencies such as China Film Cooperation, Beijing Forbidden Film City Corporation, Ermei Film Corporation and Shanghai Film Corporation are increasingly interdependent. In 1997, the nation's first limited film company run by the Government organizations was established, the Beijing Forbidden City Film Corporation; it includes the Beijing Film Corporation, the Beijing Film Television Company, the Beijing Culture Bureau, and the Beijing Radio and Television Bureau. It incorporates a chain of production, distribution and exhibition windows. In central China, another such chain was established in 1998, the Ermei Film Corporation; it consists of the Ermei Film Studio, Chengdu Film Distribution and the Chengdu Huaxie Exhibition chain. In August 2000, the Xian Film Corporation was established in response to the Government's call in July 2000 for state-owned film distribution and exhibition to be transformed into shareholding companies. It is the first joint-stock film company with 58 per cent of its assets state-owned, and 42 per cent held by private investors. Its members include the Xian Film Studio and the Shanghai Xiyu Corporation (*Renmin ribao* 17 Aug 2000). Similar limited corporations are also now developing in Tianjin. The old one-screen houses are now in the process of converting into multiscreen complexes with food and first-class amenities. Compact cinemas with foreign facilities and good quality audiovisual equipment have emerged in Changsha, Wuhan, Kunming, Shanghai, Beijing, Guangzhou, Nanjing and other major cities.

On the eve of China's entry to the WTO, the industry is anxious about Hollywood's incursions. There is a strong desire amongst professional film-makers and business people for a sound industry structure to be established promptly to halt the low consumption of domestic films, and to combat American blockbusters.

Mainstream films

> Whether we can make the 70 per cent entertainment films carry out the task of promoting the Socialist ideology is a crucial question in the transformation of the industry system.
>
> (Film scholar Ni Zhen 1994: 17)

Though Hollywood and Hong Kong blockbusters have shared up to half of China's box-office revenue since 1995, domestic films are the mainstream products in terms of quantity. Most cinemas in China exhibit mainly Mainland films, in no small part due to a regulation that no less than 75 per cent of the total screen time should be reserved for the domestic films.

Both traditional aesthetic values *wenyi zaidao* (the function of literature is to convey the Dao) and modern political mandates (art for socialism and the people), influence Chinese films. Within these twin frames of reference, they are identified and categorized as didactic cinema (*jiaohua dianying*), entertainment cinema (*yule dianying*) and a combination of didactic and entertainment cinema (*jiaole heyi dianying*). After four decades of politicized didactic cinema, economic reform provided an opportunity for the Chinese film-makers to develop entertainment cinema or make genre films. By the late 1980s more than 40 per cent of the cinematic domestic product was made up of thrillers based on the martial arts (Teng 1989: 2). The Government's demands for more pedagogic content have to take into account the fact that, in a consumer market, cinema has to contain sufficient entertainment value to assure its long-term, post-subsidy survival. The ultimate and popular criteria that the CCP, critics, and society use in their evaluation of a film are its ideological, artistic and entertainment values (*sanxing tongyi*) – though the order of priority of the three values varies!

Since 1950 the Film Bureau's annual production plan has been based on themes and subjects which are formulated in direct response to contemporary socio-political agendas. The Bureau has tended to focus on two subject areas, revolutionary history and socialist realism. Both are deployed to promote government policies. In the late 1980s and early 1990s, 'mainstream melody' films were mainly revolutionary history and war films. There was a need to reinforce social memory of the CCP's contribution to the founding of the People's Republic, in order to boost society's confidence in the Party during a period of economic transition. As most studios were on the edge of financial bankruptcy, state support was necessary to underwrite the high costs associated with high-quality historical war films. Traditionally films are made to coincide with celebrations: the anniversaries of the Communist Party, of the founding of the People's Republic or of the People's Liberation Army; as well as to promote particular political movements or policies. In the late 1980s and early 1990s, a number of big-budget historical war films were made to celebrate the fortieth anniversary of the People's Republic in 1989 and the seventieth anniversary of the Communist Party in 1991. These included *Weiwei kunlun* (*The Towering Kunlun Mountains* I and II) in 1988; *Gongheguo buhui wangji* (*The Republic Will Never Forget*) in 1988; *Dajue zhan* (*The Decisive Engagements* I, II and III) in 1989; *Kaitian pidi* (*The Creation of Heaven and Earth*) in 1991; and *Jinggang shan* (*Jinggang Mountains*) in 1993.

High-profile Communist leaders Mao Zedong, Zhu De, Zhou Enlai, Liu Shaoqi, Peng Dehuai, Lin Biao and Deng Xiaoping have all 'starred' in recent revolutionary dramas. This is quite different from earlier films that focused on lower-rank officers and soldiers: *Nanzheng beizhan* (*From Victory to Victory*) in 1952; *Dong cunrui* (*Dong Cunrui*) in 1955; *Xiaobing zhangga* (*Zhangga a Boy Soldier*) in 1964; *Shanshan de hongxing* (*A Sparking Red Star*) in 1974; and *Ah! Yaolan* (*Ah! Cradle*) in 1979. Newer films use historical footage to present an 'objective' perspective, while differences between the Communists and the Nationalists are presented through the narrative strategy *bi* (contrast). The contrast is generally drawn between Mao Zedong (CCP leader) and Jiang Jieshi (Nationalist Generalissimo), emphasizing their different ways in dealing with their children, colleagues and followers. This is seen particularly in the 1989 film *Kaiguo dadian* (*Founding Ceremony of the People's Republic*). Biopics of Communist leaders now pay attention to human characteristics instead of revolutionary spirits: *Pengda jiangjun* (*General Peng*) (1988); *Mao Zedong de gushi* (*Story of Mao Zedong*) (1990); *Zhou Enlai* (*Zhou Enlai*) (1991); *Liu Shaoqi de sishi si tian* (*Liu Shaoqi's last forty-four days*) (1991). The first time in history that the public watched an image of Mao Zedong kissing his wife He Zizhen was in *Jingsha shuipuo* (*Long March*) (1995).

Hollywood films have raised the expectations of the mainland moviegoers for high production values. This forces 'mainstream melody' filmmakers to be more aware of production values and visual effects. *Kong fansen* (*Kong Fansen*) (1996) and *Hong hegu* (*Red River Valley*) (1996) use a spectacular Tibetan landscape of snowy mountains, the vast blue sky, mighty eagles, monasteries and lakes to produce their natural glamour. Ranked 'number one' in box-office revenue in 2000, the anti-corruption film *Shengsi xuanze* (*Choice Between Life and Death*) (2000) tells the story of a Communist Party member, Mayor Li Hongzhe, who is determined to fight against the corruption that involves his wife, former colleagues and senior Party members. It is no secret that its high box-office record is partly due to the 'order' that spectators are organized (usually through the workplace) and given free entrance tickets. However, the film's high production values, narrative development, and local, contemporary political comment also contributed to its box-office supremacy over imported Hollywood films.

During the 1990s, entertainment cinema also moved closer to mainstream cultural and political ideology. Zhang Yimou's *Yige dou buneng shao* (*Not One Less*) (1998) portrays a young girl's leadership in the face of a failing school system for the rural poor. Ye Daying's two high-budget revolutionary melodramas *Hong yingtao* (*Red Cherry*) (1995) and *Hongse nianren* (*A Time to Remember*) (1998) are star-studded films with high production values that yet reinforce images of Communists who sacrifice love and families in pursuit of their political ideals. *Likai Lei Feng de rizhi* (*The Days Since Lei Feng Left Us*) (1997) is a story about the former colleague of the model soldier Lei Feng who was with him when he died in a truck accident. The film traces the protagonist's personal goal in responding to the national campaign of 'learning from Lei Feng'. The film uses the idea of a personal goal to reinforce the 'public' nature of private ideals, and the political ideology of 'serving the people' that the CCP has promoted for decades. Further, mainstream political–cultural ideologies of patriotism, anti-materialism and human feelings are expressed in recent popular and critically acclaimed films such as Feng Xiaogang's comedies *Jiafang yifang* (*Party A, Party B*) (1998), and Zhang Yang's urban series *Aiqing mala tang* (*Spicy Love Soup*) (1998).

Foreign expansion?

> 'Allowing' the import of twenty foreign films per year under the [WTO] agreement does not mean we 'must' import twenty foreign films.
>
> (Director of Film Bureau, Liu Jianzhong, 29 December 2000)

To prepare for the increasing number of Hollywood blockbusters in the domestic market after China's entry into the WTO, SARFT has planned further reforms in the industry. China will improve its cinema facilities, develop online ticket sales and establish digital film groups (*Xinhua News*, 8 September 2000). SARFT also issued a document, *Suggestions on Deepening Reform of the Film Sector*, to call for foreign and domestic non-state-owned investment. Currently foreign investors are forbidden from holding controlling stakes and operational rights in jointly funded movie theatre regulations. The document recommends relaxation of the tight controls over foreign investment by establishing a shareholding system to allow foreign capital into domestic film production, cinema construction, and technology upgrading to increase the competitiveness of the Chinese movie industry.

The SARFT document opens up another opportunity for foreign investors in China. In 1998 foreign funds began to access China's film market through co-funded projects. America and Hong Kong investors have participated in cinema construction through new joint-venture cinemas in Kunming, Changsha, Chongqing and Wuhan along the Yangze River. In

January 2001, the construction of a sixth jointly funded foreign-Chinese movie theatre in Shanghai will begin. In cooperation with the Shanghai Film and TV Group, Kodak CinemaWorld will build a four-screen multiplex with state-of-the-art projection and stadium seating. Beijing and Guangzhou will be Kodak's next target for another six to eight first-class cinemas over the next few years.[2]

While the market is opening to foreign investors, the Government's attitude towards film as a symbol of the national spirit may yet hinder the process of foreign influence in the Chinese market. In the context of the demise of the Chinese film industry, the extent to which the Chinese Government will use the Hong Kong film industry to overcome its crisis, and to assist the economic transition, will be crucial to the Mainland Chinese film industry (Pang, this volume). Meanwhile, the industry continues to operate in a shifting territory of political idealism, generic desires, and contracting box office receipts.

Notes

1 A good example of the difficulties that lie ahead for overseas film releases is the case of *Crouching Tiger, Hidden Dragon* (Ang Lee, Taiwan, 2000). The release rights in China were shared by a private production firm, Asian Union Film & Entertainment, and the China Film Co-Production Co. with the former putting up 80 per cent of the $1-million cost while its government partner invested 20 per cent. When the movie looked like becoming an international smash, state officials from China Film distanced itself from Asian Union, unsuccessfully trying to buy out the private company's majority share. Officials withdrew the movie almost immediately after its premiere in Beijing in July 2000. As the movie was the subject of bureaucratic manoeuvring it was readily available on pirated DVDs, thus killing its profitability.

2 Http://www.chinaonline.com/industry/media_entertainment/currentnews//secure/c01010456.asp, 21 January 2001.

5

THE GLOBAL–NATIONAL POSITION OF HONG KONG CINEMA IN CHINA[1]

Laikwan Pang

> We must remember that although Hong Kong is a Special Administrative Region of China, we do not receive any preferential trade treatment from the Mainland. Our role as an intermediary will be challenged with competition coming not only from overseas markets, but also within the Mainland itself. We cannot overlook the remarkable performance in recent years of some key mainland cities. We cannot sit back and wait for the opportunities to fall on to our lap.
>
> That's why we have been working with the Mainland, to help wherever we can to establish contacts, to provide up to date information, to enhance infrastructure connections, particularly with our neighbouring areas, to facilitate the movement of people and goods. And we must step up our efforts to ensure we capture the full benefits flowing from a China that will be more open to the world's markets.
>
> (Donald Tsang, Financial Secretary, Hong Kong, 12 March 2001)

Introduction

This chapter considers the current state of China's film market in relation to the Hong Kong film industry post-1997. I argue that the patterns of cinema consumption currently emerging in the People's Republic of China (PRC) are linked to the interests of Hong Kong cinema. Having been hit hard by the Asian financial crisis in 1997–98, the Hong Kong film industry is trying to incorporate the Chinese mainland into its market. In so doing it is challenging both Hollywood and the domestic PRC film industry. The recent reunification of Hong Kong with China and the development of globalization are important contextual features in this process.

The relationship between Hong Kong (Special Administrative Region) and Mainland China is complicated. Hong Kong's status as a globalized, semidemocratic territory with a mature economy works under the aegis of a developing economy in a post-socialist state. Further, the latter is struggling to establish ideological control over the former. There are inevitable tensions, and both places make sacrifices for their mutual benefit. Part of the desired benefit of industry integration lies in Hong Kong's continuing international status, which, it is hoped, will facilitate China's participation in global flows of trade and finance. The contested 'one country: two systems' principle is a platform designed to serve incompatible interests. Both the 'one-country' and the 'two-systems' tags take on different meanings at different times. In cinema, the 'unification' and 'separation' of the two film industries and markets creates a fulcrum of tension that both makes the Special Administrative Region system viable and undermines its logic. The dialogue embedded in the Hong Kong film industry reveals an anxious conspiracy between globalization and the national interest.

Hong Kong: China's global city

The cultural relationship between China and Hong Kong since 1997 cannot be understood simply as a battle between the powerful and the disenfranchised. Political issues need to be viewed in an economic macro-context, and vice versa. Hong Kong people continue to struggle with the strong sovereign state, of which they are now constitutive, for a degree of political autonomy. Economically, however, China lags far behind Hong Kong. These anomalies interact with one another, complicating cultural circulation between the two entities (Appadurai 1996: 33).

Globalization theory refers neither to uniformity nor to the unity of the world. 'The key to [globalization's] cultural impact is in the transformation of localities themselves' (Tomlinson 1999: 29). Globalization is generally understood as an Americo-centric economic and cultural imperial trajectory, on which national borders and local interest groupings are dissolved to promote the circulation of capital. In response, certain constituencies are inclined to retreat back to cultural conservatism, like nationalism, away from the so-called 'global village' (Castells 1997) The resultant tension is unique in each case. The retreat from an internationalist idealism to a much more conservative nationalism is key to the state of post-revolutionary China (Liu [K.] 1998: 170–7). Dialectic and symbiotic trajectories of globalization and nationalization epitomize the current relationship between Hong Kong and China.

Given the combined effects of China's swelling market economy and its reinvigorated nationalism, Hong Kong's reunification with its motherland is considered largely beneficial to both sides:

> On the one hand, mainland China helped solve the developmental problems of [Hong Kong] by providing them with cheap labor,

> resources, and investment opportunities. On the other hand, [Hong Kong] contributed to mainland China's development by providing employment opportunities, market stimuli to local enterprises, and vital information and contacts for re-entering the world-market'.
>
> (So and Chiu 2000: 280)

So, as Hong Kong and China merge into a more coherent economic system, it appears that their different positions on the path to modernization and capitalization serve as mutual reinforcements of the progression of each towards global market significance. Their combination is a paradigmatic challenge to globalization as a stand-alone description of world economies, when in fact many 'global' economic activities operate through national institutions and in national territories (Sassen 1999) Globalization survives on international power differences. At the same time, uneven material and power distribution within national boundaries forms alternative or subordinate systems of capital flow. Global interests exploit national economic politics, but global interests are also required to work within national power flows. There is a constant state of flux.

This scenario applies well to the case of Hong Kong. Having become part of Chinese sovereign territory, it has national obligations. This 'Special Administrative Region' belongs economically, however, to the global network. It attracts investment, regulates profits and facilitates capital flow. While China has voiced reservations on joining the World Trade Organization (WTO), as this entails endless foreign meddling, most Chinese do not see Hong Kong's reunification with China as a similar threat. Indeed, as China is anxious to join the new global order, but is hesitant about adopting free trade and levelling protectionism, Hong Kong is seen as an effective membrane to filter out unwanted elements, allowing China to take its own tack on economic development.

The cinema industry fits this model of managing change, although the situation is much more complex than the theoretical outline sketched above. Numerous collaborations between Hong Kong's and China's film industries are designed to create diverse modes of coordinating capital flow within a global market: Hong Kong and China use each other to fend off other competitors. Hong Kong plays the role of a global city for China's film scene, organizing its economic activities according to international rules. Hong Kong is also, however, one of the world's major film factories, and the city also wants a stake in the mainland's vast market potential. Between these two roles, conflict abounds. One serious issue pertaining to the development of China's film market is the changing function of cinema between political apparatus and commodity (Chu, this volume). The global–national position of Hong Kong cinema may become a useful facility through which the PRC re-creates and maintains an ideological hold over cinema.

LAIKWAN PANG

Commodity and pedagogy: the crisis of Chinese cinema

China's transition from a committed socialist state to a socialist state with capitalist characteristics has not initiated *laissez faire* capitalism, nor has it ushered in attendant principles of honouring small government and liberalism. It is a statist market with trenchant centralized motivations (Zhao, 2000: 5). After twenty years of complex development, the state and the market are now mutually constitutive of each other. The former has worked hard, however, and with some success, to achieve disciplinary dominance over the latter. Cinema is an exemplary model of this, as film is both commodity and propaganda, governed by both commercial and political discourses.

Inheriting the Leninist tradition, the PRC has always seen cinema as an effective propaganda machine. The Communist Party relied heavily on cinema to spread its doctrine to the masses long before it took control of the nation in 1949 (Pang 2001). After Liberation, one of the first tasks of the People's Republic was to claim its authority over cinema, reorganizing all existing production studios and centralizing the distribution and exhibition network into a highly regulated system (Clark 1987: 34–45). China Film Corporation (*Zhongguo dianying gongsi*) was assigned the role of coordinating all production and exhibition units to supply films to Chinese people (Wu [X.] 1999). Originally designed to maintain the central government's absolute surveillance, the new distribution network gradually evolved into a huge, inefficient and bureaucratic system detached from the audience (Jia 1999: 294–5). By the 1980s, the China Film Corporation had little idea where films ended up. Data on screenings could not be reported back to the production houses as there were just too many agencies involved. Many intermediate distribution companies survived on the little profit the films made at the local box-offices, rendering all participants involved in the production–distribution–exhibition line virtually insolvent.

In 1993, the government finally took reluctant steps to introduce market principles into the film industry. The China Film Corporation was allowed to import ten revenue-sharing foreign films per year (Chu, this volume). Before then, foreign films were screened in China, but there was no revenue-sharing option. The China Film Corporation purchased the films' full national distribution rights at a meagre bidding price, which cut out high-budget commercial films. It was only when the new revenue-sharing option was allowed that foreign film companies could taste, or fantasize about, the possible profits of the vast Mainland Chinese market. Not surprisingly, major Hollywood blockbusters filled up most of the quota, and they created uproar in China's film market, both in terms of box-office receipts and the anxious outcries of Chinese film-makers and intellectuals.[2] If the United States government forces China to further open up its film market through the WTO negotiations, there will be two likely outcomes: first, an increase of 100 per cent in imported films within three years and, second, foreign capital invested directly in China's film exhibition market in a 49–51 split with local companies. Hollywood will profit most from these changes.[3]

The enlarged quota of imported films is not actually the core problem of China's film business. A more fundamental issue for both the government and film companies to tackle is how to balance profits and ideology. Chinese cinema must become a commodity to survive in the post-socialist market environment. The government is still extremely cautious in letting cinema free from its ideological control. This predicament has generated a whole set of structural problems that are leading to the collapse of the national film industry. China's censorship system is notoriously tight, and this conservatism has led to the development of a prosperous black market in pirated movies, creating two parallel yet highly disjunctive exhibition flows. While the official cinema outlets show 'clean' movies, those prohibited – yet more entertaining – movies circulate rapidly in the VCD black market. It is this market which most accurately reflects the popular taste of Chinese movie-goers of today. They also prefer the pirated movies in terms of their price and accessibility. It seems that a more vigorous and healthy market will not be developed unless censorship is extensively relaxed.

Another problem is the indirect manoeuvring of the government through indirect subsidy. Hardly any film companies are making profits. The total sum of national investment in film production in 1999 was about three hundred million RMB (US$37,500,000), but the revenue returned was only thirty million RMB (US$375,000) in total, only one-tenth of the initial investment (Li [Shi] 2000) According to recent Web-based research by Sina.com, over 90 per cent of 50,000 interviewees consider that the cinema's ticket-price is too high.[4] Other recent research indicates that most Beijingers go to the cinema fewer than five times a year, while over sixty per cent of the same group of interviewees watch at least one film a week at home through VCDs, videocassettes or television broadcast (Dai 1999).

As a result, to survive, most of China's film companies have to rely on government aid, ranging from loans to financial awards, more than on the market. The films produced have become more and more compliant to official ideology, which further inhibits their performance in the market. Moreover, from an economic perspective, 'state intervention ... is a device to protect an economic sector from its own internal weakness and contradictions' (Guback 1987: 91). Various kinds of financial aids to the film industry are essential for the government to stay in control; yet these activities only attest to and preserve the structural problems of a system that is caught between ideological control and a capitalist market.

The current crisis of China's film industry seems to be inevitable, as a hitherto state-supported enterprise is now required to embrace the market economy and treat its products as entertainment instead of political tools.

Chinese cinema must adapt as soon as possible to the new consumer-led environment. This difficult process involves not only conflicts of interest between foreign film companies and the Chinese state, but also struggles within China's cinema industry itself. Economically mature companies in Shanghai and Beijing advocate complete rejection of all government interference and financial aid. The Oriental Distribution Company, established in 1995, founded the second theatre chain in Shanghai. A shortage of films causes the company problems, so it is highly critical of the present protective distribution system that is so hostile to imported movies (Dong 1996). Meanwhile, the peripheral film studios loudly defend the protective system and have called for social commitment defined by the state support. They would be the first to close down in the event of a free(r) market. In their defence, they argue that a complete embrace of the market would stifle all films with non-mainstream interests, such as films for China's more than fifty ethnic minorities (Wu [Kuangwen] 2000).

Hong Kong for China

The role of the Hong Kong cinema in this industry crisis is crucial, as it acts as a buffer to maintain the balance between the status quo and the new market forces. For China, the greatest merit of the Hong Kong film industry is its global structure. Its capital sources and markets spread beyond Hong Kong, and its rapid development in the last forty years could not have been possible without the full support of various Asian markets (Leung and Chan 1997; Law 2000). Hong Kong can serve as a gateway to introduce capital and marketing concepts to China's film market, while Chinese film companies can rely on Hong Kong's finance, techniques and experiences to enter the new global economy without being engulfed by it. The Hong Kong factors are indispensable for the national film industry to reform itself and combat the invasion of foreign films.

Hong Kong influence and investment has various effects on the Chinese industry. Golden Harvest, a long term prominent film production and distribution company in Hong Kong, is the main investor in Shanghai's new multiplex cinemas, Jiaxing Film City and Heping Film City. The company hopes to establish its own distribution line in China. As Helen Blair and Al Rainnie remind us, 'the Hollywood studios are basically distribution arms with a bit of production attached, a system that is set up deliberately so that distribution swallows up the money' (Blair and Rainnie 2000: 193). Hong Kong film companies are heading in a similar direction on the mainland, trying to secure their share of the market by allocating screening blocks to Hong Kong product. The chance to actualize this wish in the near future is slim, and it will be a long time before Golden Harvest turns a profit. Nevertheless the Chinese audience, or at least a small urban élite, can enjoy the new facilities immediately.

Hong Kong is also a major investor in China's film production. Under the national film importation policy, there is a separate quota for the co-production of local and Hong Kong/Taiwan companies, and through many of these collaborative projects Hong Kong has invested vast amounts of capital directly in local studios to help improve their productions. Golden Harvest is beginning to produce films in China, one example being the hugely successful *The Storm Riders* (*Fengyun xiongba tianxia*) (1998) directed by Andrew Lau.[5] There are strict laws regulating these co-productions (Chu, this volume). Most importantly, the script is carefully scrutinized by the government (2000),[6] unlike standard Hong Kong commercial films, which are thought to spread morally and politically 'corrupt' messages. Such regulations guarantee the control of the Hong Kong factor played in the reform of Chinese cinema.

Probably the most influential effect on the Chinese industry is a matter of intellectual and commercial experience. Hong Kong's production know-how and business concepts have helped the Chinese cinema to understand consumption patterns. China's film market has been structurally altered by a specific marketing concept *dangqi* (cinema seasons) in the last few years. *Dangqi* was a novel idea on the Mainland, where releases were not arranged into commercially oriented slots. There were children's films made specifically for summer vacations and patriotic films for the National Day, but these were designed mainly for social convenience and political needs. In 1995, when revenue-sharing foreign films were first introduced, Jacky Chan's *Rumble in the Bronx* (*Hongfanqu*), directed by Stanley Tong, was shown on the mainland simultaneously with seasons in Hong Kong, Taiwan, and other South-East Asian countries. The film was specifically made for the 1995 Lunar New Year period in Hong Kong and Taiwan, and it was also promoted in the mainland as a New Year celebration film. It turned out to be a huge success.[7]

For decades the Lunar New Year had brought huge box-office receipts in Hong Kong and Taiwan. Most Hong Kong film companies made specific films for this *dangqi*, usually packed with superstars, light humour, high-budget production quality and, always, a happy ending. After the success of *Rumble in the Bronx* and other New Year Hong Kong films, the Lunar New Year of 1998 saw the first systematic promotion of the 'New Year *dangqi*' for China's own productions. In the last three years, almost all of the (few) profitable Chinese productions were produced for this season. These included *Part A, Part B* (*Jiafang yifang*) (1997), directed by Feng Xiaogang; *Spicy Love Soup* (*Aiqing mala tang*) (1998), directed by Zhang Yang; and *Be There or Be Square* (*Bujian busan*) (1998), also directed by Feng Xiaogang. The *dangqi* concept has successfully conditioned the market and fundamentally changed the Chinese film culture. The Lunar New Year screenings have become the locomotive of China's film industry.

Most importantly, the new Lunar New Year films produced a new commercial genre, urban light romance comedy, which has set a new trend in Chinese cinema. This is a film form rarely seen in Chinese cinema since 1949, as the combination of petty urban stories and light-hearted romance did not fit the obsession with 'History' and the 'People' over the last fifty years. Lunar New Year films have recognized an emerging consumer culture that is unequivocally modern and metropolitan. The components in this genre might have nothing directly to do with Hong Kong films, as films like *Be There or Be Square* are clearly part of the new cosmopolitan Beijing. However, this Beijing genre is a new commodity developed for the specific marketing concept of the Lunar New Year *dangqi*. As befits this joyful and lively festival, these films intentionally avoid social or political issues. Audiences watch these films for entertainment, not information.

The *dangqi* example makes one thing clear. Direct capital investment is not enough to enable China's film market to make the transition from ideological apparatus to commodities. What Chinese cinema needs is a new marketing rationale that takes consumption practices seriously. This commercial knowledge knows how to transform the mentality and habits of both the market and the industry in face of global competition. The Hong Kong factor is particularly crucial in this regard.

China for Hong Kong

Within this happy marriage of a global city and its motherland, the relationship between the two industries is much more complicated, particularly in view of the Hong Kong cinema's desire to capture the vast market potential in the mainland population. After two decades of burgeoning development, Hong Kong cinema experienced a catastrophic recession in the late 1990s. Earlier in the decade there were more than three hundred films produced in Hong Kong annually; five years later, however, the figure dropped to around eighty. The reasons are diverse and range from a shortage of capital and an insufficiency of creativity to the existence of a flourishing pirate VCD market (Zhang [Jian] 1998: 10–14). The rapid demise of the film market (both domestic and overseas) is definitely the most detrimental one.

The recent Asian financial crisis undermined South-East Asian economies, and their capacity to purchase Hong Kong film. Hong Kong cinema had relied heavily on the diasporic audience and now needs other markets and capital sources to support a film industry which is disproportionately large for its domestic audience. The mainland film market, which was ignored by Hong Kong film companies just two or three years ago, has now become a source of fantasy for Hong Kong film-makers. They need the mainland dream to work for them, particularly as recovering East Asian countries, like Korea and Thailand, are producing their own films fashioned after Hong

Kong models. The fantasy might never materialize however. Although millions of Chinese people are loyal fans of Hong Kong films, and although these people have been watching almost all Hong Kong productions for more than a decade, Hong Kong film-makers have made no profits from this vast market. Most of the Hong Kong films have been consumed in the form of pirated VCDs and the profits have gone directly to the pirates.

The major complaint of the Hong Kong film companies, interestingly, is China's unwillingness to grant their films the status of a national product. They urge the PRC to level the revenue-sharing quota for Hong Kong films, allowing them to be distributed as national products. There are only two or three revenue-sharing Hong Kong films in each year which can enjoy the larger degree of autonomy in production and distribution, while all others are completely at the mercy of the ruthless censorship and the inefficient distribution system in China. China's position is clear: it has stated that the new WTO quota of the twenty imported revenue-sharing films also includes Hong Kong productions, and Hong Kong films will continue to be introduced and arranged by China Film Corporation alone (Liu [Jianzhong] 2000).

This unrequited desire for 'national' status, however, is double-edged. As the mainland market is so crucial for the future development of Hong Kong cinema, the unique identity of Hong Kong cinema may easily be swallowed up by the consumption needs of the mainland. *Fascination Amour* (*Aiqing mingyun hao*), directed by Herman Yau, was clearly made for China's 1999 Lunar New Year film market. According to the film's producer Raymond Wong, he included specific Chinese elements (mainland stars and China-related narrative details) in this Hong Kong production to solicit identification from Chinese audiences. Although Wong does not consider this experiment successful, he will conduct similar experiments, juggling with the Chinese audience, censorship and piracy to decode the mainland market.

It is true that the distinguished Hong Kong genre films still appeal to most of the Chinese audience,[8] but the situation is extremely volatile. According to an interview with Phoon Chiong Kit, the Managing Director of Golden Harvest, this, the largest Hong Kong film production company, will very likely move its base to China if China truly opens up its film market, as a cost-efficient and consumer-oriented priority (2000).[9] This indicates the intricacy involved in almost all post-1997 Hong Kong – China negotiations. Hong Kong is constantly trying to take advantage of its new national status to devour the huge Chinese market, yet there is a risk that the individual identity of Hong Kong will be completely assimilated by that of China.

Cinema and modernity

The reunification of Hong Kong with China has provided both the promises and threats of the merging of the two cultures and economies. However, a real integration of the two film markets has yet to be realized. In the case of cinema for example, we discover that when the national reunification of Hong Kong and China meets capitalist globalization, behind the high-toned nationalist discourse there is a complex entanglement between the cultural and the economic. Oftentimes it is the 'differences' between the two lands which are highlighted: they encourage capital flow, also promoting the exchange of cultural imagination, particularly in the case of cinema which is the prism through which 'modernity' is refracted. Hong Kong films were among the first 'foreign films' to be watched in China's film market. Chinese audiences desire to consume these Hong Kong movies mostly because of the experiences and sensibilities provided by these films, which are distinctly different from those produced by their own market. It is the introduction of 'differences' which makes modernization and globalization possible. However, there are other narratives where 'unity' between China PRC and Hong Kong SAR is stressed, especially when it is appropriate in the face of the aggressive presence of Hollywood For China, Hong Kong cinema allows for the thrill of the 'foreign' to be experienced without the danger of cultural swamping. For Hong Kong, on the other hand, the mainland is the ideal 'domestic' market to guarantee its continued development in face of the ever-expanding Hollywood cinematic powerhouse.

While such constant negotiations allow the 'two systems' to make the best of each other, they also reveal a hidden tug-of-war between China's and Hong Kong's interests. Hong Kong wants to maintain its cultural hegemony; China would prefer a filtration process to dispel the more robust aspects of Hong Kong cultural politics. Hong Kong always emphasizes its strategic global position, but the position of this 'global–national' city is complicated by Hong Kong's own economic dependence on China and its markets. A real 'unification' of Hong Kong and China's film markets, as I have suggested, might ultimately assimilate the former into the latter. Hong Kong's film companies are urging China to consider them as its own, yet the differences between the two industries are crucial if Hong Kong wishes to claim cultural superiority. Given the interdependence of cultural capital and economic organization, the desire on both sides for a 'free circulation' of capital performing under the 'one-way' flow of cultural imagination is inherently contradictory. Hong Kong films have worked for Chinese audiences mainly because of their facility in addressing the imagination of an audience on the cusp of China's modernization–globalization discursive contour. The disappearance of difference that such sophisticated hindsight produces will also dissolve market potential.

For China, the case is even more intricate. The opening of China's film market to Hong Kong requires the acquiescence of an authoritarian state, which has tended to be intimidated by cinema's ideological power. The position of the state is now at odds with its own tendencies. Film studios that are not market-ready by reason of preparation or location are raising the slogan of cinema's social commitments to society. Their complaints suggest that this social commitment manifests now simply as a glorification of the dominant state ideology. Social commitment as an issue of diverse representation is not on the agenda. Some commentators condemn the cultural hegemony of Hong Kong cinema (Li [Ding-Tzann] 1998), but the Government's priorities are also at issue here. The Xinjiang people, for example, might be more willing, both intellectually and emotionally, to watch the farcical and violent Hong Kong films rather than the 'socially committed' productions made in their own Xinjiang Film Studio.

Cinema is an exemplary case study for understanding the tensions between nationalization and globalization in the post-1997 Hong Kong – China relationship. The PRC has been careful iwith cinema because of its links to 'foreign contamination'; Hong Kong cinema presents similar dangers. Yet cinema in the PRC also needs these 'contaminated' linkages for its own survival. The negotiations between Hong Kong cinema and the mainland Chinese market bear witness to the risks for China in the global game. China plays with others/changes/globalization but it needs to hold on to its self/internal security/national profile. In this complicated manouevre China seeks to use Hong Kong for its own political interests. Hong Kong's film companies see that they have a stake in this process, and that they cannot afford not to co-operate. Sadly, the final result may be the neutralisation of the Hong Kong film industry, and the loss of the companies that took the risk at China' behest.

Notes

1 I am grateful to Stephanie Hemelryk Donald, Wai-kit Choi and Kwai-cheung Lo for their valuable comments on, and insights into, the earlier drafts of this paper.

2 There were nine profit-sharing films imported to China in 1995: one from France, two from Hong Kong, and the other six all from Hollywood. See *Zhongguo dianying nianjian, 1996* [China Film Yearbook 1996] Beijing: Zhongguo dianying, p. 211.

3 The WTO negotiations triggered hot debates within China's film industry, which worries that Hollywood will increasingly dominate the film market and further cripple the shaky local film industry. See, for example, the special issue of the Chinese film journal *Film Art* devoted to the WTO debate. *Dianying yishu* [Film Art] 272 (2000.3).

4 This research is conducted by China's Sina web in November 2000. http://ent.sina.com.cn/m/c/22840.html. According to recent statistics provided by the New China News Agency, the standard movie ticket price comprises 2 per cent of a Chinese person's average monthly income, while the corresponding figures in the United States and India are only 0.5% and 0.25% respectively. *Ming Pao*, 16 December 2000.

5 *The Storm Riders* received a record-breaking revenue of 41 million HKD (about 5.3 million USD) in Hong Kong. There are no accurate box-office records for

the film in China; we only know that it topped the box offices of many Chinese cities when it was screened. (See the data listed in *Zhongguo dianying shichang* (*Chinese film market*) 1998, Vols 8, 9 and 10.)

6 Wong, Raymond P.M. (2000). Hong Kong Film Producer, Chairman of Movie Producers and Distributors Association of Hong Kong Limited, and Director of Mandarin Films Holding Ltd. Interview with the author. Hong Kong. 8 November.

7 Once again, there are no accurate box-office data for the film in China. But there is an estimate of the film earning eight million RMB (about 1 million USD) revenue in Shanghai alone, which was considered to be hugely successful (Wang, [Hongyou] 1996: 212)

8 Among the revenue-sharing films distributed in China, almost all of the Hong Kong films are action films. In 1995 there were *Rumble in the Bronx* and *Thunderbolt* (*Pili huo*), directed by Gordon Chan; both were Jackie Chan films. In 1996, there were *First Strike* (*Jiandan renwu*), directed by Stanley Tong; *Big Bullet* (*Congfeng dui*), directed by Benny Chan; and *High Risk* (*Shudan longwei*), directed by Jing Wong. All were distinct Hong Kong genre films with major Hong Kong action stars.

9 Phoon, Chiong Kit (2000) Managing Director, Golden Harvest Entertainment (Holding) Limited. Interview with the author. 7 December.

6

'SATELLITE MODERNITY'

Four modes of televisual imagination in the disjunctive socio-mediascape of Guangzhou

Anthony Fung and Eric Ma

Context

Despite obvious fissures and rifts, the mediascapes of Hong Kong and China's coastal regions are undergoing rapid integration. The dialectic between Mainland China and Hong Kong's media has therefore become a focal point for analysis (Lee [Chin-chuan] 2000a; Fung and Lee, forthcoming) The concerns of these researchers are with the transborder mediascape that is emerging through the reintegration of Hong Kong back into Chinese sovereign territory. As part of China, Hong Kong's liberal media, although operating in a full-blown capitalistic mode, should be seen as a subsystem of the Chinese media. In Mainland China there is an overt connection between the media and the political economy. Powers are articulated across the Hong Kong – China border by more indirect and discursive means, however. The government of the Hong Kong Special Administrative Zone (HKSAR) is not legitimized by a full democratic election; it is a weak government, which operates under the blessing of the Chinese government. The Chinese government does, however, grant Hong Kong a high level of media autonomy. Honouring the promise of 'one country, two systems', China has refrained from explicitly intervening in the Hong Kong media.

Our work leads us to warn against undue pessimism. Although Hong Kong is at the political periphery, it exerts a strong influence on the media environment of Mainland China. For many years, Hong Kong has served as a template for Chinese–Western media conversations, a window through which China might relay its messages to the media in western liberal societies. Since the 'open door' policy started in the late 1970s, Western culture has been an increasingly strong presence in the lives of the Chinese people.

The most frequent exposure to outside programming is from the spillover of broadcasting signals from Hong Kong TV, which can reach a large part of the Pearl River. A study of audience-led 'border-crossing' indicates that Hong Kong programmes, including local Hong Kong productions and foreign programmes carried by Hong Kong channels, are very popular and usually attract a large share of audiences (Fung 1999). Arguably, exposure to foreign programming has created a demanding media audience, and increased the pressure for media commercialization and liberalization. Co-productions, joint ventures, visits, international fora, television and film festivals and sharing of expertise have become frequent, especially with the media industries in Hong Kong. Hong Kong and its international affiliations have become the 'demonstrators' providing Chinese media with a new discursive context in which market capitalism is the name of the game (Chan [Joseph] 1993, 1996).

Impacts on Mainland China by the Hong Kong media have been studied on institutional, reception, and contextual levels (Chan [Joseph] 2000; Gold 1993; Ma [Eric] 2001). The conclusions reached to date are not concrete, nor should they hope to be so. In this chapter we will take a direct route by 'dipping' into the televisual imagination of the Guangzhou TV audience which consumes Hong Kong TV programmes regularly. We focus on a central theoretical construct that we believe can be applied across China, but which must be researched in 'micro' case studies to carry weight. We call this the 'televisual imagination', and in the following case studies we are applying it particularly to a situation of transborder programming and reception. We are building on previous work on the transborder imagination (Ma [Eric] 2001), and on the reception of factual and fictional programming (Fung 2000). The research was organized through semi-structured, in-depth interviews. We determined to interrogate the meanings attached to fictional TV characters, as they were received, reconstructed and understood within the informants' imaginations.

It was important to us to avoid the ethnographic trap of imposing our own interpretive frameworks on our subjects. Such an approach would fail to account for the 'located politics of difference', and would not achieve 'a new sensitivity to the processes by which identities are constituted and negotiated' (Fincher and Jacobs 1998: 1). We respect and acknowledge the variable and pluralistic subjectivities of our respondents, and we certainly do not claim a homogeneous response mechanism within the rubric of transborder televisual imagination. We therefore designed the study in collaboration with a marketing research company in Guangzhou and we ourselves spent three months at the research site (Guangzhou), acclimatizing ourselves to the variable scope of the locality. Each response is a unique discursive event, based on the appropriation of the fictive and textual world of transborder TV dramas into the personal and contextual realms of the individual. These imaginative configurations are not 'interpretations' of TV dramas, but they can be aptly described as 'direct televisual imaginative structures'. In this project, we do however draw general observations from empirical mappings of the televisual imaginations of transborder TV audiences. We also accept that the media market does have the capacity to effect real change in the community (Morley and Robins 1995). Based on these mappings, we suggest a model of disjunctive socio-mediascape in the modernity project of postsocialist China.

TV colonization

Chinese TV audiences in coastal regions watch Hong Kong TV programmes which have 'spilled over' across the border. All of our fifteen informants are heavy Hong Kong programme viewers. They watch Chinese TV to glean official information and a touch of domestic and local affairs, but most of them spend more time watching Hong Kong TV for pleasure. They all name a figure from Hong Kong TV drama as their most favourite TV character. When asked to compare Guangzhou and Hong Kong TV, a few said that Hong Kong TV is trivial and too extravagant, but the majority said Hong Kong news programmes are more credible and informative, while Hong Kong dramas are more vibrant, lively, attractive and entertaining. A recurrent comment is that Hong Kong TV is of a higher level of quality, which indicates a clear hierarchy of valorization: the modernized TV programming is in general 'better' that that of Guangzhou. Adapting from Appadurai (1996), we draw from this the contention that the Hong Kong mediascape is superimposed on the socioscape of Guangzhou.

Guangzhou local TV still provides its audience with domestic programming, but it is not dominant in the audience's imagination. Hong Kong's mediated incursions and strong televisual presence meanwhile exemplify a soft colonization of its neighbours. Although Hong Kong and Guangzhou have strong ethnic, cultural and historical ties, the Hong Kong mediascape expresses a more intense form of modernity than the materialistic configuration of the Guangzhou socioscape. The Hong Kong mediascape originates from a very different domestic context. Superimposed on to the Guangzhou socioscape, it has become a window of capitalistic modernity to which Guangzhou aspires and with which it is rapidly catching up. The present audience study is thus framed in the discursive context of a lagging socioscape and forward mediascape in term of the intensity of capitalistic modernity. Here, Hong Kong's forward mediascape should not be interpreted as being in a 'progressive' stage. We are not assuming a modernization project in which 'backward' societies are developing into better ones. The conceptualization of a lagging-behind, yet forward-looking, socioscape is a descriptive framing, which reflects the political and popular desire of postsocialist China to 'leap' into global modernity. Within this Hong Kong – Guangzhou socio-media context, we have two aims in this chapter. First, we generalize dominant interpretive modes of transborder televisual imagination from concrete audience cases. Second, from these interpretive modes, we theorize the dynamics of modernity and postmodernity embedded within the disjunctive socio-mediascape of Guangzhou.

Four modes of televisual imagination

In our research account we generalized four modes of imaginative configurations from fifteen case studies. We called these the pragmatic, modernized, conspicuous and vicarious modes. These modes can be formulated within the context of the disjunctive Hong Kong – Guangzhou socio-mediascape (fig. 1).

For those who live in Guangzhou and watch Hong Kong TV, their transborder televisual imagination will be a combination of immediate experiences in the Guangzhou socioscape and imagined experiences in the mediascape as represented in Hong Kong TV dramas. This text/context dialectic is a complex hybridization refracted and structurated by this disjunctive socio-mediascape. The different patterns of televisual imagination can be categorized into four different modes. Each represents a different degree of creative mixing of the socioscape and the mediascape within the imaginary world of individuals. In the pragmatic mode, the imaginative configuration domesticates the Hong Kong mediascape within realistic social routines. In the modernized mode, the imaginative configuration lies in the overlaps between a concrete experience of modern city life in Guangzhou and similar experiences as represented in the Hong Kong mediascape. In the conspicuous and vicarious modes, imaginative modernity is inflated and displayed as a sign of social differentiation. The conspicuous mode refers to inflation and display practised

Figure 6.1 Four modes of televisual imagination

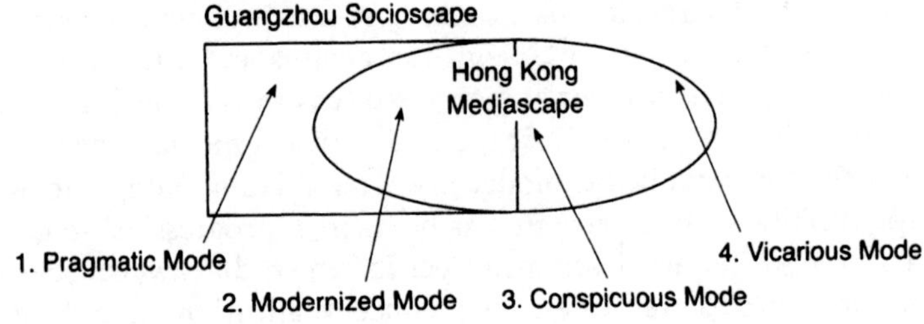

in the socioscape. The vicarious mode occurs as a pattern of wishful thinking and identification, and is not openly discernible in everyday life. We explain these modes with some illustrative cases below. In this analysis, we stress that qualitative cases are multidimensional and cannot fit nicely into these modes, or any others. Modes of imagination are theoretical constructions and analytic types. They are developed as a tool to help us understand the ways in which the fictional world of transborder TV is woven into the aspirations and experiences of actual audiences situated in a concrete socioscape.

1 Pragmatic mode

Mr Wei, a young salesman in a shopping mall, is in the lowest income bracket of our study, earning less than 1,000 yuan per month. He watches more than three hours of Hong Kong TV every day. His favourite TV character is a middle-class cop played by actor Koo Tin Lok in an action drama. What he likes about Koo is that Koo is serious, motivated and living a casual lifestyle. This is rather like Wei himself. In a game of character association, we offered our informants four different items to choose from on behalf of their chosen character: a nearby shop, a *7–11* convenience store, an ordinary (modernized) shopping mall, and an up-market department store. These four choices are in an ascending order of market position. In this game, Wei thinks that his favourite TV character Koo would go to a nearby shop to buy food. In Wei's mind, Koo wears ordinary clothing and accessories, despite the fact that this programme is considered by the Hong Kong audience to be a 'middle-class' and trendy drama.

We classified Wei's televisual imagination in the pragmatic mode. Restricted by his socio-economic location, Wei appropriates the middle-class character to the consumption pattern compatible with his own routine as a junior salesman. In this pragmatic mode, the informant domesticates those modern and stylish characters into the routines of his own less modernized world. Basic material needs are most relevant and fictional characters are discursively reconstructed to suit the lifestyles of the informants situated in lower-level lifestyles in the Guangzhou socioscape. The 'forward' mediascape is being brought down to the daily routine of the lagging socioscape. Wei may relax, expand and inflate his imagination if his own financial conditions improve, but, for now, he is pragmatic and realistic in constructing his imaginative world.

2 Modernized mode

Mr Yip, a sales manager in his thirties, watches one and a half hours of television every day. He is single and lives alone. He earns 4,000–5,000 yuan per month, which is quite high according to local standards at the time of interview. He prefers Hong Kong TV programmes because he thinks that they are of a higher general standard, are more realistic and closer to everyday life, and that the acting style is more natural and sophisticated. Similarly to Wei, Yip's favourite TV character is the middle-class cop played by actor Koo Tin Lok. It is notable, however, that while Wei associates this middle-class cop with a localized store in the association game, Mr Yip thinks that Koo would buy food, newspapers and lifestyle books in a modernized shopping-mall store. Mr Yip describes Koo as persistent, smart, modern, but casual. He says that he occasionally imitates the way Koo dresses in the drama.

We categorize Yip in the modernized mode. In this mode, Hong Kong, as a modernized world, is represented in the fictional world of TV dramas. This modernized world is not inflated and conspicuously displayed as an enviable reference point. It is neither an impossible dream nor a flamboyant model of inappropriate behaviour. Rather, its perceived modern values of work and expenditure, of efficiency and convenience, are put into practice and actively tried out by audience members. This modernized mediascape overlaps with many characteristics of the modernizing socioscape of Guangzhou. Fictional characters are flexible enough to be inflated to a higher position in cultural imaginations or recontextualized into the daily experiences of modernization. Similarly, two other informants, whom we also categorize in this mode, associate their favourite TV characters with the modern convenience store *7–11*. The imaginations in this mode are not stretching to the high end of up-market consumption associated with an imagined Hong Kong, but rather are articulated to a more down-to-earth experience of local modernity. These informants are in the middle-income group and are participating daily in the process of marketization in socialist China. They are attentive to the dress code and lifestyle of their favourite TV characters and try out their modern but mediated ways of life in their everyday life.

3 Conspicuous mode

Ms Lau, the owner of a beauty saloon, can be considered typical of an upwardly mobile and self-employed sector in contemporary China. In her late twenties, she earns between 4,000 and 5,000 yuan (500–625 $US) a month, the second-highest income bracket in our study. She watches three and a half hours of television every day, and prefers Hong Kong programmes because they are more meaningful and creative. The character she likes best is a psychiatrist played by actress Sun (Soon) in a Hong Kong middle-class police action drama. In her evaluation of the character, Lau talks about Sun being independent, professional, sporty, rational, and well organized in her work. In the association game, Lau thinks that character Sun (Soon) is coming out of a big shopping mall. When asked what she thinks about the character's lifestyle, Lau says that Sun wears good-quality clothing with well-matched colours. Lau specifically states that she aspires to Sun's lifestyle and says she has been 'partially influenced' by the drama of Hong Kong TV. She wants to be as lighthearted and carefree as Sun, not following the old fashioned lifestyles of her father's generation. If it were ever possible, she would try out different (and the best!) consumer products and services and live life to the full. She spends thirty per cent of her income on non-essential consumption and entertainment. She explains her rather high-spending pattern by saying that her professional life demands an expanding social network, for the maintenance and recruitment of clients.

We categorize Lau's televisual imagination in the conspicuous mode. The way of life in the textual world is woven into the habitus of the individual, who aspires to a consumerist and modernized life (Giddens 1991). The desire to break away from the traditions of the older generation is expressed in and through televisual character identification. The Hong Kong mediascape, as a reference frame, discursively propels the movement of the Guangzhou socioscape: to move forward and keep in line with the aspirations embodied in the Hong Kong mediascape. The people who construct this mode of televisual imaginations are those who have higher socio-economic status. The higher social location enables them to aspire to and experiment with different lifestyles.

Besides members of the new rich like Ms Lau the salon owner, we find that Chinese professionals are especially inclined towards this mode of imagination. Ms Cheung, an accountant in her twenties, earns between 3,000 and 3,999 yuan (375–500 $US) per month. She watches more than three hours of television per day. She thinks that Hong Kong dramas are more realistic and closer to everyday life. Her favourite character is a lawyer played by actress Chan Wei Shan in the Hong Kong TV drama *Healing Hands*. What she likes about this lawyer in the drama is that the character is elegant, professional, looks gorgeous, and displays good taste. Cheung thinks that her personality is quite similar to that of the TV character. To Cheung's eyes, as an audience member, the female lawyer in the TV drama lives in a classy world with a fancy middle-class lifestyle. In Cheung's mind, the TV character's daily leisure activities include shopping, playing tennis, going to the gym and the beauty salon, and attending charity events. She wears simple but expensive clothing. In the association game, Cheung thinks that the TV lawyer is coming out of an up-market store with clothing and household goods.

There are two more informants, physician Ms Mei and manager Mr Wan, who also associate their favourite characters with up-market stores and fancy lifestyles. It is interesting that the same characters, named by other informants in other imaginative modes, may position the same character in very different consumption niches. This allows us to contend that the imaginative class positions of TV characters are not determined by the narrative of the TV text, but by the flexible mixing and hybridizing of symbolic resources made available from the socioscape and mediascape (Mathews 2000).

The new rich and the professionals in China have the economic capacity and psychological need to nourish, construct, and live a middle class lifestyle (Buckley 1999). However, there are limited cultural resources and references in socialist China for such an emerging social group. The Hong Kong mediascape provides this audience group with rich symbolic resources for conspicuous identity differentiation. The term 'conspicuous' alludes to the theory of conspicuous consumption which argues that the new rich are using explicit material and symbolic markers to assert their newfound identity. The desire for identity formation and assertion is framed within the discursive contexts of China's great leap into marketization. Here, the thesis of conspicuous consumption is applied to the cultural formation of televisual imagination, which is reworked and structured by the impulse of differentiation in China's modernity project.

4 Vicarious mode

Ms Pei, a clerk in her late twenties, watches three and a half hours of television every day. She prefers local TV programmes because they are more familiar and contextual. Earning 1,000–2,000 yuan per month, she is not interested in trying out the high-class lifestyle depicted in Hong Kong TV dramas. However, when asked to identify her favourite TV character, she still names a supermodel played by Hong Kong actress Chow Heir Mea in a Hong Kong TV drama. Despite her strong admiration for Chow's high-class tastes and great ability in the business world, she explicitly states that she is not Chow. They are two different kinds of people. In the association game, Chow is seen going out from an up-market department store. She wears elegant business suits and expensive evening gowns. In Pei's words, she is different, distinguished, trend-setting, and has an unattainable status and unique style of her own. Despite her strong admiration for the character, Pei insists that her experiences of fictional and everyday worlds are very different. The ways of life represented on television will not work in real life.

We categorize Pei's imagination in the vicarious mode. The extravagant life in televisual discourse is seen as an entertaining fantasy. There might be strong or weak character identification, but the attachment and admiration are restricted to the imaginary and are not considered to be realizable. In fact, of all our fifteen informants, Pei uses the most vivid and extraordinary terms to describe her favourite character. Restricted by her socio-economic location, her inflated imagination is contained within the vicarious pleasure she finds through watching the unrealizable world of the impossible. The term 'vicarious imagination' suggests the theoretical subtext of escapism and vicarious pleasures in watching TV. In this mode, the more inflated the transborder imagination, the more intensive the vicarious pleasure it generates. In sum, informants categorized in this mode exhibit a few similarities. First, the configuration of the televisual imagination is inflated with a heightened sense of hyper-reality. Second, the informants are vicariously attached to, but realistically detached from, their favourite characters. Third, the informants are in restricted socio-economic positions.

The above are analytic modes into which all empirical cases may not easily fit. There are overlaps, but still these modes have distinct analytic boundaries. The pragmatic modes domesticate the transborder mediascape. The modernized mode contextualizes it into concrete experiences of the modernizing socioscape. The conspicuous mode inflates the symbolism of modernity in order to manage and perform identity differentiation. Finally, the vicarious mode exoticizes the imaginary and unattainable vicarious pleasures. These modes are predisposed, but not determined, by socio-economic locations. The lower status groups are predisposed to operate in the pragmatic mode, or the vicarious mode of exoticizing the imaginary. However, they may also take on the other two modes. The middle and upper status groups are predisposed to take the modernized or conspicuous modes but may also shift to the pragmatic or the vicarious. Thus the formulation of these modes is not to be taken as a predictive of the interpretation tendencies of individuals, but rather to understand the patterns of imagination formation.

Disjunctive socio-mediascape and the trajectory of modernity

From these interpretive modes, we theorize the dynamics of modernity and postmodernity embedded within the disjunctive socio-mediascape of Guangzhou. Modernity, as Giddens (1990) argues, is inherently a global project. It spreads across boundaries by political necessity and, increasingly, by economic logics. The role of transborder media in the spread of modernity has been formulated in the media imperialism thesis and in various globalization theories. However, most of these theoretical forms take a 'macro' and general analytic approach. We attempt a mid-range analysis by theorizing the dynamics between a transborder mediascape and a domestic socioscape, describing and exploring the disjunctive socio-mediascape and its consequences (fig. 2).

Figure 6.2 Disjunctive socio-mediascape and the trajectory of modernity

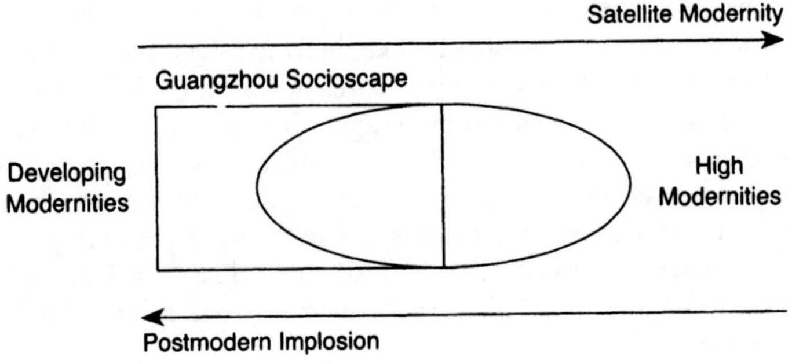

Satellite modernities

Hong Kong, as a satellite metropolis of global capitalism, is 'colonizing' the political centre of China with popular media filled with consumerist and capitalistic ideologies. In China, the proliferation of Hong Kong popular culture, especially in the coastal provinces, has impacts at various levels (Gold 1993). It lures audiences away from Chinese media, it appears to have changed their frame of reference in their evaluation of Chinese media, and it also exerts strong pressures on the institutional practices of coastal media organizations (Chan [Joseph] 2000). Apolitical music, TV, soap operas, and weekend consumer reports are carrying values such as individualism, consumerism, and scepticism of authority. These popular texts have opened a modest, albeit tentative, space outside the power of the state, where audiences can explore their dreams and aspirations. In this contingent and historical conjuncture, the media become cultural intermediaries, which introduce new ways of life and cultivate desires for individual freedom. As China moves away from collectivism to 'market socialism', individual fulfilment has been re-prioritized as a culturally correct and politically legitimate pursuit (Litzinger 2000).

The Hong Kong mediascape, superimposed on the Guangzhou socioscape, fuels an imagined conception of Hong Kong's satellite modernity, and extends the interlocking discursive networks which relay Hong Kong and global capitalism to Guangzhou (Ma [Eric], forthcoming). Here, the term 'satellite' refers to the nexus that relays sites of high modernity and developing modernities. Transborder media have become a driving force in attracting and relaying satellite sites to centres of high modernity. The 'lagging' domestic socioscape is motivated by the imagined modernity proposed through the transborder mediascape (McCraken 1988). The local consumption of this imagined modernity is a creative hybridization and contextualization of the mediascape and socioscape by active audiences, resulting in the push and pull of the imaginary and the practical.

In our conceptualization, the most dynamic mode of imagination is the conspicuous mode, in which the Guangzhou audience members improvise their own micro-versions of satellite modernity in their everyday practices. These improvisations are mediated by the Hong Kong mediascape. The disjunctive socio-mediascape may either encourage migration to countries with a high intensity of modernity, or the individual, mobilizing the discursive resources of the transborder mediascape, may modify his or her domestic habitat and lifestyle. The practice and conspicuous display of these mediated behaviours produces an indigenized version of modernity. We also contend that this process also involves opportunities for expansions of collective deliberation and responsibility for the mitigation of inequality, of values of freedom, and of human rights in the long term (Waters 2001: 232).

The postmodern implosion

Imaginative versions of satellite modernity push ever forward. The other worlds that travel across borders are only meaningful as ambassadors of the new, the newer and the newest. However, transborder televisual imagination working in high modernity can rebound. If, as in the case of Guangzhou, the local is both modern and less modern (inevitable in a period of transition), then there are crucially uneven rates of change across the imaginative worlds of many and the performed desires of the few, those given to conspicuous display. This unevenness is of course exacerbated by the actual pace of economic development; by welfare collapse, and by daily financial disappointments. The effects of these differences produce something more than simple tension between unequal groups. We suggest that the state of change may be described as a postmodern implosion between the modern and the less modern.

Recently, cultural flows across the Sino–Hong Kong border have become much more reciprocal and complicated. Since the 1990s, material cultures from all over the world have been flooding into the Chinese market and the exchanges between Hong Kong and China have been more frequent (Kwok and So 1995; Ong 1999; Smart 1998). In this period of dialectic interaction, transborder cultural imaginations have become unstable and even demonstrate some postmodern features. There is an almost physical crush of modernities pushing for actual and imagined space in the new territory of conquest – China. Each operates with different levels of intensity, and the inevitable contradictions and incoherencies produce mediated and social symptoms that look like fragments of postmodernity. Hong Kong consumerist modernity – the image, the imagined, and the imaginary[1] – is dislocated in its passage to the Guangzhou community via the Hong Kong media. It is disruptive, but also by now an embedded feature of the everyday. The cultural imaginations of Guangzhou citizens, especially in the modernized and conspicuous modes, have become an organized field of social practice. A dislocated and disjunctive mediascape dissolves into life, hybridizing traditional and modern imaginations and practices.

This process will repeat itself until some level of satiation and stability is achieved. As modernization and marketization become official policy, so consumer products become available in China. So too is the discursive power of Hong Kong culture released in various parts of China, reproducing social practices based on imaginations of western modernity relayed through the satellite modernity of Hong Kong. That is the pattern which we have come to recognize, and which we traced in the responses of our informants. But the field changes quickly. If not satiation, then at least some osmotic balance is beginning to take over. In the 1980s and early 1990s, China modelled itself on Hong Kong. Recently, it has developed its own cultural edges and economic power to complicate Sino–Hong Kong exchanges. As China catches up in the race to modernize, the cultural boundary between Hong Kong and China become fuzzy and unstable (see Pang, this volume).

The sovereignty transfer in 1997 was particularly instrumental in softening the cultural boundary of the two places. Now the Sino – Hong Kong territorial border has become more administrative than political. Hong Kong culture has been 're-sinicized' (Ma [Eric] 1999), while Hong Kong's brand of modernity is exported, reproduced and localized in other parts of China. More and more Hong Kong entrepreneurs and opportunists are exploiting the possibilities offered by the developing Chinese market (Ong 1999). But here, postmodern theories are not in full purchase. Postmodern features – symbolic simulation, hybridization, and blurring of boundaries – are phenomena that can be framed within the disjunctive socio-mediascape in multiple satellite modernities. They arise in the gaps between the overlaps of high modernity and a developing modernity. The discursive fragments refracted from the headlong collisions between two or multiple modernities exhibit postmodern features, but they remain within the fold of a compressed and asymmetrical process of modernization. (Lash 1999; Wittrock 2000).

The informants in our study live in the midst of this dynamic but exhausting set of changes. They consume branded versions of modernity through the media and through their lifestyle choices and necessities. They also make their livings in ways which are new for their generation. They are pioneers of a new modernity in the postsocialist space that is the People's Republic of China. Meanwhile, the satellite modernity that is exemplified in the HKSAR sits on their doorstep, both inside and outside of China. It offers an image of where they might go, and how they might model the performance of that journey. It also offers itself up as a target for a competing modernity that they are currently constructing on their own behalf. The hybrid modernity that grows from the HKSAR and Mainland Chinese relationship is itself a production and intervention in the meaning of trans-border media.

Notes

1 In this context, Benedict Anderson's imagined community (1983) can be extended to include the dislocated imagination of a faraway 'satellite community' of modernity.

7

SEND IN THE CLONES

Television formats and content creation in the People's Republic of China

Michael Keane

Over the past decade the concept of 'entertainment' (*yule*) has become a defining factor in the shaping of television programming schedules in China. At the same time it has gained acceptance within the echelons of political power as a strategic means for ensuring the placement of soft propaganda messages. Not surprisingly, the concept of entertainment has become a target for criticism from many of China's conservative intellectuals, who see it as having the kind of homogenizing effect formerly attributed to the 'culture industry' or consumer culture by the Frankfurt School (Xie 1996). A certain academic and semantic fuzziness seems to congeal around the term 'mass culture', most notably an assumed relationship between it and the public culture of the Chinese Communist Party from the 1940s to the 1970s. Both commercial consumer culture and public culture are expressed as *dazhong wenhua* and exemplify a culture imposed from above rather than a holistic culture born out of autonomous production. In the minds of conservative critics, the 'culture industry' of the Frankfurt School, the heavy-handed public culture of the Maoist era, and the contemporary cultural industries of television, advertising, and cinema are seen as bedfellows, complicit in denying people real choice in their cultural consumption (see Yin Hong, this volume).

Suspicion of commercial culture often distracts us from a dispassionate account of the role that entertainment plays in everyday life. Mass entertainment spectacles such as the CCTV Spring Festival 'party' (*wanhui*) and formats such as Arts Kaleidosope (*Zongyi daguan*) have a social function of community bonding. In recent years, however, new entertainment formats such as game shows and chat shows have been acquired from neighbouring television systems and have spread in a virus-like fashion throughout the Chinese television landscape. There are many reasons for this: these programmes are relatively cheap to produce, they have demonstrated audience success, and they can incorporate pedagogic characteristics where necessary to appease cultural police.

Television formats illustrate the machinations of contemporary television industries. Copying successful ideas gets audiences, although, as I argue in this chapter, it can also stymie industry development if cloning becomes the dominant strategy. There is also the vexing question of format copyright, made even more complex by the pandemic of intellectual property piracy in China. Whereas many television systems worldwide abide by industry agreements that formats are the intellectual property of their originators, in China format appropriation is opportunistic and rampant.

The positive aspect of television formats is that they enable technology transfer and cultural hybridization. Whereas Chinese producers have borrowed ideas from foreign television systems over the past two decades, the mass exploitation of formats is a recent phenomenon. In the context of increasing 'copy-catting', it is worth noting that producers are often reluctant to discuss questions of format origin, and that Chinese viewers are generally unaware of the extent of format flows. What does this say about Chinese audiences and television producers? Probably nothing more than the fact that copying is deemed good business, a legacy of a social system in which everything belonged to the state, and therefore to the people.

Aside from the many revealing cultural insights that can be gleaned by submitting formats to textual scrutiny, there is another aspect that informs my research: that is to view formats not simply as mass cultural artifacts but as 'packages of ideas'. The chapter will therefore provide a theoretical perspective on format flows, which rather than simply emphasizing ideological or stereotypical representations encoded in finished programmes – as has been the dominant mode of 'content' analysis – will consider formats as a 'cultural technology'. In this sense, the propagation of formats has the capacity to add value to television systems' diversity in programming menus. The second part of the chapter will deal with a particular manifestation of format cloning: the Chinese dating show (*zhenghun jiemu*).

Formats and new trade routes

The travelling format is a well-recognized cultural artifact in Western television landscapes. Audiences have been exposed to a seemingly endless supply of reality TV scenarios devised by dedicated European format specialists like Pearson, the BBC, Distraction Formats, GMG Endemol, Action Time, and Celador (Moran 1998). It can be argued that working with formats is a legitimate survival strategy for television producers operating outside of the cashed-up American television system. Ready-made formats are a cheap option for television stations operating in undercapitalized markets unable to compete with the high-budget offerings of foreign providers. Copying formats saves R & D and obviates the risks associated with new programme development.

In a global environment of television industries confronting change from state subsidy to privatization, from mass delivery of content to customized service industry models, any content that captures audience segments without necessitating huge outlays of investment is manna from heaven. It is in the commercial environment of generating audiences to sell to advertisers that the mutation of entertainment formats is most visible. Aside from the pedagogic pull of 'how to' info-tainment formats, the banality of *Blooper* and amateur video shows, it seems that relationships, personal transformation, and wealth generation fulfil the requirements of good television programming. One of the popular attractions of formats therefore is the identification of cultural variations that occur when formats mutate from country to country. Clever manipulation of cultural dynamics also adds value to the product in non-native markets as viewers identify with the foibles of ordinary people revealed on the small screen.

With television producers in China now moving from genre imitation to format appropriation in order to maximize audiences with a minimum of programme development cost, the medium-term future of Chinese content development looks distressingly uninspiring. A number of questions need to be asked. Can Chinese television stations gear up for new media environments by simply copying formats? What is 'good television' in China? Is it programming that is innovative and challenging, or simply that which delivers audiences to advertisers? What happens when formats pass their relatively short shelf life? What are the economic and moral implications of plagiarism? Should there be more stringent policies to combat the epidemic of copyright infringement? Should television stations pool their resources to improve the quality of content?

These are issues that confront China's media industries as they enter a new competitive phase following entry into the World Trade Organization. Format appropriation might just be a stopgap measure as the industry gears up for competition and shakes down its excessive channel structure (see Redl and Simons, this volume). Knowing which formats work, however, does not necessarily translate into market success. Television concepts and ideas are swiftly copied, modified, and exploited by neighbouring stations desperate to put together successful programmes to keep their station leaders happy. However, despite the practice of cloning without permission, there are already a number of formats under licence to major television stations in China. Shanghai Television's adaptation of *Sesame Street* is the most notable in this regard. The transfer of the format to Shanghai Television from the parent Childrens Television Workshop (CTW) began in 1996, taking the producers and a team of eighteen educationalists and psychologists two years to put together a 'Bible' (*tianshu*) – the package of licensing procedures agreed to by both parties. The programme was finally screened on 14 February 1998. Another project, *Joy Luck Street* (*Xingfu jie*), a co-production format funded by Granada Television in the United Kingdom, produced by Hong Kong-based Yahuan Cable Company and directed by leading lights of the Beijing Broadcasting Institute, began screening in 2000 on 90 cable channels. Devised as a remake of the English 'soap' *Coronation Street* the Chinese version soon found local audiences somewhat bemused by the Anglicized soap opera format, resulting in the sacking of the director and his replacement by locals (see Keane 2001b). Another example of a licensed format is a version of *Entertainment Tonight* broadcast on Shanghai Television.

When there is not the revenue base to enact a formal licensing agreement, it is often simply a case of taking a format and pretending that you originated it. The example of Hunan Satellite Television's *Kuaile da benying* (*The Citadel of Happiness*) is a good example of successful format adaptation combined with self-reliant management strategies. The show consists primarily of apolitical entertainment content, based around social issues, youth lifestyle, and popular music. According to management at Hunan Satellite Television, this variety game show was of domestic origin and was conceived in 1996 in response to viewer dissatisfaction with the pedagogic content of existing variety formats such as CCTV's *Zhengda Variety* and *Arts Kaleidoscope* (*Zongyi daguan*).[1] The Hunan programme was piloted and subsequently refined. Confident that it had a winning format, Hunan Satellite Television then spent a great deal of money promoting the show, bringing in celebrities from Hong Kong and Taiwan. Indeed, the show became so successful that advertising rates exceeded expectations. Within a short space of time the programme's own format had been cloned into more than 100 local variants within China itself, none attaining the heights of the original – a fact attributed to its youthful hosts Li Xiang and He Ling, and its constant evolution in order to distance itself from its imitators. Furthermore, whereas many cable stations exchange programme packages based on the concept of reciprocity, this does not apply to *The Citadel of Happiness*. Despite its Hunanese origins and the criticisms of it emanating from Beijing, many cable providers in China carry the show.

Not surprisingly, Hunan's new breed of television executives soon attracted the displeasure of CCTV stalwarts who claimed that the programme was a rip-off of Taiwanese formats. Producer Wang Bingwen was called to defend the integrity of *The Citadel of Happiness*. Wang refuted claims that the programme was appropriated from Taiwan, and cited a long pedigree of similar variety formats in the United States and Japan. In order to negate the criticisms of the programme's lack of educational (*sixiang*) content, he drew attention to programme themes like the 105th annual celebration of Mao Zedong's birth, environmental protection, and sensitive issues of unemployment (*xia gang*) (Wang [Bingwen] 1999).

Cultural exchange: theoretical parameters

The neglect of formats in scholarly accounts of China's media industry is testimony to the potency of cultural imperialism models that presuppose a flow of values from a stronger to a weaker media environment. Central to our study of format cloning, however, is a theorization of cultural exchange. While cultural imperialism has proved to be a rather crude paradigm to explain often-complicated negotiation of meanings that occur in processes of cultural exchange – in this instance when foreign programmes are introduced to China – it nevertheless retains a kind of commonsense attraction for communication scholars. This is no doubt due to the steady stream of moral panics that seem to reinforce the consensus that popular culture has determinate and detrimental effects on passive populations. The use of the term 'hybridity' has likewise served as an antidote to simplistic media effects and it can be useful in explaining how texts (programmes) are creatively appropriated and reimagined. However, it is important to bear in mind that the term 'hybrid' implies a pure origin. This is something that is unmasked when we examine such phenomena as the traffic in television formats. By the time a television format is 'adapted' to Chinese audience tastes it may have travelled across several continents and traversed an equal number of linguistic systems. As we shall see, the formats that 'take' in the Chinese media market are often those that are successful in places like Taiwan and Hong Kong, even though they may have come to the Middle Kingdom via Western television trade routes.

The route that formats take leads us into an examination of the relationship between form and content. With ideological limitations on expression in the People's Republic of China, the format functions as a 'Trojan horse' for the infiltration of bourgeois content. The concept of the 'mediasphere' is a useful heuristic device to illustrate this point. John Hartley developed the idea of the mediasphere from the work of the Soviet semiotician Yuri Lotman (1990). Lotman's original concept, the 'semiosphere', referred to the universe of symbolic content. Hartley sees the 'mediasphere' existing inside the semiosphere as a repository of mediated content that is potentially lubricous. He calls it 'the whole universe of the media – both factual and fictional, in all forms (print, electronic and screen), all genres (new, drama), all taste hierarchies (from art to entertainment) in all languages in all countries' (Hartley 1999: 218). The mediasphere can also be seen as comprising national mediaspheres. To take this line of thought further, we can say that the Chinese mediasphere was until the past decade extremely impoverished and sterile. This was due to the limited archive from which its content was drawn – the deeds of model citizens, war heroes and great villains, and traditional culture certified as 'healthy' by the Ministry of Culture. Added to the problems of impoverishment and sterility was governmental control over forms. A limitation on forms and genres (e.g.

socialist realism, mainstream melody productions) worked to limit what was said, how it was said, and how it was circulated. That is, as the form (e.g. socialist realism) pre-existed it was often a case of the content being made to fit. The news was written before it was published, the TV drama was already scripted before the writers came to the table.[2] An increase in the number of media forms/formats resulting from the commercialization of the media thus creates a demand for new ideas and challenges the hegemony of official media forms. Diversity of forms creates problems for the disciplining of content. The Chinese mediasphere thus expands and begins to overlap with, and feed off, other globally promiscuous mediaspheres.

The diversification of formats can also be illustrated by a recipe metaphor. If there are more recipes available there will be a corresponding demand for more ingredients. In industry parlance the relationship between format and content is that of 'pie and crust', whereby 'the 'crust' is the same from week to week but the filling changes' (van Manen cited in Moran 1998: 13). Michael Rodrigue of format specialist Distraction Formats offers another spin on the gastronomic metaphor:

> A TV program format is a recipe, which allows television concepts and ideas to travel without being stopped by either geographical or linguistic boundaries. To achieve this, the recipe comes with a whole range of ingredients making it possible for producers throughout the world to locally produce a television program based on a foreign format, and to present it as a local television show perfectly adapted to their respective countries and cultures.
>
> (Rodrigue 2000)

The format is a recipe, a package, or a combination of technologies that enables change in media systems. The idea of cultural technology transfer presents an interesting shift from text-based explanations, and allows us to take into account the dynamics of flows whereby measurable economic benefit accrues to the appropriator, often at the expense of the originator of content. At the same time, ideas, policies and organizational practices are introduced into the receiving system. The idea of cultural technology transfer thus has two edges. In a material sense a cultural commodity is formed; in the other sense the success of commodity – its consumption, or in the case of a television programme, its ratings – leads to further appropriation of the technology.

This idea of cultural technology entails looking at content from the increasingly mutually porous production–consumption relationship rather than through the legacy of 'effects' models. The format is thus a 'cultural technology' that can be used to add value to the recipient industry. Whereas knowledge of audience taste and predisposition garnered by market research is used to originate programmes, a package of associated technologies is traded (under licence) or appropriated without permission. As van Manen has pointed out, format transfer (in the formal sense at least) can include the provision of computer software for programme credits, animation sequences, designer blueprints for such things as programme sets and studio filming, film footage for insertion in the new programme version of the format, and scripts for individual episodes (van Manen 1994: 15–23) Other technologies may also constitute a part of the transfer package. These include ratings information derived from audience surveys, programming details, and polls associated with the broadcast of the earlier programme version of the format. Within the industry these are collectively referred to as 'the Bible' (*tianshu*). Another technology that is frequently added to the value of the format itself is a consultancy service, wherein a production executive associated with the earlier programme will act as adviser to a new production of the format (Moran 1998: 14).

Case study: Who does your heart beat for?

Television dating shows have a kind of universal and mass voyeuristic appeal. Witnessing simmering libidos and overreacting egos on the small screen can be compulsive viewing. Until the Internet's recent takeover of the matchmaking sweepstakes, television presented the ideal medium for the presentation of one's self to one's soul mate (and to a mass audience of judges). Dating shows of all hues have been around almost as long as television and still hold their place in the ratings. For instance, in Ireland a self-styled 'daring' dating game show format, *Perfect Match* currently rates highly for its commercial broadcaster TV3. Aimed at the demographic 16–35, *Perfect Match* is aired weekly in the Friday 9 p.m. slot. According to Distraction Formats, the originators of this programme:

> This edgy format attributes its success to its unique format, daring questions and raunchy liaisons! Each week, the audience gets to make their Perfect Match with the three boys or girls by matching them to their cars, best friends, and by asking revealing and cheeky questions. Only the quickest and shrewdest survive and once all three of the boys or girls are paired off, the audience must vote for the winning couple!

Western dating programmes are less about bringing two star-crossed strangers together, as providing an opportunity for contestants to vie for prizes such as holidays, jewellery and cosmetics. The Chinese dating show, on the other hand, provides us with a distinctly collectivist matchmaking game. In contrast to the overtly sexual and individualist nature of most Western dating shows, the Chinese clones embody multiple match-offs, contestants' attention to detail, moralist commentary by hosts and audience, and the technological infallibility of the resulting match-offs.

The forerunner of the mass entertainment dating format on Chinese television screens was a simple matchmaker format (*zhenghun jiemu*) in which the desperate and dateless, often well-educated, unmarried, middle-aged men and women, sought lifelong soul mates. In a manner similar to Internet sites that offer relationship 'services', this format – best exemplified by Beijing TV's *Tonight We Will Become Acquainted* (*Jinwan women xiangshi*) – presented participants' photographs, personal attributes, and expectations of relationship to the wide viewing audience.

This televisual personal introduction service failed to capture the imagination of Beijing audiences and was soon left on the shelf, like many of its participants. Several years later Hunan Satellite Television hit on the right formula with its popular dating show, *'Xizhilang' Romantic Meeting* (*Meigui zhi yue*).[3] The sponsor 'Xizhilang' is a Japanese food company that produces among other things, jelly. What is distinctive in *Romantic Meeting* is a carefully planned group format culminating in a match-off that often brings together several couples. Audience participation also features with family members, friends and workmates barracking and influencing the judging. This programme is a prime example of format cloning. The group-date format had originated in Japan in December 1975 on NET (now ANB) on a programme called *Propose Dai-Sakusen*.[4]

But it was the Taiwanese programme *Special Man and Woman* (*Feichang nannü*) that ultimately had the biggest impact upon mainland audiences. First broadcast in China in July 1997, this programme was distributed by Phoenix Television (Hong Kong) to Chinese cable stations as *'Yajia' Special Man and Woman* (*Feichang nannü*). Yajia is a brand of cosmetics. A year later Hunan Satellite TV's *Romantic Meeting* was up and running (Luo 2000). The success of the group-date format soon spawned a rash of clones including Shanghai Television's *Saturday Meeting* (*Xiangyue xingqiliu*), Hebei Television's *The Square of Kindred Spirits* (*Xinxin guangchang*), Beijing Television's revised version of *Tonight We Become Acquainted* (*Jinwan women xiangshi*), Beijing Cable TV's *Everlasting Romance* (*Langman jiujiu*), Shandong TV's *Golden Meeting* (*Jinri you yue*), Shanxi TV's *Good Man, Good Woman* (*Haonan haonü*), Nanjing TV's *Who Does Your Heart Beat For?* (*Wei shei xindong?*), Nanjing Cable TV's *Conjugal Bliss* (*Huahao yueyuan*), Hainan TV's *Talking marriage* (*Nannü danghun*), and Chongqing Satellite Television's *Heavenly Fate* (*Yuanfen tiankong*) (Luo 2000; Yang [Bin] 2000) As well as being ubiquitous on Chinese television networks, these dating and matchmaker shows range from the tragically amateurish and underproduced to slick productions featuring special guests, music, and segments filmed outside the studio. Contestants likewise are not confined to good-looking twenty-somethings. Older contestants whose values are more conservative provide balance and often a more serious demeanour.

Making out on the small screen

> I used to think that all people in Taiwan were Guomindang (Nationalist Government) and if it came to conflict I would be the first one to fight them to the death, but after watching *Special Man and Woman* I have had an about-turn in my thinking. I saw a group of young people across the sea who were just like me, and who struggled hard to have a happy life.
>
> (Correspondent to the TV show *Feichang nannu*, cited by Luo 2000: 3)

The format for *Special Man and Woman* provides the template for numerous imitators. Twenty participants are seated facing each other. The programme is introduced by a male and a female host, following which participants are introduced and audience members, including family and workmates (*qinyoutuan*), provide additional information about the contestants, their personalities, abilities, and moral values. Contestants then play a round called 'fall in love at first sight' (*yijian zhongqing*). Based on the information provided, the participants cast a primary electronic vote on whoever they feel might be an ideal partner. This is followed by a round called 'special topic' (*feichang huati*) in which contestants are quizzed on their opinions on a range of themes such as premarital relationships, extramarital relationships, marriage tribulations, homosexuality, and romance. The show's compères freely ad lib as well as seek the opinion of an invited expert on marriage and relationships. A secondary vote follows and the most popular couples are revealed on a backdrop screen, as well as the persons who voted for them. Following this, participants engage in a cross-examination of potential partners. The final vote is conducted and couples who match up take the stage and exchange gifts while those unlucky in the love game are able to make a statement about their availability to members of the viewing community.

Hunan Satellite TV's version of television dating adopted many of the formal characteristics of the Taiwanese original, while differing in some aesthetic factors. According to one critique of the two shows, *Romantic Meeting* is more down-market and frivolous than *Special Man and Woman*, with the mainland contestants engaging in more banter and blatant self-promotion than their Taiwanese counterparts. This he attributes to the fact that Taiwanese people subscribe to a more ethical code of self-presentation based upon Confucian principles (Ye 2000). The broadcast of *Special Man and Woman* in China has even contributed to the fostering of international relations. In fact, the widespread cloning of dating show formats might well be attributed to the power of television in liberating the mainland Chinese population from collective capture by socialist morality, a code of ethics in which people could not publicly admit individual desires, or discuss sexuality and love. Taking into account the stigma and social protocols associated with forming partners in China (and Chinese societies elsewhere), it is not surprising that dating/relationship formats once broadcast should develop loyal audiences. Traditional Chinese society placed a heavy emphasis on finding a partner, not so much for love, but for practical reasons, such as social status. Nowadays Chinese youth are less restrained about expressing emotions, a consequence of exposure to the cultural traffic of 'assertive' Western pop culture and hybrid pan-Asian cultural identity formats carried by Japanese, Hong Kong, and Taiwanese music videos, television dramas, and cinema.

Moreover, the very fact of appearing on television and baring one's innermost feelings to millions of people suggests that Chinese people, often stereotyped as reserved, can overcome inhibitions. An illustration of this occurred on *Romantic Meeting* a year after its inception when it opened its studio doors to three participants from Beijing who had registered on-line. One of the three, Wang Shaodong, an employee of the Dow Jones joint venture in Beijing, gave his reasons for wanting to go on the show as wanting to expose himself to a national audience and become a national celebrity (Luo 2000: 9). Wang and his two companions did become mini-celebrities due to their humorous antics. We can only conclude that Andy Warhol's famous statement about everyone having fifteen minutes of celebrity status travels well. Participants' reasons for appearing on dating shows vary from simply wanting to be seen by a mass audience to genuinely seeking a romantic relationship. The competitive nature of dating shows now means that producers seek out the bold and the beautiful to appear rather than the despairing and dull. If contestants can sing and dance, engage in repartee and self-parody, and have good teeth to boot, they are most likely to make it on the small screen.[5]

Conclusion

Notwithstanding the criticism directed at entertainment formats by critics we have to acknowledge their role in filling out the viewing schedules of China's television broadcasters. With multi-channelling and increasing audience fragmentation beginning to bite in China, television stations increasingly look for the cheap proven formula to gain their ratings figures. This sends mixed signals about the state of China's domestic industry. Formats add value by introducing new ideas, technologies, and production skills. They also appease audience desires for affective content while incorporating necessary pedagogic elements. However, there is something fundamentally parasitic about cloning which is detrimental to the reinvigoration of the Chinese mediascape. We can certainly expect a new wave of format appropriation in the near future, whether these formats come from Taiwan, Hong Kong or Japan, or travel the longer trade routes from the

West. Perhaps the next killer format in China will be a combination of reality-TV shows *Survivor*, *Big Brother* and *The Mole*, in which a dozen or so Chinese cadres will be forced to struggle for scarce resources in a work unit, warding off the threats of corruption, spiritual pollution, and back-door politics.

Notes

1 *Zhengda zongyi* (literally 'the upright arts magazine') is a format co-produced and sponsored by the overseas China Zhengda consortium based in Thailand that specializes in livestock and agricultural fertilizers.
2 See Hartley and McKee (2000) pp. 49–50 for a discussion of this in relation to indigenous media.
3 The word *meigui* literally means 'rose'.
4 The dating programme concept was developed by Fuji Television a year earlier – a one-on-one scenario called Punch de Date. Incidentally *dai-sakusen* literally means 'big operation'. (It comes from the Japanese title of *Mission Impossible* which was very popular at that time. The Japanese title of *Mission Impossible* was *Spy Dai-Sakusen.*)
5 Chen Kuan-Hsing (2000) makes a similar point in relation to the Chinese acceptance of karaoke and KTV. See also Chua Beng-huat (1999) for a discussion of the use of self-parody in public space as a means of obviating potential embarrassment.

SECTION 3

POLITICS, IMAGE, AND THE NICHE MARKET

8

ROCK IN A HARD PLACE

Commercial fantasies in China's music industry

Jeroen de Kloet

> If you understand the production part, it'd be easier to talk, or if you knew about publishing, marketing and promotion. But in China, nobody understands that system. Musicians in China don't know anything about how the industry works, ... they just play the music and want to make a name. People from outside [China] or some local Chinese would like to collaborate, but they don't know how to help them, so in the end there's nothing.
>
> (Dickson Dee, Manager, Sound Factory, Hong Kong)

Seductive narratives

In the mid-1980s, rock singer Cui Jian stirred up the waters of popular music in mainland China with his hit 'Nothing to My Name'. The adoption of the song by the students' movement in 1989 fed well into the subversive aura of rock 'n' roll. The early 1990s witnessed a growth of Chinese rock culture. Investments by record companies from Taiwan and Hong Kong provided, arguably, a fertile soil for rock to grow on. Both musicians and journalists complained in the mid-1990s, however, about a creative crisis, a decreasing popularity of Chinese rock. Seduced by the sounds of pop from Hong Kong and Taiwan, infected by the spirit of money, rock was not 'hot' any more among Chinese youth. After 1997, however, rock regained its position in the market, due mainly to investments from local, Beijing-based companies. Rock is now a fairly stable genre *within* the pop music industry, but it has not proved the huge money-earner that some had hoped it would be.

Attracted by the provocative poses of some mainland bands, most academic work concentrates on Beijing rock culture rather than on the music industry (Jones 1992, 1994; Steen 1996; Kloet 1998, 2000). Here, I analyse the developments of the music industry in China in the 1990s. I consider economic trends, concluding that the Chinese music market, contrary to popular belief, has declined over the decade. The market is anything but big, despite the size of China's population. Having sketched this rather gloomy picture of the music industry, I discuss the role of regional investors in the production of Beijing rock. In particular, Magic Stone from Taiwan (part of the larger regional record company Rock Records) and Red Star (*Hong xing*) from Hong Kong are believed to have taken over the production of Chinese rock. Barmé (1999: 133) notes that 'contacts with the Hong Kong and Taiwan music industry went from strength to strength'. Huot (2000: 170) makes a similar point.

Chinese pop culture is perceived to be in the grip of a process of rapid commercialization. This perception is linked to the regionalization of media industries in general, and to the wider context of global 'industry' flows. The role of the regional music industry is sometimes interpreted as proof of common popular culture in 'Greater China', in which Hong Kong and Taiwan are considered to be the key cultural producers (Gold 1993; Harding 1995). I argue that, whereas the 'Greater China' narrative suggests that economic and cultural ties between Hong Kong, Taiwan and China have strengthened over the 1990s, Chinese rock underwent a reverse trend: at the end of the 1990s, local companies expanded at the expense of regional competitors. To single out commercial factors for these developments would offer inadequate explanation. My study shows how investments from regional companies as well as the subsequent 'local turn' are grounded in embedded cultural aspirations. The pop–rock divide, in which pop (from Hong Kong and Taiwan) is perceived to be commercial and inauthentic, and rock (from Beijing) is considered truly authentic, informs investment policies from record companies (Kloet 2000). A concept such as commercialization is far too sweeping to grasp the particularities of the Chinese music industry. It also foregrounds the financial at the expense of specific cultural considerations that inform the market policies of record companies.

The present argument is based on existing literature, figures from the industry, provided by the International Federation of the Phonographic Industry (IFPI – the representative of the major record companies), and in-depth information obtained from interviews with record companies, publishers, managers, producers, musicians and journalists between 1997 and 2000. The necessary incompleteness and inconsistencies of the information gathered can be interpreted as symptomatic of the chaotic state of the Chinese music industry. The sheer impossibility of developing an encompassing organizational-economic model for the Chinese music industry forces us to look for contextualized and fragmented interpretations.

Asian records

The size of China's population invites an easy exaggeration of its market potential, especially in comparison with other parts of the world. Even if

Table 8.1 1999 world music sales ranking

Country	*Retail value US$millions)*	*Ranking*
USA	14,251	1
Japan	6,437	2
UK	2,909	3
Germany	2,832	4
Australia	656	8
Netherlands	522	12
Taiwan	307	16
India	175	24
Indonesia	127	29
Hong Kong	99	34
China	94	36

one only reaches a small part of the youth market of China, profits are 'bound' to be huge.[1] A best-selling artist might well sell millions of albums on the mainland. Table 1 presents an overview of the world music sales ranking of both Western and Asian countries (source: IFPI 2000).

The United States and Japan are currently the world's biggest music markets. The retail value of 'Greater China' – that is, the total retail value of China, Taiwan and Hong Kong put together – amounted to US$500 million in 1999, a market comparable in size to that of the Netherlands.[2] China's market amounts to only 14 per cent of the Australian market and 0.7 per cent of the United States market. For the time being, although the mainland music market might be huge in terms of potential customers, it is less so in terms of its retail value. Indeed, the Chinese market gradually declined through the 1990s (Table 2).

Table 8.2 Retail value of selected music markets (US$ millions) since 1995 (IFPI 1999, 2000)

	1995	*1996*	*1997*	*1998*	*1999*
China	(178)	(188)	127	103	94
Hong Kong	(183)	231	175	118	99
Taiwan	336	415	427	320	307
'Greater China'	**(697)**	**(834)**	**729**	**541**	**500**
United States	12,100	12,298	11,906	13,193	14,251
Australia	680	815	739	607	656

Note: The figures for China for 1996–97 and the figures for Hong Kong for 1995–96 are not comparable, which is why these figures are placed in parentheses in the table.

The Hong Kong market reached its peak in 1996 and then declined. The Taiwanese market underwent gradual growth until 1997. Celine Cheung, manager of the publishing unit of Rock Records Hong Kong, explained to me how Cantopop sale figures decreased in Hong Kong during the 1990s (pers. comm. 19 July 1999):

> There is a great difference between now and the past. When I entered this industry in 1988 I worked with the company of Anita Mui. A good album would sell 200,000 copies. Now a top one like Leon Lai only 50,000 to 80,000. Most artists sell around 2,000 to 3,000.

The 1999 sale figures and the development of the Chinese market during the 1990s both present a depressing financial picture. The narrative goes that over the 1990s the spirit of money took over control in China. It proves to be a fragile spirit when it comes to the music industry.

Open doors – closed regulations

There are four factors, which go some way to explaining the situation: the Asian financial crisis, the supremacy of the (cheap) cassette tape, high piracy levels and the role of the state. First, the Asian crisis has impacted badly upon the regional music industry. This contradicts assumptions that the Asian crisis – which began in 1997 and spread from Thailand, Indonesia and Malaysia to, among other countries, Taiwan and Hong Kong (Hamlin 2000: 1–16) – has had comparatively less impact on Mainland China (Saywell 1999). The figures (Table 2) show a steady decline in the music market in China, Hong Kong and Taiwan, suggesting that in this industry the crisis has caused problems across 'Greater China'.

Second and third, there are delivery problems. Citizens consume at a low rate and, when they do, the potential income for the industry is dented by piracy as well as by the cheapness of the dominant music carrier – the music cassette as opposed to the CD. In 1999, 69.9 million cassette tapes were sold in mainland China, against 8.4 million CDs. For Hong Kong these figures were 0.2 million and 10.3 million respectively, which helps explain why Hong Kong ranks higher on the world music sales list (IFPI 2000). China ranks first in the world on the retail value of domestic piracy; this has been calculated to be approximately US$620 million, giving a piracy level of around 90 per cent (IFPI 2000). Cut CDs (*dakou*) exported to China from the West (to be used as surplus plastic), enter the illegal market, further undermining the profits of the record companies. Nevertheless, both pirated copies and cut CDs open up a sonic space for audiences that would otherwise remain closed due to censorship and import quotas, or simply because legal CDs are too expensive for most Chinese. Pirated and illegal cassette tapes and CDs may be considered both productive and destructive for music cultures in China.

Finally, the structure of the music industry in China is not conducive to financial success. A distinction must be made between music publisher and record company. A record company contracts the artist and records the master tape. It takes care of the design and is responsible, sometimes together with the publisher, for the marketing. Foreign record companies are not allowed, yet, to set up an independent office in China; only joint ventures are legal. Record companies cannot release albums on the market, they can only do so through a music publisher. By definition, the music publisher is a government-owned company. It often arranges the duplication of the master tape and is responsible for its distribution throughout the country. The gatekeeping role of these publishers affects the 'openness' of the Chinese music market. Meanwhile, foreign companies license their product to an internal distributor. According to Gene Lau from ZOOM music, a Hong Kong company with an office in Beijing (5 November 1997):

> For the international record companies, if they cannot handle the distribution directly, they are not really interested. Many foreign companies hold offices in China now, but they are just using a very small budget and trying to learn how to manage a company in China. Their main purpose is to sell their foreign products to China.

Thus, *all* sound carriers in China are being released by one of the 250–300 publishing houses, all of which are affiliated to the General State Administration of Radio, Film and Television (SARFT) (*Guojia guangbo dianying dianshi zongju*) or to the Ministry of Culture (*Wenhuabu*). The publishing houses are relatively independent entities. They can be considered to be state-owned companies aiming for a firm position in the market. The publisher receives a comparatively large share of revenue. Roughly, the shares of revenue from a 10 RMB purchase (roughly US$1) are divided as follows: the record company receives 15 per cent, the publisher/distributor 60 per cent, and the retailer 25 per cent. It is a sheer impossibility for record companies to cover the costs of production.

My sketch of the Chinese music industry shows that it is too simple to group developments in the 1990s under the concept of commercialization. Manager Edward Ko from Rock Records Shanghai concisely summarizes the crucial obstacles (27 July 1999):

> The problem is that the CCP controls all the publishing houses; they don't allow record companies to publish their own records, because they think it is dangerous. Now they are ready to enter the WTO, they must at least open their cultural market. ... If that happens, the whole structure will change. Promotion, publishing, everything will change. The market will become a normal one and piracy will be reduced. At the moment the publishing houses are doing a bad job.

World Trade Organization membership may indeed benefit the cultural industries. Meanwhile, it seems justifiable to adopt the jargon of the Party and speak of 'commercialization with Chinese characteristics'.

Commercial pilgrimages

Seventy per cent of the global music industry is in the hands of five major record companies (Laing 1998: 339). Global capital plays a predominant role in the production of local and regional music cultures. Global record companies are deeply involved in the production of the idea of a 'Greater China'. They recognize the need to localize their products in order to gain a considerable market share. Rather than excluding one another, the global, the regional and the local are mutually embedded. Global record companies penetrate the well-developed markets of Japan, Hong Kong and Taiwan, but are far less part of the less-developed Mainland market. In the mid-1990s, the transnationals had a market share of 90 per cent in Hong Kong, but only 14 per cent in China (Laing 1998: 339). Apart from Universal, none of the transnational companies has contracted a Chinese rock band. The obvious explanation for this is that China does not allow independent record companies yet to enter the market; only joint ventures are allowed to operate in China.

Rather than one of the big five, it was regional record companies that entered the Chinese rock market in the early 1990s. At that time, the financial picture seemed promising given the popularity of rock music. After the decline in retail value in the early 1990s, what motivated producers Magic Stone from Taiwan and ZOOM Music (*Zhimu changpian*) and Red Star, both from Hong Kong, to stay? Presumably, the answer is 'optimism':

> Maybe in three years the market will be open, and if we hadn't started two years ago, we wouldn't have a chance to survive. If we can produce one classic album a year that people will still buy ten years later, we just hope [...] Nobody wants to give up the Chinese market, you know, because it's so huge, but to survive will be a long march, it isn't easy.
>
> (Leslie Chan of Red Star, 5 July 1997)

> I feel that in China there are no rules of the game, so you can still start your own company, even if you don't have so much money. But in Hong Kong and Taiwan, it's all controlled by big record companies; independent companies can't do the same kind of things. ... In China there are still many chances to do independent business.
>
> (Gene Lau, of ZOOM music and formerly in charge of BMG's China trade, 5 November 1997)

The absence of the major record companies provides space for small companies to enter the market. Apart from their desire to fill the vacuum left by the absence of the big companies, discontent with the pop music they grew up with was often quoted as a consideration:

> I don't like Hong Kong music, although I am a Cantopop lyric writer.
> (Gene Lau)

> The more time I spend in China, the more I realize that Cantopop has a big problem; it has no spirit, the music is not music. ... It's like drinking water, it has no taste at all. ... But for the music in China, especially the Beijing artists, they really come up with something.
> (Leslie Chan)

> Our long-term goal is to export music to Hong Kong and Taiwan, rather than having Cantopop pushing into the mainland, which is really sad. Everybody sings the same kind of music, about love and relationships, 95% is the same. Chinese music may have something different, the contents, the lyrics are more sophisticated, something that is from the heart.
> (Louis Chan, Red Star, 28 August 1997)

The perceived authenticity of Chinese rock music and discontent with 'commercial' Cantopop were then incentives to enter the market. Added to the perceived authenticity of the music is the image of Beijing as the cultural centre of 'Greater China'. Beijing is an important signifier. Along with the Great Wall it is *the* dominant symbol of 5,000 years of Chinese history and tradition. As such, the appeal of Beijing rock to regional record producers can be interpreted as an imagined cultural pilgrimage. The Hong Kong and Taiwan producers return to their imagined cultural roots and thus merge with 5,000 years of history. Rock singers play on this:

> I love Beijing because it is a city of culture, you can always feel the culture. In Hong Kong, all you feel is money, just the commercial thing, everybody is living in a supermarket. ... In Beijing it's different, we think more about music.
> (Folk-rock singer Zheng Jun, 2 July 1997)

These factors support Negus's argument that 'what are often taken to be straightforward business decisions are actually based on a number of culturally specific beliefs and assumptions' (Negus 1998: 367). These beliefs and assumptions are not necessarily shared by all the parties involved. Musicians are often highly critical about record companies, and smoothly retreat to the grounds of national–cultural essentialism in order to make their point:

> I don't know how a record company should be, but to me, the Taiwanese like to cheat people. The Taiwanese are good at making fake things.
> (Gao Wei from pop-punk band Underground Baby (*Dixia yin'er*), signed by Taiwan-based company Magic Stone, 13 October 1997)

Red Star gives me very small royalties; it's very unfair, but they are Hong Kong people, you know ...

(Zhang Qianqian, female singer contracted by Red Star from Hong Kong, 28 October 1997)

I don't believe in Taiwanese people, I just don't like them. ... I know some singers who were contracted by Magic Stone, they have big problems.

(Wang Feng, lead vocal of *Baojiajie 43*, a band contracted by Beijing-based company Jingwen, 10 September 1997)

These opinions suggest that the commercial links do not necessitate the emergence of a deeper common culture. Commercial imperatives motivate cultural struggles in which 'national characteristics' are articulated in order to strengthen one's own position. Producers often react in a similar manner. Rock Records manager Celine Cheung from Hong Kong complained about how lazy Chinese rock singers are, and that they constantly had to visit Beijing to inquire about the progress of Dou Wei. Others consider them simply as having been brainwashed by communist propaganda.

The production of rock can thus be interpreted as a struggle over and for culture. Boundaries – that is, markers of cultural difference – are both drawn and contested. The commitment of producers to Chinese rock can be traced to a complex and contradictory set of factors. It is a cultural pilgrimage, yet for producers the final destination of this pilgrimage – Beijing – simultaneously signifies repression and unpredictability. Commercial aspirations are strongly fuelled by social and cultural considerations.

During the latter half of the 1990s, as the expected profits failed to materialize, certain regional record companies – Magic Stone from Taiwan and Red Star from Hong Kong – did gradually pull out of the Chinese rock market. They left a gap that was filled by local companies like Jingwen, Modern Sky (*Moden tiankong*), and New Bees (*Xin feng yinyue*). The production of rock is now characterized by a decrease (rather than increase) in economic ties between China, Hong Kong, and Taiwan.

The local turn

In the popular mainland press the local turn in the production of rock is considered to have resulted in the emergence of the New Sound Movement (*Xinsheng yundong*) (Yan [Jun] 1999). Modern Sky plays a pivotal role in rock's rebirth, with at least ten new titles a year. The same company also publishes its own monthly music magazine – *Modern Sky Magazine* – which contains, like other magazines such as *Music Heaven* (*Yinyue tiantang*), a compilation CD introducing both Chinese and Western bands with an accompanying booklet explaining the tracks. It also has its own rock venue, Bar 17 in Sanlitun (a street of bars located in the diplomatic area of Beijing).

Shen Lihui, manager of Modern Sky, has set a trend in the music business of China. Although both Jingwen and Modern Sky are local, they are strikingly different. Jingwen resembles very much an old-style work unit or *danwei*: It is located in a grey apartment block, is directed by older men and, given its status as a music distributor, has close ties with the official structures. Modern Sky works more independently: it is run by young people and is housed in a chaotic office where the most recent computers (i-Macs, of course) are used. Shen Lihui is profiting from what he calls 'a relaxed attitude towards music publishing on the part of political authorities' (Steen 2000). Modern Sky has been labelled by Guo and Su (Steen 2000) a 'typical postmodern PRC paradox' because it uses different tactics to circumvent regulations.[3]

Modern Sky signifies a break with the old system; it shows how new, young entrepreneurs have created a space that operates more independently from the state, a space filled by young entertainment and Internet companies. But, however promising its start, the financial picture drawn earlier in this chapter has not changed. There are rumours in the rock culture that Modern Sky's financial problems are getting worse. Various foreign companies have shown interest in buying the company, with Sony named as the most likely candidate (Virant 1999: 12). To label Modern Sky a local company might shortly prove inaccurate. The local turn marked a specific moment in China's modern history. It remains to be seen whether local or regional companies are strong enough to compete with the big foreign record companies that will most likely move in when China joins the WTO.

Cultural factors are again named by managers of the local companies to explain why the regional competitors didn't really get a foothold in the Chinese rock market.

> The problem is that the managers were not Beijingese, so they had little knowledge on how to operate in the mainland market, and operated as they do in Hong Kong and Taiwan.
>
> (Fu Chung from New Bees, 11 April 2000)

Modern Sky is particularly clear in positioning its products vis-à-vis the earlier rock bands produced by regional companies. Manager Shen Lihui constantly stresses that he wants more diversity.

> One irresponsible shouter is leading a group of headless shouters; this is today's situation of Chinese rock music. At present, the irresponsible shouter has already turned into an chattering old woman. Today, without understanding anything, he is still recovering from the complaints of his childhood. In fact, apart from affirming Freudian

> science, this doesn't say anything to us. This world has already started to change, and the things he is talking about don't have anything to do with us. ... I think he or they should go into a museum and get some sleep!
>
> (Shen Lihui on the Web site of his band, Sober (*qinxing*), quoted by Steen, 2000)

Clearly Shen Lihui is talking here about Cui Jian and his generation. Cui Jian responds to this by labelling the new generation as 'charlatans without culture' (Yan [Jun] 1999: 31). With the depoliticization of everyday life, Cui Jian is framed as a voice from the past. The early generation is downplayed as comprising screaming, long-haired individuals. The new generation is said to reflect contemporary urban life: They are more playful and less rebellious. New Bees boss Fu Chung gives similar descriptions of the new generation and refers to his company's pop-punk band The Flowers (*Huar*) as one of its examples.[4] Such characterizations of the New Sound advocated by Modern Sky cover up the fragmented state of Beijing's rock culture. But in employing such a chronological framework, Modern Sky and New Bees position themselves as the new brand names for rock. It is a clever marketing tactic:

> I think that if we can produce music that can meet the standard of international music, many overseas Chinese will be proud of it. ... [Taiwan and Hong Kong rock musicians] lack an idea or spirit in their music.
>
> (Fu Chung of the New Bees, 11 April 2000)

Ironically, the local turn signifies a desire to become global. Regional companies motivate their activities in terms that reflect a cultural pilgrimage, whereas a local company aims to conquer the world by adopting to the perceived global (that is, Western) standards of rock. Whereas regional companies are at pains to articulate the local, the Chinese-ness of rock, local companies stress the global characteristics of their products.

> I feel it makes no sense. When I listen to a Dutch band, I don't question what its Dutch characteristics are. What matters is whether the music moves you. Since rock comes originally from the West it is obvious that musicians play Western instruments. If they insist on integrating Chinese elements, the music becomes unnatural and is not successful. Music is all about authenticity and sincerity.
>
> (Fu Cheng)

What links the motivations of regional and local record companies is that both express a desire for a strong Chinese culture, a desire that that is packaged in the sound of rock. A desire, incidentally, that resonates uncomfortably with the nationalist policies of the CCP during the 1990s.

Savings

My account of the music industry shows that the complex processes of commercialization during the 1990s have led neither to the disappearance of the state nor to a financial boom. In the 1990s, the music industry witnessed a commercialization with Chinese characteristics. Because of state regulations against independent foreign companies, limitations on the import of foreign releases, relatively low revenues, and poorly enforced copyright regulations, China is largely excluded from a global music market that is dominated by a few transnational record companies, whereas Hong Kong and Taiwan are not. Instead, regional record companies from Hong Kong and Taiwan have entered the music business in China.

The rock industry in China is rather small in terms of the number of new releases each year, the number of albums sold, and – especially – the revenues it generates. The power of state-owned music publishers frustrates the development of the Chinese music industry considerably. The role of music publishers sets the Chinese market apart from other such markets around the globe and indicates that it is still too early to speak of an 'open market'. Regional record companies have commercial motives for entering the market, but these are embedded in specific cultural considerations. The investment in rock from Beijing by producers from Hong Kong and Taiwan is related to a strong discontent with the pop music these producers grew up with. It may also be interpreted as an imagined cultural pilgrimage.

But the commercial and cultural links established by Hong Kong and Taiwanese record companies with the Beijing rock scene do not imply the emergence of a common culture. The assumed emergence of a 'Greater China' covers up cultural struggles that proliferate between companies and artists, struggles in which 'national characteristics' are articulated in order to explain perceived local and regional differences and strengthen one's own position. 'Greater China' turns out to be both more fragmented and less great than is often assumed. The local turn signifies a move away from a focus on making rock with Chinese characteristics, towards making rock that meets global – that is, Western – standards. It reflects a desire to become truly cosmopolitan, which is coupled to a desire to have Chinese rock enter the global music market. Whereas the regional companies focus on making rock with Chinese characteristics, the local companies aim at making international rock that comes from China. In both cases, 'Chineseness' remains the key signifier to articulate a sonic difference with the West. Yet, the seemingly safe grounds of perceived cultural differences are likely to shift considerably after China enters the WTO. Only then will it become clear whether and how the local can challenge the global.

Notes

1 This image of the Chinese market is not restricted to post-1978 China. Already in 1842, when the Sino–British Treaty of Nanjing was signed to end the opium war and open up China, Sir Henry Pottinger, who designed the treaty, assured the textile factories of Manchester that their capacity would be insufficient to make even one pair of stockings for each Chinese citizen in only one province. Thus the business opportunities were considered to be extremely promising (Osterhammel 1989: 171).

2 Copyright income over, for example, karaoke or radio airplay is not included in these figures. Neither is the piracy market included in these figures, nor the informal recording and circulation of music. Sale figures thus present a distorted view on musical activity in 'Greater China' (see also Negus 1992: 12–13).

3 Unfortunately, both Jingwen and Modern Sky were deliberately vague when I inquired about their specific legal status, and no one else active in the culture industry could tell me more. Consequently, I cannot explain precisely how both companies are tied to the official structures. Shen Lihui did point out, however, that because their company is involved in the publishing of the music, they have more control and lose less money compared to record companies, which rely on the official publishing houses. Again, he remained vague about precisely what this involvement entailed.

4 Because 'The Flowers' sold well in Taiwan (50,000 copies in one month), where it was released under the Magic Stone label, New Bees managed to earn a lot more money than they did in China.

9

'WE ARE CHINESE' – MUSIC AND IDENTITY IN 'CULTURAL CHINA'

Lee Tain-Dow and Huang Yingfen

Andy Lau's album, *Chinese*, is marketed by BMG(HK/Taiwan/Singapore/Malaysia). Lau, who is one of the most popular male singers in Asia, released *Chinese* in March 1997. The album was heavily promoted as the first so-called 'shaped CD'. It resembles a map of China (including Taiwan). The lyrics are revealing:

> It has been windy and rainy here for five thousand years, dreams have hidden/
> yellow skin and black eyes, smiles have never changed/
> the landscape extends for eight thousand miles, like a song/
> no matter where you come from and where are you going to, the same tears and pain, all in our mind/
> the same descent and heritage, there are dreams in the future/
> we will be together hand in hand, you and me, let the world know – we are Chinese.

'Five thousand years' is a number chosen to appeal to a feeling for Chinese history and a general sense of ethnic descent ('yellow skin and black hair'). These commonalities apparently unite the nation(s) of Chinese. The song *Chinese* retreats from current political boundaries; as the lyrics say, 'no matter where you come from and where are you going to'. At the end of the chorus, an intriguing call to integration and a proclamation of an essential belongingness 'let the world know – we are Chinese', combine to confound state-nationalism conceived outside the borders of the motherland. Clearly, the song identifies a pride in being Chinese, claiming to offer a way forward from the frustrated histories of the past. At the same time, the shape of Chinese territory appears as a spiritual symbol signifying 'a cultural China', and presenting itself as a totem for Chinese all over the world.

The album was extremely successful in Chinese communities, particularly in Hong Kong where it evoked a 'feel good' response to the 1997 hand-over of sovereignty. It evoked a collective sense of Chinese nationalism, enunciated by a Hong Kong singer. For the public of Hong Kong, Lau's *Chinese* reduced the collective struggles of political identity in the Greater Chinese region to a nostalgic process of delocalized root-seeking.

Jeroen de Kloet has argued in the previous chapter that Beijing rock is fast asserting itself as a local industry, albeit one with problems of its own. Here, we argue that the popular music scene in the region, and specifically in territories that might describe themselves as 'culturally Chinese', is an increasingly transnational operation. We describe this regional-global nexus as the regional turn in the economics of globalization. Within this terminology, the field of music production and marketing is a cultural battlefield on which politically diverse territories sing out their differences, without genuine acknowledgment or validation of areas of incommensurability. Local contexts are debated in the same moment that they are flattened out for the purpose of extending commercial reach. A non-socialist territory, such as Taiwan, confronts the meaning of its value system as it engages with China, a socialist market, in commercially grounded practices: cultural sharing, syncretism and de-territorialization.

This is not unusual. Global cultures, informed by the logic of capital, have long struggled with, and incorporated, local cultures around the globe. Globalization is not a one-way process of homogenization, Westernization and modernization, as it is generally understood in Western scholarship. Rather, we argue that in the Chinese region, commercial practices produce regional and internal responses, and that these are sustained by older discourses of regional and ethnic belonging, cultural memory, and social habitus.

Identity

The concept of identity receives considerable attention in psychology and sociology. In general, the production of identity is associated with interaction with the external world. This can be understood in rather different ways. Hall (1992) distinguished three very different conceptions of externally factored identity: those of the Enlightenment subject, the sociological subject and the postmodern subject. The Enlightenment subject was based on a conception of the human person as a fully centred, unified individual, endowed with the capacities of reason, consciousness and action, whose 'centre' consisted of an inner core that first emerged when the subject was born. The notion of the sociological subject reflected the growing complexity of the modern world and the awareness that the inner core of the subject was not autonomous and self-sufficient. Identity bridges the gap between the 'inside' and the 'outside', between the personal and the public. The postmodern subject is conceptualized as having no fixed, essential or permanent identity. This subject assumes different identities at different times, identities which are not unified around a coherent 'self'. Within us are contradictory identities, pulling in different directions, so that our identities are constantly shifting. Accordingly, social structure determines the construction of subjectivity. A change in social structure shifts the establishment of subjective identification.

Identification is also invoked as a psychological mechanism, and different subjective interactions produce different degrees of identification. P.W. Preston (1997) suggests that identity can be categorized into three levels: locale, network and memory. The locale level refers to the ways people live their lives, with routinized practices, interactions and meanings. Based on the locale level of categorization, people form their sense of identity when they interact with other people. This identity is stored in the memory of their subjective revisions. Therefore, an individual first identifies with the locale, and then identifies through interaction with other habitants, and finally selectively commits these identities to memory. There may be conformity or contrast across different levels. In this formulation, national identity may conflict with individual identity.

Furthermore, identity must be examined in terms of its practice. Preston has pointed out (op. cit.: 54) that identity studies focus on how agents acknowledge themselves as members of a political ensemble, how this acknowledgment is expressed in routinized practices, and how it is legitimized in the public sphere. Identity lies in words, behaviour and consumption; it also lies in interaction with agents such as family, school, and media signification and discourse.

In the latter regard, Benedict Anderson (1983) also speaks of the materiality of the imagined community which lies within the process of media signification. Media serve as carriers of identity construction and are alive with various symbols and meanings. Media as cultural commodities become bearers of meanings which consumers absorb and which thus dominate identity practices. Spatially too, media and communication technologies restructure identity formation, as they literally speed up interactive associations between people, and facilitate quick and phenomenologically convincing communication across borders. Social relationships move from rationalized modernity to polysemic postmodernity. Industrial production moves from the mass-productive Fordism of the early twentieth century to a decentralized post-Fordism on a global scale. Communication media under such circumstances move from public broadcasting systems to commercial systems focused on capital accumulation and profit-making. It is significant that most global audiovisual productions are controlled by a few (Western) transnational media conglomerates. They determine the rules of the game and dominate the whole media 'ecology'.

The mediasphere thus established by transnational media conglomerates tends to an absence of local images in a local setting. The term 'cultural sharing' gives this phenomenon a positive spin. Taiwan boys wear T-shirts emblazoned with Nike or Michael Jordan icons and use notebooks with the television show *X files* trademark on their covers. Taiwan girls imitate the hairstyle and dress of Japanese teen idol Namei Amuro, while reading the Japanese teen magazine *Non-no*. Japanese animation series such as *Slam Dunk*, *Chibi Maruko-Chan* and *Crayon Shin-Chan* are all the hottest topics of discussion among primary school students. Younger students typically own a set of Disney-made *Lion King* stationery (at least in 2000). McDonald's has come to represent the typical Taiwan youngster's birthday party. Drinking is epitomized by Japan's Kirin Ichiban beer and Taiwan residents shout, 'bottom up!' as they raise glasses of Japanese beer. The logic of capitalist globalization results in these routine human interactions, which in turn lead to a segmented, floating, and complex perspective of national–local–international identity.

Offshore cinema, which has been used to promote non-Taiwanese political identities since Japanese colonization (Lee [Tain-Dow] 1997b: 46) continues to corner the mainstream cultural imagination. The American film *Men in Black* (1999) inspired all kinds of spin-off products; the name has even been adopted by a popular Taiwan singing band, a trio called 'Music Is Back'. In 1997, they filmed a music video in which three middle-aged men, dressed in Star Wars costumes, wearing Ray-Ban sunglasses and holding high-tech memory sticks, sang Taiwan folk songs of the 1970s and 1980s. In these multiple hybridizations, Preston's familiarity of the locale is blurred, as Taiwan citizens know more about Amuro than they do about their neighbours and drink more Kirin Ichiban beer and Left Bank Café than Wooloong Tea.

Memory loss

The nature of identity is therefore unstable in a market field dominated by transnational media. Satellite technology, cable television, cinema, and other international media commodities interfere with human geographic recognition; mediated human interactions even take over popular memory. The national myth is re-narrated by transnational commercial interests. The 'postmodern' subject described by Hall becomes concretized: segmented and fragile structures determine the segmentation and fragility of national and cultural identity.

What is worse, from our perspective, is that the historical environment of Taiwan has itself caused Taiwan's cultural memory to weaken. Between 1895 and 1945, Japan colonized Taiwan for fifty years. In this period, Japan interfered with the regulation and institutions of Taiwan's political, economic and cultural arenas. At first, Japan adopted an estrangement policy but later inclined towards assimilating Taiwan's residents to incorporate Taiwan with Greater Japan. From 1945 to 1987, Taiwan's national identity was once again distorted and reshaped. The newly established KMT (*Kuomintang*, *Guomindang* or Chinese Nationalist) administration claimed the role of decolonizer. With such slogans as 'Overrule the continent, restore the homeland' and 'Defence against Communist spies is everybody's duty', Taiwan was engaged in a political tug-of-war with Mainland China. This entailed a reinvented national identity structured around nostalgia for the five-thousand-year-old culture of Greater China. The political reality on the Mainland was denied, and in so far as it operated figuratively as a homeland, China was 'imaginary'. At the lifting of martial law in 1987, Taiwanese consciousness and the pro-independence movement emerged. Taiwan's largest opposition party, the DPP (Democratic People's Party), challenged the KMT-propounded view, 'fifty years of the history of China', which defined Taiwan's national/state construction. The DPP called for a 'Republic of China on Taiwan'. Again, any hope of an organic politico-cultural identity for Taiwan was undermined. From the 'Great Japan' consciousness during Japanese occupation, to the 'Great China' consciousness under the KMT administration, to the Taiwan-independence consciousness promoted by the political opposition party, the axis of Taiwan's identity shifts continually. Yet these shifts do not fit neatly into the Enlightenment, sociological, postmodern categories elaborated by Hall. Rather, Taiwan exhibits political, spatial and cultural vulnerability on the cusp of its own reliance on global markets and regional trade. In the 1980s economic growth in the highly urbanized Taiwan produced a culture of mass consumption. American-dominated audiovisual products started to take over the market. Japanese-produced mass cultural forms, comics, videos and idol systems, were also widely accepted around the island. The pressure of transnational capitalist forces undermined spatially bounded history and myths and popular cultural memories that defined Taiwanese consciousness as a distinct identity marker.

When dealing with the dialectic relationship between globalization and localization, many Western scholars argue that the two are not opposed. They suggest that the latter is one dimension of the former, and that globalization is involved with interspersion between the global and the local, the universal and the distinctive (Robertson 1995). However, globalization is by no means a simple matter of cultural hybridization and penetration. Existing power structures are still reproduced and sometimes reinforced in the interchange between the global and the local. We have to think of the inequality and unbalanced proportions of different cultural elements in such a process of cultural hybridization.

Taiwan, as a member of the non-dominant non-Western world, needs to be concerned not only for itself but also for other countries in the region: Indonesia, Malaysia, and Thailand. Under the flag of globalization, local materials throughout Asia tend to be incorporated into transnational institutions. As we argue further below, that process promotes inter-regional access to 'culturally similar' product, through cultural sharing, cultural syncretism and de-territorialization. It also, of course, enriches the abundance and the market penetration of global cultural production. The dominant Western and Japan media conglomerates become the only viable channels through which to communicate unvoiced local material on a global scale. Spanish-language macarena dance music goes global via the American recording industry; Aboriginal music is piped into the mainstream through Western marketing beats; while the international 'Free Tibet' spirit is supported by Hollywood's cinematic web, a few links away from Disney's *Mulan* claim on a Chinese classic story of filial piety! As these networks share out and syncretize local culture, do they also destroy the integral spatially bound memories that produced it in the first place?

'Taiwan' as a geographic term exists on the world map. 'Taiwan' also exists as a political entity. But 'Taiwan' as a discrete cultural sociological perspective is losing its meaning in the international community. In the world system, 'Taiwan' is culturally invisible. It is submerged under other hegemonic cultures, in danger of becoming an empty geographic term and memorialized on the altar of political struggle.

Globalization is more than convergence. It entails memory loss, and the re-imagining of spatial realities. Taiwan's national cultural identity suffers particularly from the memory of colonization, decolonization, and anti-authoritarianism, while its current identity choices are constantly reshaped by the logic of capitalism. We contend that in the process of construction, deconstruction, and reconstruction, local culture in Taiwan is brushed away. This bleak version of the impact of culture, and in particular of cultures associated with media delivery and communication systems, is exemplified in the case of popular music. In this example, the global is symptomatically assimilated into a regionally manipulated 'cultural Chinese-ness'. The regional turn serves both major producers (many of which have parent companies in Japan and the United States), and dominant political interests in the Chinese world.

Music and 'cultural China'

There is a complicated discourse of identity in the Greater Chinese region. The operating paradigm is a time–space construction of China, which produces identity through music. In some ways, this echoes earlier constructions of China as the imagined homeland, although now it must always be understood within the context of multinational media interests. It is also sedimented through competing accounts of Chinese-ness which demonstrate local histories, cultural excellence (Hong Kong Cantopop), and sheer scale (People's Republic of China). In this identity market Taiwan has a reputation for scattered innovation and entrepreneurial investment (de Kloet, this volume), as well as for flights of great creativity (the film-maker Hou Xiao-xian and the singer Theresa Teng).

As we saw with the Lau song, *Chinese*, popular music works in the disputed territories of Greater China as an open text where identity is negotiated within specific historical and political conjunctures. The notion of conjuncture refers here to 'the exact balance of forces, state of overdetermination of the contradictions at any given moment to which political tactics must be applied' (Althusser and Balibar 1970: 311). This concept articulates the 'enunciative strategies' of de/reterritorialization and cultural syncretism in constructing the idea of 'cultural China.' Zhu Yao-wei contends that China has contained a self-orientated conception of political geography since antiquity – China (*Zhongguo*) is a cultural entity which refers to 'Middle Kingdom' and which considers herself to be located at thc centre of the world (Zhu [Yao-Wei] 1996: 150). This concept of absolute superiority was not challenged until the mid-nineteenth century, when China experienced the anxiety of decentralization due to the invasion of Western colonists. The Chinese observed that European technologies and military power far exceeded their own. The invasion of Western colonists both destroyed the unassailability of Sinocentrism and stimulated the rise of a defensive nationalism.

Nationalism did not become enmeshed in state politics, however, until the conflict between the Nationalist and the Communists took hold in the 1930s, and solidified over the Taiwan issue after 1949. In 1949, both the KMT in Taiwan and the Chinese Communist Party-led government in Mainland China proclaimed themselves the only orthodox Chinese government, both referring to the Middle Kingdom as their cultural base. The Middle Kingdom became a signifier, which now stands as the motherland of Chinese in the past, present and future. In this imagined Kingdom, all Chinese people have shared the same civilization, language, culture and history. In the actual kingdoms of everyday politics and identity formation, the situation is, as we have suggested earlier, more fragile, and fractured by a series of disjointed versions of national alliance.

Within the market of the Greater Chinese region, Hong Kong and Taiwan own the most prosperous and established music production industries, which incorporate popular artists, composers, and producers. Artists who do well in these two places are repackaged and promoted by global music corporations to other Chinese communities in this region, to Mainland China, Singapore, and Malaysia. The representation strategies used to promote these artists mediate between complicated cultural identity issues and national boundaries. In the construction of 'China-as-music', it is only harmful for the circulation of goods to be too politically exact. The concept of 'cultural China' has therefore been very freely adapted by the global music industry to shape the identity of its products. 'Cultural China' does not refer to any political entity; however, it does conceive an abstract cultural concept. Benedict Anderson's notion of 'imagined community' is relevant here: 'Cultural China' becomes a musically imagined cultural community.

The central contention of David Morley and Kevin Robins's *Space of Identity: Global Media, Electronic Landscapes and Cultural Boundaries* (1995) is that space and place are central to identity. Media transform the surfaces and frontiers which define the space of nationality and identity (Morley and Robins 1995: 72–5). Through Dupuy they argue: 'Through their (media) capacity to transgress frontiers and subvert territories, they are implicated in a complex interplay of deterritorialization and reterritorialization,' We understand this process as a commodification of identity, and suggest that 'cultural China' is being assiduously developed under the same principle.

The Chinese singer

The 'Chinese singer' as a uniform label for artists working across different Chinese cultural and political borders conforms to the market principle of 'cultural China'. Within this marketing logic, the nationalities and the local characteristics of artists are not stressed. Eric Moo (signed to EMI, Taiwan) originally comes from Singapore. Mindy Ke (BMG, Hong Kong) is a Malaysia-born Chinese. Coco Lee (Sony, Taiwan) was born in Hong Kong, grew up in Los Angeles and runs a successful career in and out of Taiwan. Faye Wong (EMI, Hong Kong) comes from Beijing. These performers use Mandarin (*putonghua, guohua*) as the common language for regional distribution. Love is the most common theme of their songs. When focusing on the individual experience, there is no need for these popular love songs to refer to any specific social context that has facilitated their own circulation. Thus, the trope of 'cultural China' in popular music has abandoned the profound sense of political-geographic meaning of 'Middle Kingdom.' Chinese singers are recognized by capital mostly in terms of the language they use regardless of their national or territorial origins. That said, there are telling occasions on which the local reasserts its market prerogative through identity communality.

Ai Jing, a mainland singer, is an example of anti-de/territorialization. Ai's first single *My 1997* (Sony, Hong Kong) was a failure. Released in 1996, the song articulated great expectations of the coming of 1997. As a mainlander, Ai 'looks forward' to visiting the city, Hong Kong, which will soon be reunited with China. Although the song praised the modernity and prosperity of Hong Kong, it did not win over the Hong Kong market. By singing 'My 1997, going to Hong Kong', Ai was perceived by Hong Kong as an 'invader' from the mainland who coveted Hong Kong's commercial benefits. Unlike Andy Lau, whose *Chinese* struck a chord with fellow Hong Kongers, Ai discovered that when her work strayed into the territory of local political memory and anxiety, her Mainland status mattered.

We have referred to the idea of cultural syncretism, and regard it as a key aspect in the regional turn within the global music scene. While some artists incorporate themselves into an umbrella of 'cultural China' by de/reterritorializing their localness; some other artists have attempted to syncretize the cultural differences between different political entities of China and Greater China. Cultural syncretism promises a flexible identity for Chinese in different spaces. It supposes locally inflected work by musicians, which is syncretized with more broadly conceived Chinese attributes and reference points. Cultural syncretism is represented by the use of different dialects in albums. Although Mandarin remains the official language in the Greater Chinese region, local dialects such as Taiwanese and Cantonese are still widely used in Taiwan and Hong Kong. In Hong Kong, the 1997 hand-over increased the use of Mandarin in business and government circles (mostly at the expense of English). In the domain of popular music, however, Cantonese is dominant. Many artists from Beijing and Taiwan have to first learn Cantonese in order to produce a Cantonese version of an album especially for distribution in Hong Kong.

Taiwanese singer Sheu Ru-Yun (Warner Music, Taiwan), Cheung Shin-Zhe (Sony, Taiwan), Faye Wong and Eric Woo have been trained in Cantonese in order to add more Hong Kong-ness to their performances. Similarly, in order to respond to the rise of Taiwanese sentiment, some singers add Taiwanese songs to their albums. Eric Woo released a Taiwanese dialect album in 1995, which was marketed by his previous agent, PolyGram. In his 1998 album *Imprint Your Love on My Mind*, Andy Lau included his first and heavily promoted Taiwanese hit 'I am the First Rank' (which is composed by a well-known Taiwanese musician).

The success of Dadawa (Warner Music, Hong Kong) is another example of syncretism within the logic of 'cultural China.' Dadawa (real name Zhu Zheqin) is native to Shanghai but is portrayed as a Tibetan singer. The lyrics and rhythms of her songs are inspired by Tibetan religion and daily customs. Her album, *Sister Drum*, demonstrates a great sense of Tibetan culture. In an international arena of global and glamorous popular politics, the syncretism of a Chinese star masquerading as a Tibetan singer is reasonably ironic. In entertainment circles, Hollywood regularly shows her support for Tibet's anti-Communists by making films such as *Seven Years in Tibet* and *Kundun*, both of which are banned in China. At the same time, global capital desperately makes efforts to syncretize the two cultural entities – Tibet and China – as interpreted by a Shanghai singer whose album features both Mandarin and Tibetan songs. The album incorporates the very local Tibetan culture into the space of 'cultural China' in order to erase the memory of old geographic boundaries, and of the massacre in 1954. Dadawa has had her Tibetan name created in order to fabricate her Tibetan identity. Like Taiwanese and Cantonese pop songs, Tibetan songs in Dadawa's album serve as a second string to Mandarin.

The content of songs also reflects the trend of syncretism. Li Ming (PolyGram, Hong Kong) was born in Beijing and immigrated to Hong Kong when he was five years old. In his 1992 hit, 'I Came from Beijing,' Beijing is analogized as a benevolent mother:

Imagining you in a distant place, your face is still clear/
The memory remains yet it was so long ago/
We are a thousand miles apart, yet our two hearts are
  brought together/
We are apart, yet your image is hidden in my dream/
One day we will meet again, your love is a great gift to me,
  my song will be my only baggage.

The poetic mother China is envisioned in this language of nostalgia as a departure of contact, exploration, and syncretization. The lyrics 'one day we will meet again' announce the anxiety of exile and the expectation of homecoming for numerous Hong Kong and Taiwanese people. In 1987, the ban on Taiwanese visiting China was lifted. This has increased concrete cultural and personal ties between Taiwan and China. Further, the lifting of martial law in 1988 paved the way for new possibilities within the cultural frame of both places, and for the sound of music such as 'I come from Beijing'.

The hit 'One Night in Beijing' of Taiwanese singer Chen Shen (PolyGram, Taiwan) refers to an ancient Chinese legend: inside the gate of a city wall an elderly woman is sewing embroidered shoes and waiting for the return of her lover who went to war. Outside the gate of the city walls, a soldier, wearing rotten iron armour is calling for the gate to be opened. For a thousand years, they have been waiting for each other. The lyrics are stylishly laden with historical and legendary emotional connotations, rather than national or political ones. The composer has utilized the rhythms of Beijing opera and Taiwanese folksong as the basic melody, which is an unusual combination of features for a popular hit. The Taiwanese folksong is used not to contrast with, but to modify the abstruse qualities of Beijing opera. By the same token, Hong Kong singer Cheung Eric's PolyGram album *Wish to Walk with You Again in the Wind*, contains tracks which refer to Taipei and Beijing: 'Taipei: A City of Sadness' and 'A New York Taxi Driver is Dreaming of Beijing'. The syncretic intention is clear in the combination of these titles. In 'cultural China', Taipei and Beijing occupy a complementary spatial imagination, in sharp contradistinction to the exile represented by New York.

From cultural fragmentation to synthesis, the Chinese singer works on desires for cultural integration and interpretive translation across Chinese communities. He or she is a dynamic figure in the regional turn of global capital, an embodiment of 'cultural China' attempting to break the boundaries of political identity in consumption. He or she does not, as Ai and Lau have illustrated, transcend the context of place and belonging, but does traduce it through reduction, nostalgia, and tokenism. The meta-discourse of Chinese identity is mobilized along an axis of partial and generalized cultural memory, and it is that, the sheer vagueness of *Chinese* which sells it so successfully. For Taiwan, this vagueness is however a marked threat to local cultural identity. When a multiply occupied space is again colonized by the dream factories of foreign capital, it is hard for creativity to do much other than fragment with style.

10

SEMIOTIC OVER-DETERMINATION OR 'INDOCTRITAINMENT'

Television, citizenship, and the Olympic Games

Wanning Sun

Soon after the 27th Olympics Games in September 2000 in Sydney, I visited Beijing from Australia. The Games were the inevitable conversation starter. People in Beijing talked about the Sydney Olympic Games with keen interest, expressing memories as though the Games had just been held in their own city. Although the Chinese only saw the Games on Chinese television, there was little mention of the lack of direct and immediate access to the event, in spite of their not being there (Rowe 2000: 12). Moreover, an almost default association was made between the Chinese athletes' performances at the Sydney Games with the chances of Beijing's winning the bid to host the Games in 2008.

From my conversations, I got the impression that television had played a crucial role in this global sports event and that the Chinese people had just spent a couple of weeks watching television intensely, 'gazing' rather than 'glancing' at the television (Hartley 1992). My Beijing trip made me wonder about the relationship between nationalism, the state and the local construction of a global media event. It raised questions on television's pedagogic role in the formation of cultural identity and citizenship through media consumption. The Sydney Olympic Games was the most globally televised sports event ever; yet the imagery and symbolism deployed in the media coverage of the Games were culture- and place-specific. How were images and narratives constructed for and, consumed by, national audiences in China? In addressing these questions, I discuss the Chinese government's investment and involvement in transmitting and producing television programmes about the Games. I look at the construction of meanings associated with the Games, via some interviews with television viewers in

Beijing, to demonstrate the impact of media consumption on the construction of cultural citizenship.

These questions refer to the nature of the relationship between national culture, which is time-bound and location-specific, and global culture, which is memory-less and de-territorialized (Smith 1990). In work on media consumption in the context of the globalization of electronic journalism, Gurevitch (1986) points to the issue of 'openness'. He suggests that, although news materials are disseminated globally, these materials are 'open texts' since they are subject to local and regional treatment. Audiences are more likely to increase their dependency on local decoders in making sense of the images and narratives from faraway places and cultures. There needs therefore to be a shift from a concern with the content and flow of news and images to a concern with the activity of constructing local meaning from globalized events. Although images of media events like the Olympic Games are globally televised and open to polysemous interpretation, the meaning of these images, once relayed into the realm of what John Hartley calls 'national semiosis' (Hartley 1999: 161), can become over-determined, rather than self-determined. The formation of citizenship in this case is not entirely about how to 'do it yourself', but about how to keep the balance between being interpellated by the state on the one hand and asserting one's rights as a consumer in the market economy on the other. This is certainly the case with Chinese television viewership and the Sydney Olympic Games.

Nation, state and media event

The involvement of the state-controlled Chinese media in the transmission and production of the Sydney Olympic Games was unprecedented. This was true in terms of the size of the media entourage, the diversity of modes of information transmission, the ways of interactivity with spectators, and the depth and scale of coverage of specific sports media and individual athletes. Chinese Central Television (CCTV) sent 110 people to Sydney to cover the event.[1] Many other news organizations, including local newspapers and television stations also sent their own reporters to Sydney. Beijing Youth Daily sent eleven people.

The team of China's official news agency in Sydney, the Xinhua News Agency, consisted of thirty-nine people. Their contribution, however, produced only a small percentage of Xinhua's total coverage. Rather than relying on Sydney-based Xinhua reporters exclusively to supply news dispatches, photos and stories, Xinhua's management required its 160 branches scattered around China and the world to contribute to the coverage of the Games from local perspectives. This catered to broad interest in the Games as well as to audience curiosity about Chinese athletes. Local branches provided a large amount of coverage on Olympics-related events and individuals prior to, during, and after the Games, in a plethora of columns, in a variety of genres, including features, people profiles, comments from audiences, and anecdotes. These materials were supplied by Xinhua to television and print media, both at national and local levels (Xu 2000: 34–5)

CCTV's decision to send many people to Sydney to cover the event ensured that the media would not need to rely on syndicated materials from Western agencies. In return, this allowed the transmission of images from the event to serve the political and cultural agenda of the Chinese state. Xinhua's strategy went further. The agency maximized the impact of the Games by transmitting the sports news, and also by generating localized stories that related to the events themselves. This suggests that although the Olympic Games fitted the category of 'global media event', the production of the ideology, not just the transmission of the event, warrants closer scrutiny. The presentation formats of the coverage ensured an effective combination of live transmission and regular news updates. The content feasted the audience, sandwiching live transmissions with pre-match speculation and forecasts, and after-the-event discussion and retrospective analysis. These programmes were interspersed with frequent segments of Chinese audiences' greetings to the Chinese athletes in Sydney.

Xinhua's Web site also provided an alternative information outlet, benefiting not only domestic audiences who could not watch the Games live on television, but also the Chinese in diaspora who had difficulty accessing information about the performances of Chinese Olympians.[2] Feeding news to the Web sites also meant that, for the first time in covering a global media event, Xinhua staff had to work around the clock instead of simply meeting the deadlines of morning and evening papers.[3] Digitized camera technology facilitated quick transmission. The Xinhua Web site published more than 100 Games-linked news dispatches a day (Xu 2000: 35) and over 200 pictures of the opening ceremony (Pu 2000: 37).

Glorious China

The government's investment in reporting the Games was apparent in the volume of news, but was also evidenced in the careful planning to achieve the desired balance between entertainment value and ideological impact. The close correlation between political agenda and selection of news angles is best seen in a programme outline for *Oriental Time and Space* (*Dongfang shikong*). This high-rating CCTV news and current affairs programme devoted a special segment *Glorious China* (*Guangrong zhongguo*), focusing exclusively on the Sydney Olympic Games. An episode outline stating the aim of each of the nine episodes from the production team is telling:[4]

1 'Triumphant return'. Beijing residents' warm welcome to our athletes coming home.
3 'Exciting moment'. The moment of glory and victory of individual athletes when they win gold.
4 'Legends'. The emotional world of some of our legendary athletes.
5 'Hope'. Young, upcoming stars, who symbolize the bright future of China's sports.
6 'Eternity'. Gold medals bring the nation confidence, courage, joy and respect.
7 'Backstage'. Unsung heroes who work hard and make sacrifices for the achievements of our athletes.
8 'Ping Bo'. Chinese fight hard not just for their own respect and glory; but for the dignity and honour of China.
9 'Sydney'. The patriotism of Chinese communities cheering our athletes on in Sydney.
10 'Glory'. Results of the Chinese team. Campaigning for Beijing to host the 2008 Games.

The close relationship between sports, state and nation is well documented. The direct intervention of the state in television markets, especially during nationally significant sports events, is common in many countries in the West. Every nation-state has a political agenda – promoting nationalism or a specific version of cultural citizenship – in the media coverage of such events. Each negotiates with commercial and public television in order to deliver these narratives free and live (Rowe 1999). Nevertheless, the level of political determination is particularly high in the Chinese state. This is partly due to the factor of ownership. Despite deregulation in the structure, funding and revenue generating mechanism, television, like Party newspapers, is expected to function as the 'throat and tongue' of the Party and the Government.[5]

In this context political determination in the coverage of sports events may have occurred not in spite of, but because of, economic interests in media production. State-owned and -controlled media operate within political and ideological parameters set by the Party and the Government, but their survival is contingent upon their capacity to generate financial sponsorship from business and to generate advertising dollars (Zhao [Yuezhi] 1998, 2000) Unlike some of the public broadcasters in the West which accept only limited sponsorship and advertising, CCTV sees no paradox in allowing the commercial logos of some products or companies to promote the socialist ideology of the state. While the media must do propaganda work, they also have to deliver their message in the most palatable and entertaining way possible. All international sport, but particularly the Games, is an occasion for 'commodified nationalism' (Rowe 1999: 23). A good example of the happy marriage between revenue generation and nation-building is the product logo on the T-shirts of Chinese spectators in the Homebush Stadium of the Sydney Olympic Games on global television. The Chinese company which produces Wuliangye, a hard liquor, was allowed to advertise its product on T-shirts given free to Chinese cheering squads during the Games, in exchange for covering the cost of their tickets.

There are reasons why the state wanted to get as much political mileage as possible out of covering this particular global sports event. One might recall the humiliating moment when the International Olympics Committee President Samaranch uttered the word 'Sydney' rather than 'Beijing'. The Chinese government, anxious to repair the tarnished image to the international community following the June 4th Incident in 1989, had desperately wanted China to win the bid to be the host of the 27th Olympic Games. The loss to Sydney was a blow to the credibility of the state and to the nationalist pride of its population. A win for 2008 would benefit China domestically and abroad (Sinclair 2000: 37). China realized that to increase China's chances, it should take advantage of the international platform at the Sydney games to score some points. A competitive number of gold medals would establish China as a major sports player in the international arena, an essential criterion for consideration as a potential host of such events. It would boost patriotic sentiments among the population as well as among Chinese communities overseas, generating populist support for China's bid. Ultimately, it would signal to the world that China is a globalizing nation with political and social stability suitable for transnational interests. By the same token, it would instil in its own people a national cohesion, racial pride and faith in the Government.

During the Games, Chinese television visualized the centrifugal power of the People's Republic of China (PRC) with images of patriotic expatriate Chinese. One interviewee in Beijing remarked that what moved her most was seeing the Chinese national flag hoisted on Sydney's Opera House by the Chinese communities in Sydney. Another interviewee was still visibly moved when recalling the Chinese badminton players' medal ceremony. According to his description, the Chinese had won gold, silver and bronze, and spectators at the Stadium were mostly Chinese, many of whom were holding the Chinese five-starred national flag. These emotional interviews demonstrate the power of televisuality in instilling nationalistic pride in the population. Images from entertainment worked much more effectively than political sermons from the state propaganda machinery. My mother mentioned many times the moving scenes of the 'ocean of red flags' and the drowning chorus of cheering for the Chinese at the badminton games. When I asked her what exactly it was about these images that moved her, she said, 'I can't help feeling emotional when I see our national flags raised and our national anthem sung again and again in a foreign country.'

'Good' patriotic overseas Chinese were sought after by the cameras. 'Anti-China' elements were left out of the visual sphere. On 27 October

2000, the *Beijing Youth Daily*, one of the most widely circulated newspapers in China, ran an article (on p. 7) 'The Falungong Followers Make Fools of Themselves in Sydney During the Olympics'. Written by a reporter from Xinhua News Agency, the report detailed numerous attempts by Falungong followers to gain international media exposure and support during the Games. According to the account, Falungong is the black sheep of the Chinese communities. Its activities and its posters appeared on a number of occasions when local Chinese in Australia celebrated PRC gold medal achievements as an expression of support for Beijing's bid for the 2008 Olympics. The article ends by saying 'Falungong is a heretic cult organization which has become a political weapon of the anti-China elements in the West. It seeks to disrupt the social stability and economic reforms processes in China and to finally overthrow our socialist system'.[6]

Media Consumption and national imaginary: Sydney games and Chinese viewers

Watching the live transmission of the opening ceremony of the Games on commercial Channel Seven in Western Australia and knowing that my parents and family would also be watching it in China, I could not help wondering how these icons of Australian-ness were being interpreted by folks back at 'home'. How could they read Ned Kelly, the Aboriginals, the corrugated iron, and the lawnmowers? Would they be 'put off' by these performances if they did not have the decoding mechanism to make them meaningful? I imagined millions of television sets beaming exotica into Chinese homes, a spectacle signifying nothing. My cross-cultural anxiety was not shared by most people I interviewed in Beijing. Most of them thought the opening ceremony was a great success. Mostly without prompting, they told me that the opening was terrific and that Sydney did a good job hosting the show. I was also told that China would have done even better. Furthermore, I got the impression that everyone – ranging from my family to a taxi-driver on the way to the airport – wanted Beijing to win the bid for 2008. Repeatedly, it was confirmed to me that 'everyone' watched the Games, sports fans or not, and that 'everyone' wanted China to win.

Three factors were unanimously mentioned to account for the success of the opening ceremony in Sydney: artistic innovation (*yishu chuangxin*) – typified by the ocean; national characteristics (*minzu tese*) – embodied by Aboriginals; and sophisticated use of science and technology (*keji hanliang*). When I asked respondents if they had difficulty 'reading' the Australian-ness of these icons, most answered that it was not a problem since CCTV provided a running interpretive commentary. Chinese television viewers thereby learned that these were icons of work, life and history in Australia. I also figured out that the 'three reasons for the success of the opening ceremony' were formulated by the sports commentator of Channel 5, CCTV's official Games channel.

When I asked people what the lawnmowers meant to them, some said that they did not notice or remember seeing them, while those who did notice tended to interpret it within a 'development' framework. One interviewee read it as a symbol of Australian early settlers' attempts to conquer wilderness. Another speculated around the country's effort to utilize vacant land, for which Australia is famous in the Chinese imagination. None noticed or recognized the significance of the corrugated iron. Most conspicuously absent was an appreciation of the contested importance of Aboriginality to Australian political and social life. Note the following conversation between three retired science academics and myself in Beijing over lunch:

> WS: what do you think of the opening ceremony?
> Mr Lu: I like it. It's nice. Starting with a little girl and an Aboriginal old man.
> Mr Zhong: China can do much better. We have a much longer history of civilization and 56 nationalities. Ours would be much more spectacular. All they have is one Aboriginal race.
> WS: But they are not just one race. They have different languages, skin colors and laws.
> Mr Xiao: They all look the same. Anyway, I don't like the look of them on the television.
> WS: Why?
> Mr Zhong: They look so …
> Mr Lu: So primitive (*yuanshi*).

The official interpretation of Aboriginality in Australia by Channel 5 consisted of a brief commentary which informed the audience that Aboriginals predated European settlers in the continent, and that the appearance of Aboriginal figures is an act of respect and a recognition of the cultural contributions of Aboriginal peoples to Australian society. Interviews with viewers suggest to me that the interpretation of 'Australia', an unfamiliar country of which the average Chinese know little (except for its kangaroos, sheep and clear air), reveals most about the dominant Chinese ways of thinking. The reluctance, if not unwillingness, to engage with the idea of the diversity of the Australian Aboriginals is particularly pronounced. This response is consistent with dominant perceptions of, and attitudes to, the non-Han communities in China, which in spite of comprising 55 different ethnicities, are usually conveniently lumped together under the umbrella of 'ethnic minorities' (*shaoshu minzhu*). State discourse of nationhood privileges unity but discourages diversity. Official policy on ethnic affairs tolerates ethnic difference but assumes the supremacy of the Han nationality and the rule of the Chinese Communist Party. This provided a convenient if inaccurate framework within which to make sense of Australian Aboriginals: they are minorities and make the nation spectacularly 'colourful' and hence form an essential part of a 'nice' image.

Aboriginals, like the 'ethnic minorities', are not only relatively few, but are also deemed 'primitive'. The deployment of descriptions such as 'primitive' resonates with the frequently made comment that the 'minorities' in China are 'backward' (*luo hou*), and 'in need of enlightenment' (*bu kaihua*). Modernity, a discourse widely adopted in China at both official policy-making level and that of the popular consciousness, is sometimes premised upon an 'internal orientalism' (Schein 1997), which operates upon a homology of the ethnic 'other' as underdeveloped, uncivilized, and hence unfit to participate and produce modernity. Such a discourse of modernity assumes the unquestionable advantage of development, of the conquest of nature by culture, of the opening up of the vast areas of unused land in the remote regions – where many minorities live – by those from the centre.[7] A recent example of the prevalence of the discourse of development can be found in the hyperbole in the current nationwide drive for 'opening up the west' (*kaifan xibu*) [8]. It is not so much the lack of cultural knowledge or the cultural chauvinism on the part of Chinese spectators, as the ease with which one's own way of thinking lends itself to an understanding of the 'other'. This is one dimension of the Chinese television spectatorship which contributes to what I call a 'semiotic over-determination' – to distinguish it from the 'semiotic self-determination' in John Hartley's argument on the formation of 'do-it-yourself' citizenship (Hartley 1999: 159).

'*Pingbo*' – the Chinese spirit

This tendency for 'semiotic over-determination' is also evidenced in the spirit (*jingsheng*) in which people watched sports events during the Games. I do not refer to the tendency of Chinese television to transmit only events which were likely to win China gold medals: badminton, ping-pong, platform-diving and weightlifting. Nor do I mean the Chinese media's practice of giving favourable and sympathetic treatment to Chinese athletes. Every country does that. Television has the pedagogic function of teaching the population who we are (Hartley 1999). In the Chinese case, television allowed the Chinese audiences to learn not simply information related to sports events but more importantly to mark out China's allies, friends and enemies on the international stage. The over-determination lies in the linking, almost by default, of the achievement of individual Chinese athletes with that of the nation, and a collective desire to read the sports events as both metaphors and metonyms of China's greatness in an international context.

Most of the people I interviewed saw the Games as a platform on which China's strength as a nation was demonstrated. Mr Sun, a middle-aged senior public servant in Beijing (no relation to this author) told me that he had watched most of the shows transmitted by the CCTV, although he did not play sports:

> What the Games displayed was a spirit and resoluteness (*zhiji*) of the Chinese people. Many of our gold medals came when chances of winning looked really slim. Our athletes were prepared to give themselves completely to fight to the last second, fight to the death (*pingbo*). We used to be the 'sick man of Asia' but now we realized that there is nothing super-powerful about the foreigners.

Many of the people I talked to in Beijing used the word *pingbo* – a word which has no ready equivalent in English – to describe the spirit of the Chinese athletes. While *ping* literally means 'death-defying', *bo* means 'fight to the bitter end', 'fight with a very strong opponent and persevere through adversity'. To Mr Sun, it is this *pingbo* spirit that enabled the Chinese economy to boom. Pointing to the fridge next to him, Mr Sun said:

> In the 1980s, Japanese electronic appliances filled up the Chinese household. Nowadays, they have been mostly replaced by domestic products. Our Hai'er fridge is selling so well in Europe that it has acquired the status of inspection-free production. Some Western commentators say that China is becoming a threat to the West in the twenty-first century, and I think this is true, and it is really great!

The broadcasting of the Sydney Olympic Games in China provides a perfect case study of local constructions of global events. Chinese national television produced and transmitted images directly from Sydney, producing materials even more 'pure' and 'raw' than the scenario described by Gurevitch. This means two things. First, the images, such as of the opening and closing ceremonies, which were globally transmitted, were broadcast with Chinese commentaries within the ideological parameters of the dominant discourses. Second, the enormous Chinese media entourage, both electronic and print, ensured that the Chinese audiences were fed with a continuous diet of sports events and activities which the Chinese media saw as relevant to Chinese audiences.

Semiotic over-determination: some explanations

In watching the Olympic Games the Chinese audiences received a 'package deal', with meaning processed and delivered to effect a 'semiotic over-determination'. This does not mean that Chinese audiences have been duped, nor that the Chinese media are nothing more than a part of the state propaganda machinery. To think this way would be to fall into the trap of both the docile audience argument and the theory of the omnipotent state, hence ignoring the complexity and dynamism which mark the relationship between media consumption, cultural citizenship, commercialization, and nationalist state ideology in contemporary China. To understand this complexity, we need to consider a number of factors, which conspire to ensure the semiotic over-determination we see in the case of the Olympic Games in the Chinese media.

In China as elsewhere, sport lends itself easily as both a metonym and metaphor in discourses of nationalism. In the absence of war, sport comes closest to the acting out the dynamics of battle (Elias and Dunning 1986), with its lose-or-win inevitability, its us-versus-them binarism, and a 'beginning–development–finish' structure. Sport is sometimes described as the symbolic representation of war, and global media sports events, like the Olympic Games, have become 'orgies of both nationalism and commodification' (Rowe 1999: 22–3). The Olympic Games, the most significant international sports event, naturally become the most spectacular and significant space where nations are metaphorized – through the raising of national flags, the playing of national anthems – and embodied – through medal winners saluting national flags and diasporic Chinese spectators singing the national anthem. All this is effective because it is entertainment. Sports events are presented as drama rather than politics.

Incidentally, the Sydney Games took place between the Chinese Mid-autumn Festival (mid-September) – a family reunion season – and the National Day (1 October) – the longest public holiday in the year, giving the Chinese audience three weeks' non-stop adrenalin-flowing excitement. Such high drama on a global scale, once mediated through television, became the highly palatable spiritual food (*jingsheng shiliang*) consumed in domestic and public settings. Many interviewees described how they also watched the Games in public places; restaurants, street stalls or shops. Donald's (2000) argument[9] on 'publicness' and the centrality of cinema as a public cultural space is also useful in studying television viewership in this case. Publicness refers to the spontaneously formed spaces of viewing among friends, relatives and family members, and bears no resemblance to official spaces of organized meetings or viewings. The notion of voluntary publicness is crucial to understanding the relationship between media spectatorship and citizenship formation. Semiotic over-determination is effective because of familial and private modes of consumption. The Olympics Games on Chinese television seemed to offer a mixture of didactic teaching and pleasurable info-tainment.

Semiotic over-determination would not be possible without the live transmission of technologized images, which visualize the nation and create a spectacle effect. This is seen in repetitively played images of the kissing of the Chinese national flags by Chinese gold medallists, the spectacle of many national flags in the stadium, and sounds of cheering enthused with patriotic sentiments among the overseas Chinese spectators during the badminton matches. Live television brought the Games to the audiences and made television viewers feel that they were also participating in the cheering. Writing on the power of technologized images, Rey Chow (1995) discusses the ways in which an electronic medium such as film allows the entire nation to be visualized. I would add that live transmission of important events such as the Olympics Games allows the entire nation, its history, culture and people, to be visualized and made spectacular. It also contributes to the formation of a modern subjectivity, characterized by a deterritorialized sense of cultural identity. The identification of Chinese television spectators with their counterparts in Sydney in the Homebush Stadium points to the power of electronic images to enhance a collective cultural identity. As people in Beijing remarked to me more than once, the most effective ideological lesson of patriotism was given outside China. As the Chinese journalists say, the most effective propaganda message to the international community about Beijing's suitability to host the 2008 Games was delivered from the gold medal podium (Yang [Taoyuan] 2000)

China went to the Games confident in the knowledge that China, along with Russia and the United States, would be a strong gold-medal winner. This meant that these Olympics Games were likely to create many moments of glory and triumph, which could be easily made into political spectacles for audiences at home and abroad. This, in turn, would accumulate political capital for the Chinese government for its various strategic needs, including promoting patriotism, increasing its political legitimacy and scoring points for Beijing's bid for the 2008 Games. This justified the dispatch of an unprecedented number of Chinese journalists, reporters, camera crew and technical supporting teams to Sydney.

The globalization of electronic journalism has not led to a homogenization of world views. Nevertheless, my findings suggest that a combination of political, economic, technological and cultural factors conspired to result in an over-determination of meaning for the Chinese viewers in 2000. This over-determination does not point so much to the disempowerment of the Chinese audience as to the growing capacity of the Chinese state to deliver propaganda while at the same time giving people what they want. I call this phenomenon 'indoctritainment', the 'happy marriage' between state agendas and popular social desire.

Notes

1 Information comes from *Focal Point* (*Jiaodian Fangtan*), CCTV's highest rating show, September 2000.
2 See Xinhua's Web sites: aoyun.xinhuanet.com
3 For instance, Xinhua is proud to record that it dispatched the news of the winning of gold medals for Chinese men's gymnastics four minutes after the event. See Shi 2000, No. 10, p. 74.

4 This blueprint 'Glorious China – Special Olympic Games Program, Oriental Time and Space' (*Guangrong zhongguo - Dong fang shi kong aoyu tebie jiemu*) appeared in the 42nd issue of the Zhongguo Dianshi Bao (Chinese Television News), p. 23. My translation.

5 A good example of the use of media for political mobilization in China is the way in which media events are televised on the Chinese television. See Sun [Wanning] 2001.

6 Information regarding this incident comes from *Beijing Youth Daily*, 27 October 2000. See Li Shufeng, 'Falungong xini yan chouqu' (Falungong's clown's Performance in Sydney), p. 7.

7 I am grateful to Zhao Bin for calling my attention to this point in an earlier version of this article.

8 'Open up the Big West' (xi bu da kai fa) has been a constant topic in the Chinese media since the turn of the twenty-first century. The 'west' here refers to some of the provinces in the western part of China such as Sichuan, Qinhai, Tibet and Xinjiang, which are, in comparison to the greater part of China, undeveloped and sparsely populated.

9 Donald argues (2000: vii) that before we settle on the 'national' or 'transnational' dimension of cinema, it is crucial to acknowledge the publicness of cinema.

11

CRAZY RABBITS! CHILDREN'S MEDIA CULTURE

Stephanie Hemelryk Donald[1]

A crazy rabbit stalks the landscape of computer technology in China. It enters children's brains, driving them mad and sending them on to the streets to commit unnaturally antisocial acts. Or rather, it did in 1997, when the film *Crazy Rabbit* (*Fengkuang de tuzi*) was released to popular and critical acclaim. Dealing with adult fears of technology, change and the young, the subject is strangely suspicious of its target market. Most successful children's drama gives children the roles of heroes and heroines, for once powerful in a fantasy version of an adult-dominated universe. In *Crazy Rabbit* it is the children, corrupted by an alien virus, who threaten the safety of the sensible world. What then is the position of children's media product in the People's Republic of China (PRC) and whose interests does it serve?

Children in education

> Chinese children have their own cultural style. They tend to be more introverted. And, as they come from one-child family units, I think they have special psychological needs and characteristics. But in the 1990s the films always portray the children as extroverted. There are exaggerations, and the children have foreign interests, foreign characteristics and foreign issues to deal with ... children are just objects in the adult imagination. What films should depict is the child's imagination.
>
> (Chen San, film critic, Beijing Film Academy, 1999)

Chen San's critiques of films of the 1990s (especially those produced at the Children's Film Studio in Beijing) arise in part from their concern to address private social issues (divorce is a staple topic), as opposed to public moral issues (exemplified in early realist drama for children pre-1949, and post-1949 revolutionary expositions on courage). In the same conversation, Chen referred to *Chicken Feather Letter* (*ji maoxin*, 1954) as an excellent example of a film that understood children and the ways in which they make emotional connections. The film is about a small boy who carries a letter over enemy lines during the Sino–Japanese war in the 1930s. The letter is tied to the underbelly of one of the sheep that he herds, and the emotional punch of the narrative is carried in the relationship between boy and sheep.

Chen also premises his opinion on generalized assumptions about the nature of Chinese children. His reading of children as 'introverted' certainly does not tally with observations I have made of primary school (*xiaoxue*)-age children in the PRC. Some are introverted and some are not. Arguably Chinese children are as diverse across families, regions and the urban/rural divide as any other large population of young people. However, Chen San's remarks are interesting in that they conflate a description of children themselves with his understanding of the influx of consumption and commercialism into the hitherto ideologically bounded world of media for children. His comments also reflect the concern over children and media and media effects, which informs debate worldwide. Furthermore, he speaks for a generation which finds the self-confidence and self-containment of contemporary children's culture hard to swallow. The world of animated 'commercial supersystems of transmedia textuality' (Kinder 1991: 122; Gibson 2000) does not fit easily with conformist expectations of socialist citizenship and national regeneration. Nor does an entertainment-led content revolution tally with the still huge importance of education (*jiaoyü*) to Chinese families (especially urban families with disposable incomes for increasingly expensive schooling, but also in a wider sense of education through public media, political engagement and social modelling). As a group of (urban-based) third-grade teachers said to me in 2000:

> (T1) Although we have never experienced war, we have heard so much about wars from our parents' generation. But for the children, war is too far away, they can't understand, they have become very commercial.
>
> (T2) Yes, few children nowadays can be stimulated by watching film stories like Lei Feng [a model soldier from the early 1960s]. It is very hard to get them interested on an emotional level in class. For example, when I told them the story of the Five Soldiers at Langsha (*Langya shanshang wu zhuangshi*) they were not moved in the slightest.
>
> (T1) I remember in the 1970s a film from North Korea, *Flower Seller* ... when it was screened in China all the children cried and cried. Look at them now! Contemporary children are rather emotionally cold.
>
> (Teachers, Qinghua Linked School, 2000)

The teachers went on to describe the sense of individual preservation (over and above patriotism and selflessness) that drove the moral decisions of their students. One could doubtless suggest that adults are prone to nostalgia, and especially in their descriptions of earlier modes of child behaviour in comparison with current trends. The further they grow from the state of childhood, the more likely they are to forget their own weaknesses and their own refusal of adult standards. Indeed, it has been suggested that one of the reasons for the huge 'success'(the word is advisedly in 'scare' quotes) of the GPCR (Cultural Revolution) was the delight of youth to have an excuse to break free of endless authoritarian teaching methods and political monitoring at school.[2] If children in the 1990s and 2000s are unfamiliar with the passions of their parents' generation, it is surely due to chronological distance rather than to inherent coldness on their part. Their parents heard war stories from *their* parents, but have no similar stories to tell themselves. No one is publicly enthusiastic about the Cultural Revolution period (1966–1976), unless through retro-art and food in metropolitan centres in the east, or through recurring adulation of Mao Zedong. It is required of teachers to pass on revolutionary history to their students, and in so doing to map out patterns of behaviour consonant with social norms and expectations. They must do so, however, with students who are also expected to participate in normality-as-consumption. As the Billy Graham-esque hero Li Yang of the documentary *Crazy English* (*Fengkuang yingyü*, Zhang Yuan, 2000) shouts out to his adult and child audience (while teaching them English en masse), 'Don't be hypocritical! Why do you really want your children to learn English? To MAKE MORE MONEY!!'.

The prerogative for socialization through education is ideally very high, but the ideal does not translate into high levels of education across the nation. Girls receive less education than boys in rural areas for social and financial reasons (Rosen 1995: 130–8), although participation has risen significantly amongst girls in remote provinces since 1979 (Shi [Jinghuan] 1995: 145). Illiteracy is still much higher amongst women than men. In Sichuan 70 per cent of illiterates are women, and the proportion rises to 78 per cent in Beijing, and 83 per cent in Guangdong. That said, literacy levels are generally good in metropolitan areas (China Statistical Yearbooks 1997–2000). In the remote and rural regions in central and western China, however, less than 50 per cent of children go on to senior secondary school at the age of 15. This is a distinctive statistic when one realizes that the highest progression rate, in Beijing, is 87.3 per cent, and the lowest, in Guangxi, is 18.6 per cent (Benewick and Donald 1999: 68–9). These figures remind us that the media-sphere in China is highly differentiated. The need for local content or locally manipulated formats is clear where the population has such widely differing levels of education, and thus of socialization. I suggest in the following analysis that there are at least three ways of reading the Chinese media-sphere for children. None is likely to explain the situation entirely, but awareness of the possibilities may allow us, as analysts and producers, to think clearly and creatively about children's consumption practices and desires. First, we can examine children's reactions to content, the choices they make and the pleasures they derive from those choices. Second, we can look at children's media as a top-down process by which the population is induced to develop along certain national, political and cultural avenues. Third, we consider ways in which the internationalization and subsequent domestication of children's culture feeds on the creative autonomy of the children's market place. I suggest that children represent a formidable target audience for content provision and associated merchandising, but that they nonetheless remain central foci of the state's objective to reproduce itself and its values through education and mediated messages.

Chen San judges (and here I would agree with him) that mediated entertainment for children must endeavour to find ways of addressing their concerns, their interests and their expectations, and, I would add, in their time, place and circumstance. Cinema, television, multimedia products and Web sites must take their audiences' preferences and taste structures seriously if they are to succeed as spiritual or as commercial messengers.

Children as consumers

In late 1999, 25.4 per cent of the population of China was reportedly under 14 years old. These children are catered for by television, films, and a thriving magazine culture.[3] There are about 640 television stations broadcasting to children. CCTV alone runs up to eight hours of programming per day, as well as broadcasting family films on CCTV 6 (the movie channel). These are often produced under the auspices of the Children's Film Studio (Beijing). The Studio caters mainly for under-twelves, and acts as a training ground for directors and producers in the field. It is hard to say whether or not these films are actually popular. Overall, the Children's Film Studio has produced ninety films over the past two decades, and almost one-third of those have won prizes (Liu [Huizhong] 2000). However, it seems that the most popular pre-release pirated VCD in early 2000 was the Pixar/Disney digital-animated production, *Toy Story 2*.[4] Children are not watching, or their parents are not purchasing, the films that the state sponsors on their behalf. Policy-makers are not ignorant of this, and there is a great deal of pressure being exerted to develop the market for local, especially animated, content. The Shanghai Animation Studio is the most visible domestic brand name for cartoons, and has become the model for the General State Administration of Radio, Film and Television (SARFT) for expansion of the domestic industry. From June 2000, SARFT required that all foreign animation should be approved directly by SARFT's social administration department, and that animation targets for 2001–05 should include a requirement that ten minutes of domestic animation be screened per day, per broadcasting station. Seventy-five per cent of all animation screened must be domestically produced. Any foreign imports must be submitted to SARFT for approval and a release licence before broadcast. These measures will be unlikely to squash the pirate trade in internationally distributed movies, unless the quality contends with international products. Nor will they help the broadcasters, who point out that domestic production remains low although they are expected to broadcast ten minutes of material a day.

There are some points of optimism however. Chinese animation fell out of touch in the 1970s but it has an honourable tradition of craftsmanship and cultural finesse, and also of appealing to children's tastes. In the early 1960s, Xie Tian in *Little Wooden-Top* (*Xiao ling dang*, 1964, Beijing) used puppetry to tell the story of a 'doll' that played with children and got them into mischief. The beauty of *Little Tadpoles Look for their Mother* (*Xiao kedou zhao mama*, 1960, Shanghai) lies in the use of ink-wash painting to create the images before animation. Ink and water have been superseded by the clean glint of computer animation, the stuff of *Toy Story* 2. Nevertheless, the painterly style of the film echoes additional ink-wash techniques that are still propounded in children's painting and drawing manuals widely available in popular bookstores. If Chinese animators develop local styles in international modes, especially the computer generation and manipulation of images, and if the industry as a whole can support them on this, then there is a future for domestic product.

The Children's Film Studio has already sought to breach the gap between 'trace and paint' and fully computerized image generation. They work with the encouragement of government, which has asked for at least five children's films per year, but also within its constraints; these five productions must keep to a total budget of 7 million RMB (yuan) (875,000 $US). In 1997 the studio produced *Crazy Rabbit*. The sci-fi story gives a nod to a computer-literate, or computer-aware, audience. The rabbit in question is infected by aliens with a computer virus, and sent out to damage human intelligence. Each time a child opens his or her PC, the rabbit jumps from the screen and destroys part of the victim's brain. The children then become disorderly and a menace to society. It would be interesting to gauge audience reaction to the film. Does the audience respond to the horrific messages about techno-invasion and social disorder, or do they just enjoy the craziness of the rabbit, and the ensuing furore caused by their damaged peer group? Given that the rabbit is digitally mastered and the rest of the story is shot on location, it might well be the latter.

The film includes forty-eight shots of digitally generated montage (320 seconds in total). The innovation persuaded the government to increase funding for the feature from 1.2 to 1.5 million yuan, 0.25 million of which was used to fund the fully digitized sequences. This is not a huge budget for a technically ambitious movie, but the response did signal some state-level understanding of the need for Chinese studios to deploy new technologies in their efforts to regroup their audience. The studio was also inventive in its financial management. It sought to make the film a co-production with a partner institution that could offer access to editing equipment. The deal was stuck with the Computer Centre at the Institute of Science and Technology. The film also won an award at the 8th Bronze Ox Film Festival for outstanding animated design (Liu [Huizhong] 2000). Liu Huizhong, a media professional at the Children's Film Studio, also claims that the film brought social benefit. In this claim he is following in the wake of Yu Lan, the founder of the studio, who has always argued for entertainment together with spiritual health in children's films.[5] In 2000 another co-production was in the planning stage, on this occasion between the Children's Studio and Beijing Wisdom Image Co. This time a fully digitized feature *Stories of a Strange Forest* is under way. Again the project aims to combine high-quality production goals and methods with appropriate local content.

Children as proto-citizens

State studios are wise to argue that their work provides social benefits as well as entertainment. Subsidies need to be justified under the rubric of the national interest. It is not clear, however, whether audiences derive the 'intended' messages from their favourite shows. In 1999–2000 a great children's favourite was CCTV1's latest version of *Journey to the West* (*Xi you ji*).[6] This animated series was also sold on VCD for fans, and for those who could not make it back from school by 5 p.m. to see the next episode. The merchandising associated with this programme was fairly intense, and pricey. At the same time, the series complied with the need for domestic treatment of Chinese material. *Journey to the West* is a classic of vernacular story-telling, combining folk Buddhism with martial arts, anti-establishment innuendo and stock characters (all of which make great toys).

Without merchandising, Chinese domestic animation is unlikely to expand and build on its digital experiments. Merchandising is 'par for the course' for high-quality contemporary cartoons. At least two-thirds of international animation cost/profit budgets are covered by associated merchandise. A Disney film is as much an advert for its retail outlets, toy promotions, Happy Meal deals with McDonald's, staggered video releases[7] and online commerce, as it is a work of creative entertainment. So, does children's consumption of contemporary television programmes and associated merchandise encourage them to develop different ideas about political socialization and belonging from those propagated by the Chinese state? Does children's access to television programmes, toys, and the multiple models of belonging that are implicit within them, affect the ways in which they grow and develop as citizens? SARFT's insistence on foreign licensing is mainly a protectionist measure for the industry. Underlying that priority, however, is a continuing worry about the role of children's media in social reproduction.

But does it actually matter if children see the show, buy the toys and then play Monkey-style martial arts in the playground – or perhaps confuse Monkey with a *Pokémon* power and make them play together (Chu et al. in press)? The teachers at Qinghua Linked School certainly thought so. They unhesitatingly blamed media products for children's 'cold emotions', and for their unwillingness to act unselfishly on behalf of others. They also expressed concern over the inappropriate body images offered in the elongated heroes and heroines of Japanese animation. They felt that 'children's faces on adult bodies' offered a confusing self-image to young audiences. Japanese animation is often referred to as the 'bad guy' in the war on imported cartoons. Small Chinese boys, or at least those of them who can afford the luxury, trade in *Pokémon* cards much as their peers do across the rest of the urban world, and they attract similar levels of criticism and antiglobal anxieties. However, while in the West *Pokémon* tends to be seen as just one more super-network of media merchandising, in China it is seen as a specifically Japanese phenomenon (see also Hooper 2000).

Perceptions and programmes of political socialization (or modes of citizenship) in China differ from those articulated in liberal democracies (Chih 1999; Unger 1996). John Fitzgerald (1995, 1996; see also Tang [Xiaobing] 1996 and Duara 1988) argues that membership of the nation was once strategically determined by political leaders in their struggles to build a sovereign socialist state. 'Belonging' required that people accept the duties, responsibilities and codes of conduct approved by the state. Citizens' rights were limited to the economic, social and cultural benefits bestowed by the state upon virtuous members of the nation. Part of that virtue always lay in correct identification of enemies, and those enemies tended to be Japanese, British and American. Even today, children are quick to point out their preference for Chinese shows on television in clearly patriotic terms. One little girl told me that she loved cartoons, but was visibly upset when others in the group informed her that her favourites were all Japanese imports. The three bogeymen are still at work in Chinese national preoccupations. British pre-school children's shows are now hugely successful in the Asian region (*Teletubbies* and *The Tweenies*), but are not so visible in China. It is the Japanese and American imports which apparently threaten the integrity of the Chinese child's animated national imagination.

As the vehicles for, and measures of, the nation's progress and cohesion throughout the twentieth century, children have been the subjects of intensive programmes aimed at inculcating norms of citizenship, however that socio-political relation to the state was defined. The educators, film-makers and print media artists of the 1920s and 1930s paid especial attention to the plight of street orphans as a metonymic of the dismemberment of the nation

(Farquhar 1999). In the anti-Japanese and civil wars of the 1940s, children were depicted in films and comic books as mini-nationalist and revolutionary soldiers. This was viewed as an appropriate performance of their national duty in a time of great danger (Donald 2000). Following the revolution, under the direct control of the victorious Chinese Communist Party, the structurally integrated Chinese media and education systems played a crucial role in popularizing civic virtues among young audiences (Liu [Alan] 1971; Chan [Anita] 1985). Film plots and school primers emphasized the contribution made by revolutionary children to the identification and elimination of class enemies, post-war socialist reconstruction and the formation of collectives. During the Cultural Revolution, Mao Zedong and Lin Biao harnessed the energy of the young to invent a new version of citizenship, one that explicitly centred on collective expressions of correct class attitudes and sacrifice for the nation, working class or peasant commune (Chen [Xiaomei] 1999). That version continues today under the auspices of collective democracy, and collective consumption habits (Chih 1999).

In the post-Mao era, the state continued its efforts to instil in the population an understanding of its civic obligations (Pan and Chan 2000). However, the ideals of citizenship promoted by the state were transformed along with the economy itself. The 1982 Constitution and subsequent market reforms made membership of the nation conditional upon merit – measured in observance of the law, productivity, independence and entrepreneurship (Shirk 1984; Solinger 1999; Keane 2001c). In the midst of this, children were again given iconic status as cultural emblems of a modernizing nation. In the press, state poster campaigns and television soaps, children feature as agents and repositories of pride, cohesion, hope and concern (Donald 1999, 2001). News and chat shows display children's anger at 'acts of aggression' toward China and their enthusiasm for national reunification. Despite mini-documentaries on China's west, where many of its minority populations live, children are still addressed as a singular generically Han national group. The use of regional dialects is actively discouraged through televised Mandarin-speaking competitions between schoolchildren. Environmental awareness is built around the billboard image of a child picking up waste; use of new technology is encouraged by a child, schoolbag over her shoulder, racing toward a computer screen. In 2000 the Beijing Dunhuang Cartoon Co. offered two titles that gelled with this trend: *I Love Animals* (*Wo ai dongwu*) and *I Love Nature* (*Wo ai ziran*).

The animated drama *Lotus Lantern* (*Baolian deng* 1999–2000) was also very successful. *Lotus Lantern* tells the story of a little boy who loses his mother and spends his youth fighting evil powers in order to regain her. His mother, the bearer of the powerful Lotus Lantern, has been tricked into giving it up to the evil *jiujiu* (wicked uncle) on the promise of the return of her kidnapped son. Of course, as she lets it go, she is cast into a vortex of entrapment and despair, from which her son must finally release her. On the way, he enlists the help of the now beatific *Sunwukung* (Monkey King), a smaller and cuter monkey helper, a beautiful *Pocohontas* look-alike (whose father has been similarly 'disappeared') and, when he retrieves it, the lantern itself. As he nears his objectives a song cuts in, assuring the audience that he is on the 'road home'. This theme is the most overtly sentimental fragment in the narrative, and is reminiscent of the Disney trope of using a song to mask time while a central character grows up in montage (*Tarzan, The Lion King*). The film is otherwise action-packed, with the main character excelling at elegant fighting, and at spectacular falls through space from one firmament to another. His final reunion with his mother takes place on a cloud, bringing them close to Nirvana and the transcendence offered through the Lotus Lantern, and demonstrated by *Sunwukong*'s transformation into (a rather truculent) Boddhisattva.

This show was named in a questionnaire administered through Beijing primary schools (a sample of seventy children) as one of the most popular cartoons of that year.[8] Apparently the familiarity and excitement of Monkey's 'guest' appearance, the attractiveness of the main character, and the speed and kinetic excitement of the narrative combined to produce a smash hit. The action is punctuated by abrupt movement between earthly and ethereal (and hellish) locations separated by black space. The characters fall, whirl and slide through space as though they were ciphers in a computer game, their animated nature taking precedence over their mortality. Indeed, no one in these stories is truly mortal. Even on the rare trip to recognizably human locations (there is one scene drawn in a 'someteenth' century market place), we do not stop long enough to cathect with characters. They are ciphers of human interaction in service to the swift pull of the narrative. One such cipher is an old lady, who reciprocates a small act of kindness with a free *mantou* (steamed bun). She must have realized that this boy, who has already been through screen years of misery and aggression, might be *hungry*.

The story is thus deeply embedded both pictorially and in terms of narrative detail in local cultural references and aesthetic styles. That said, it draws heavily on the Disney film *Pocahontas* to describe the leading lady/primitive heroine and 'her people', and there is a significant element of the action which mimics computerized game technology. The film is also, however, socially specific. It plays on themes of internal colonialism (expressed as a magical journey of mutual self-discovery between boy (colonizer/saviour/hero) and girl (colonized/saved/beloved), that feed back into the discourse of Han hegemony and national unity.

Meanwhile the feature film *Not One Less* (*Yi ge ye bu neng shao*, Zhang Yimou, 1999) celebrates the civic virtues of honesty, hard work and loyalty to be found among village children. However, there is also heavy coverage of child slavery and the kidnapping of urban youngsters by rings of 'peasants'. These latter, self-flagellating stories are notable because of the divide they depict between the progressive cosmopolitanism of cities and the backward parochialism of rural cultures (Cohen 1993).

Changing representations of citizenship go hand in hand with a broad appeal to children as consumers. The one-child policy has produced an élite generation surrounded by adults keen to spend money to ensure their physical and intellectual development (Anagnost 1997). Exceptions to this rule of thumb notwithstanding, the budgets of provincial and local television stations have come to rely on advertisements that encourage parents' purchase of education, vacations, beneficial foods and vitamins, personal computers, toys and clothes (Yu and Green 2000; Zhao and Murdock 1996). Although the appeal to consumption for a child's welfare is aimed at the parent, this is abutted with references to children's culture and popular children's programmes. Domestic productions and merchandise continue to represent model children performing meritorious deeds for the nation, neighbourhood and village. But do the heroes of American and Japanese cartoons convey the same ideas about civic virtue to their young audiences?

Conclusion: the international market place

The production of media for Chinese children is entering a financially dangerous but potentially thrilling stage of development. Although the animated industry is generally deemed to be in crisis, there are people taking risks and forging new ways of working. They may also need to forge an international view of their audiences. Co-productions with European and Australian production houses and broadcasters allow new audience tastes and new technologies to intermingle with Chinese styles and narrative structures. www.chinanim.com is a Web site devoted to China Animation, an alliance of three organizations[9] devoted to enhancing the reputation of Chinese animation and improving collaborations and communications across the industry networks. A judicious mixture of professional communications, co-productions, technological investment, and stylistic flexibility would go a long way to preserving China's hold on the imaginations of its own children.

Notes

1 Parts of this paper were developed in discussion with Sally Sargeson and David Brown (Asia Research Centre, Murdoch University), Andrea Witcomb and Yingchi Chu. Fieldwork was supported by the Australian Research Council.

2 This argument was made by GPCR participants in a closed seminar at Indiana University in 1999.

3 In a survey carried out by the author amongst Beijing teenagers in 2000, over 40 per cent named the comic-joke magazine weekly 'Master Joker' (*youmodashi*) as their favourite media item.

4 Web sites have also sprung up to promote and extend the reach of the movie, for example: http://movie.bdinfo.net/toystorytwo
5 Conversation with the author, December 1998
6 ACNielsen audience ratings place the show top in Beijing (18.2 per cent) and third in Shanghai (12.5 per cent).
7 Discontinued in 2001.
8 Questionnaires administered June 2000, by the author and researchers at Tsinghua University.
9 Chinese Cartoon Society, Beijing Dison Computer Graphics and Image Ltd, US Animationworld Network.

12

'WHAT CAN I DO FOR SHANGHAI?'

Selling spiritual civilization in China's cities

Steven Wayne Lewis[1]

Shanghai's Nanjing Road presents an eye-popping array of visual advertisements. Enormous neon signs and vivid window displays mark the fronts of department stores. Shop banners flap and snap overhead in the wind. Large billboards painted on spare walls, small backlit postings mounted on poles next to curbs, and signs tacked on to pedestrian bridges, bus shelters, and anti-jaywalking barriers hawk a dizzying array of goods from across China and around the world. Colourful commercial murals cover the sides of buses and taxis slowly wheezing down the congested street. Handbills, flyers and product samples frantically thrust into the hands of unwary passers-by by gangs of costumed corporate mascots and uniformed store clerks peddle still more goods and services.

Nor is the commercial odyssey merely visual. Jingles floating out of department store doorways and hip pop tunes blaring from trendy clothing boutiques grab the ear. Curried lamb and chestnuts roast on grills in doorways. Fragrant soft drinks and juices pour out of tanks mounted on carts and backpacks. And of course the tantalizing smell of food frying behind the counter at Kentucky Fried Chicken (and its personal corporate nemesis lurking nearby ... the Ronghua Chicken) wafts into the air. The nose is jerked back and forth across the street. As with any major commercial street in Hong Kong, Tokyo, Taipei, New York or London, the entire body is drawn to play in this materialist circus of the senses.

And yet there is a unique spiritual presence in China's urban outdoor consumer mediascapes. Here and there are advertisements for a distinctly local product: Socialist Spiritual Civilization (with 'Chinese Characteristics') *shehui zhuyi jingshen wenming jianshe*. A large mural on a wall exhorts, 'Strengthening Socialist Spiritual Civilization is the Grand Strategic Goal!' (*shehui zhuyi jingshen wenming jianshe shi yixiang zhongda zhanlue renwu!*)

A small billboard tucked in among the trees lining the boulevard quietly implores, 'Persist in Reforms and Opening Up to the Outside World: Safeguard the Stability of Society'. (*jianchi gaige kaifang/weihu shehui wending)* Bright red banners hanging from street lamps advise passerby, 'Liberate Your Thinking: Expand and Strive for Self-Improvement' *(jiefang sixiang/kaituo jinqu),* and 'Study the Spirit of the 15th Party Congress: Advance the Development of Jing'An District' (*xuexi shiwuda jingshen/ tuijin jing'an qu fazhan*). A bus shelter poster urges commuters to, 'Pitch In and Keep Shanghai Clean' (*renren dongshou qingjie shanghai)*. Small back-lit billboards mounted on poles and glowing with visions of a sparklingly clean, forested and skyscrapered metropolis ask all, 'What Can I Do For Shanghai?' (*wo wei shanghai zuo dian shenme?*)

The modern Chinese state has always been a prominent player in the urban outdoor commercial arena. From 1949 to the late 1970s, and through banner and bullhorn, dance and drum, it drove the masses to build the nation through class struggle and hard work in the *danwei*, the state-owned workplace. Now, however, the state is asking people to develop Shanghai – or Beijing, Chongqing or Guangzhou – through selfless individualist efforts to solve local problems. Consumer/citizen and locality are replacing class and nation-state in these appeals. The socialist sermon of spiritual civilization can still be heard loudly and clearly, but the call is being made by local preachers trying to capture mobile flocks of 'born-again' capitalists. And now there are new choirs of communication technologies to make the spiritual message heard above the din of the urban marketplace.

We must wonder: how has the sermon of socialist spiritual civilization (*shehui zhuyi jingshen wenming*) survived the growth of a seemingly overpowering material civilization? In this chapter I argue that state political propaganda has survived because the combination of economic liberalization and political decentralization has forced the local state – the organs of the Chinese Communist Party and urban government – to adapt, innovate and experiment with new messages and new technologies. Contrary to the conventional wisdom of Western social scientific theory, the state in China's transition central planned economy has not disappeared or withered away with the emergence of a public sphere and the gradual growth of the institutions of civil society. It is actively engaging an increasingly transnational consumerist movement in order to marshal resources for distinctly local political and economic goals. The state is still preaching the sermon of China's socialist state authority and yet in doing so it indirectly – and perhaps unintentionally – fosters local, individualist political identification and consumerist notions of citizenship.

In the following sections I briefly present evidence from pioneering surveys of outdoor political advertisements in Shanghai and Beijing to demonstrate that the local state in China has indeed adapted to marketization by selling a version of spiritual civilization that serves its own development needs. I then discuss how the decentralization of political authority has forced the local state to become innovative and to experiment with new messages that may foster the creation of civic identities that transcend the nation-state and yet tie individuals to localities.

Selling socialist spiritual civilization

What is this product called 'Socialist Spiritual Civilization'? As one expert has neatly observed, socialist spiritual civilization is a concept both 'vague and complex' (Lynch 1999: 242, footnote 22).

The term truly is vague because although frequently invoked by China's top Party leaders it is never defined in detail. At the Fourth Session of the Ninth National People's Congress in March 2001, Premier Zhu Rongji pledged to 'vigorously promote socialist spiritual civilization' as he advocated ethical and moral behaviour that would serve the needs of a socialist market economy (Xinhua Foreign News Service 2001a). But in his report on the 10th Five-Year Plan to the Congress he did not define it, simply calling for moral behaviour by cadres and masses and government policies that would promote 'better' cultural products and more scientific knowledge and education (Xinhua Foreign News Service 2001b).

At a 1997 meeting to establish the Party Central Guidance Committee on Socialist Spiritual Civilization Construction (CGCSSCC), President and Party Secretary Jiang Zemin seemed to define spiritual civilization construction (*shehui zhuyi jingshen wenming jianshe*) as the catch-all sum of numerous, uncoordinated efforts to promote morals and ethics that would facilitate China's drive toward economic development:

> We must persistently use the party's basic theories and basic line to educate cadres and the masses; firmly establish a common ideal among all the people on building socialism with Chinese characteristics (*you zhongguo tese de shehui zhuyi*); comprehensively carry out educational programmes on patriotism, collectivism, socialism, and hardworking pioneering spirit; make greater efforts to promote public spirits, professional ethics, and family virtues whose principal objectives are to serve the people; strive to cultivate a new generation who have revolutionary ideals, sound morals, good education, and a strong sense of discipline; improve the whole nation's ideological, ethical, scientific, and cultural standards; and strive to provide powerful spiritual driving force and intellectual support and to create a favourable social environment for China's reform, opening up, and modernization drive.
>
> (Xinhua Domestic News Service 1997)

Finally, Ding Guangen, Politburo member, head of the Communist Party's propaganda department and director of the CGCSSCC, emphasized at a December 25, 2000 meeting of its plenary committee that the goal of spiritual civilization work is to create better 'spiritual products' that can help the Party 'win the hearts of the people' as they cope with the problems of economic reforms:

> We must uphold economic development as the centre, and integrate spiritual civilization construction work with city and rural development work, as well as with business work for all industries and trades. We must put efforts into raising the ideological and moral quality of people, and also their science and cultural quality, thus providing spiritual motivation and ideological assurance for modernization construction. We must uphold the guiding position of Marxism, expand the socialist cultural front, and use even more and even better spiritual products to satisfy the increasingly multi-faceted spiritual and cultural needs of our citizens ... In our spiritual civilization construction, we must do more work to win the hearts of the people, comfort the people, and stabilize the people, thus enabling the masses to gain real benefits.
>
> (Xinhua Domestic News Service 2000)

As with the use of the term 'socialism with Chinese characteristics', 'socialist spiritual civilization construction' is a vague ideological justification for a vast array of central Party and government propaganda campaigns designed to obtain popular support for policies to develop China economically while maintaining one-party rule.

Socialist spiritual civilization is also a complex term because it has been used throughout the 1990s to justify the call for dozens of specific campaigns promoted by many central Party organs and government agencies. These include campaigns on AIDS awareness, anti-dumping, consumer rights, anti-counterfeit goods, drug prevention, the promotion of the Eighth National Games, fire prevention, family planning, literacy, flood prevention, afforestation, cooperation among nationalities, polio prevention, the registration of non-governmental organs, legal education, anti-crime efforts, the promotion of sports and fitness, the teaching of science and technology, the maintenance of control over internal migration, anti-corruption, and the celebration of the return of sovereignty over Hong Kong and Macau, to name just a few.[2]

Changes in the content of the spiritual civilization construction campaign(s) over time are thus a useful case for the study of changes in political communication in China in general. As a vaguely defined, omnibus ideological campaign it is capable of reflecting the needs of all state organs in all localities in China in the reform era.

But the promotion of socialist spiritual civilization in China's urban outdoor mediascapes is a particularly important case for the study of changes in political communication media. Urban outdoor political advertisements are important not only because they are ubiquitous and yet costly – which suggests that the state believes them to be influential – but because they are one of the few media that allow us to understand the effects of the decentralization political authority on China's transition to a market economy. Most propaganda media are either relatively easily controlled by constraints on the capital, labor and technologies of production – the publishing and film media – or by the fact that in addition to these constraints they are public goods that also require government coordination for their effective use – television and radio, because they are broadcast over a limited amount of public airwaves. As such, they are most likely to present propaganda work that reflects the interests of that part of the state that can most easily control them: the central Party and government. Urban outdoor advertisements are one of the few media that are capable of reflecting the local state's needs and interests. In the next section I will discuss the importance of considering the role that local state actors play in theories of transition in China and other Socialist central planned economies.

But what brands and formulas of socialist 'spiritual products' are local Party and government organs trying to sell? I conducted surveys of outdoor political advertisements on commercial and residential streets in ten urban districts in Shanghai in 1997 and 1998, and Beijing in 1998[3], looking for the range of themes of spiritual civilization emphasized and their importance over time as reflected in the durability of the format in which they were presented.[4]

As discussed above, central organs called on 'all levels' to develop propaganda campaigns in at least 40 issue areas during this period, but basic content analysis[5] suggests that China's urban localities only promoted some 16 themes:

1 Afforestation and the protection of the environment;
2 Model citizen conduct and civilization, both in general and in specific residential and work units;
3 Crime awareness and education about new laws and regulations;
4 Support for development and modernization;
5 Disaster relief;
6 Knowledge about various elements of the local economy;
7 Knowledge about international affairs;
8 Standardization of the written and spoken language;
9 Study of the thoughts of China's leaders, including Mao Zedong, Deng Xiaoping and Jiang Zemin;
10 Designation of residential and work units as 'model units' (*shifan danwei*) of civilization;

11 Knowledge about current events in general, through the use of notice boards and display cases containing official newspapers;
12 Knowledge of upcoming, major political events, including district-level people's congress elections and such one-time sporting events as the national games;
13 Public health, sanitation and family planning policies;
14 Knowledge about and compliance with tax rules and regulations;
15 Traffic safety education and compliance signs, but not common traffic coordination and directional signs; and
16 Establishment of ties between individuals, work units and the People's Liberation Army (PLA) in order to support veterans and demobilized soldiers, as well as PLA actions in disaster relief.

The number of messages for many of these issue areas, and the temporary nature of their presentation (cloth banners and paper posters), suggest that they are not high priorities for local state propaganda organs. This is particularly true of campaigns to disseminate knowledge about political events, the thoughts of national leaders, and new laws and regulations. But as seen

Table 12.1 Top issue areas and durability of political advertisements for Shanghai 1997: 143 ad messages total

Issue Area	*Number of messages*	*Number of durable ads*
Public Health and Family Planning	31	16
Traffic Safety	26	17
Citizen Conduct and Civilization	24	10
Afforestation and Protection of Environment	17	15
Political Events	15	6
People and Army Support Campaign	10	1
Development and Modernization	5	0
Model Units	5	5
Leader Thoughts (Deng Xiaoping, Jiang Zemin)	3	2

Table 12.2 Top issue areas and durability of political advertisements for Shanghai 1998: 244 ads total

Issue Area	*Number of messages*	*Number of durable ads*
Afforestation and Protection of Environment	48	35
Citizen Conduct and Civilization	46	35
Public Health and Family Planning	35	26
Traffic Safety	23	8
Model Units	21	21
People and Army Support Campaign	19	16
Development and Modernization	12	6
Leader Thoughts (Deng Xiaoping, JiangZemin	11	4
Features of Local Economy	10	6

Table 12.3 Top issue areas and durability of political advertisements for Beijing 1998: 332 ads total

Issue Area	*Number of messages*	*Number of durable ads*
Citizen Conduct and Civilization	54	42
Afforestation and Protection of Environment	51	30
Political Events (Including NPC Elections)	42	9
Public Health and Family Planning	42	31
Crime Prevention and Legal Education	29	8
Features of Local Economy	27	25
Traffic Safety	26	23
Development and Modernization	19	17
Notice Boards and Newspaper Displays	14	14

in Tables 1, 2 and 3, district and municipal governments in Shanghai and Beijing seem to have invested many resources in campaigns designed to generate individual contributions to solve urban public good problems common in all societies: environmental protection, civilized behaviour in public areas, and public health and safety.

This agenda is most clearly seen in several series of ads. 'What Can I Do For Shanghai?' urges citizens to find new ways to keep Shanghai clean, develop green spaces, and support economic development projects (including taxation to pay for urban infrastructure). The same goals are reflected in signs promoting compliance with the 'Seven Do Nots' of model citizen behavior in Shanghai, and its 'Ten Dos' corollary in Beijing.

That the state is creating more and more appeals to promote these issue areas, and is presenting them in more durable and costly formats, also suggests that they represent valued policy goals. The data from Beijing support this conclusion, with the high number of political event messages here reflecting the fact that elections for the people's congress were conducted during the survey period. In general, these surveys show that the local state in China has clearly found ways to use those elements of the national socialist spiritual civilization campaign(s) rubric that are most beneficial for its development needs and interests. The sermon can still be heard above the roar of material civilization.

Decentralization as the mother of adaptation, innovation, and experimentation in political communication

The conventional wisdom of Western social science theory holds that marketization necessarily leads to the collapse of political systems in socialist central planned economies as Communist Party control is destroyed by competition from new values, norms and technologies. First, liberalization is said to generate incompatible disparities in the values and beliefs of masses and elites, creating an ideological legitimacy crisis.

Second, marketization is said to transform the norms of organization of both state and society, disconnecting them. Finally, marketization is said to lead to changes in the technologies of communication, making traditional propaganda methods and messages obsolete, and further disconnecting state and society.[6]

All of these explanations assume that the socialist state that built the central planned economy and one-party rule is incapable of adapting to competitive forces. And yet there is no reason a priori why the socialist state in transition cannot recruit new elites, establish ties to new forms of economic and social organization, and use technologies to promote its development goals and maintain one-party rule at the same time. In this section I argue that these theories of the withering away of the state make these dubious assumptions as they over-emphasize the centralization of political communication in socialist planned economies and posit a clear dichotomy between authoritarian and liberal political order.

The transformation of political communication in post-Communist systems is commonly exclusively attributed to changes in central Party organizations and popular values (King and Cushman 1992; Zhao and Shen 1993; Goban-Klas 1994; Downing 1996). Reform-minded top leaders are said to lead these societies down the path of reform, and in doing so undermine both the ideological justification and organizational strength of propaganda organs. Here, the Communist Party withers away as its vocal organs find that they simply have nothing relevant to say. Meanwhile, populations are said to discover or re-discover values incompatible with those that were successful under the old order.

Such theories of communication in transition societies discount the causal relevance of local actors and overdraw the distinction between state and social organizations in socialist systems. Changes in political communication in the former central-planned economies are not simply the product of new directives from central authorities but rather represent the transformation of the local 'information environment', including all local political and economic actors (Sanders 1992: 158). As such, communication may be subject to the same forces of decentralization that are transforming the array of Chinese political, economic and social institutions.

Extensive research has demonstrated that local governments, entrepreneurs and firms are not merely passive actors in the transition process, but are instead often those who give impetus to central-level reforms: in fiscal organs (Oi 1992; Wong et al. 1996) privatization experiments (Lewis 1996), local economic development zones (Lewis 1997), collective farming (Kelliher 1992), bureaucratic hierarchies (Zweig 1992), cadre retirement systems (Manion 1993), nomenklatura systems (Burns 1994), local election committees (O'Brien and Li 2000), dispute resolution systems (Li and O'Brien 1996), industrial enterprise organs (Naughton 1992; Walder 1995) and agencies that regulate foreign investment (Su [Shaozhi] 1994).

Such transformations not only decentralize political authority. They also foster economic growth by imparting credibility to investment in a political system with few formal-legal means to resolve disputes over property. In such a system, there is competition between centre and locality, and between localities. As with federalist political systems in which fiscal relations between levels of government create similar competition (as in the United States and the United Kingdom, but not in such nominally federalist systems as Germany, Brazil or India), leaders at the local government level in particular know that if they do not create favourable environments for business, investors will simply move to other localities. (Montinola, Qian and Weingast 1995; Lewis 1997).

Local Party and government actors thus have a strong incentive to use the spiritual civilization campaign to promote issues that are important for their goals. And, as seen in the surveys of political advertising in Shanghai and Beijing, they are similarly forced to adapt and experiment with new propaganda messages and technologies.

First, they are adapting to competition from other localities by imitating and adopting political communication strategies used by neighboring localities. The 1997 survey of Shanghai's urban districts shows that Jing'An and Huangpu presented many political messages, many issue areas and a wide range of formats on their commercial streets. In other districts, outdoor political advertising seemed to be less frequently used, and almost non-existent. By 1998, however, Xuhui, Luwan and Changning had also turned their commercial streets into political mediascapes. The transformation was particularly clear for Luwan District's section of Huaihai Road, one of the oldest and largest commercial streets in Shanghai. In 1998 it began to see the proliferation of the same array of messages and formats as used on Nanjing Road in Jing'An and Huangpu Districts.

Interviews with an official of the municipal propaganda committee suggest that the mechanism for this transformation was Luwan District's 1998 incorporation of land development companies. This created not only long-term leasing contracts for stores and entrepreneurs, but also accompanying long-term leaseholds for such advertising formats as billboards and sign postings. Such incorporation followed the model of development started on Nanjing Road by Huangpu and Jing'An Districts.

The local Party seems to be taking advantage of its programmes for privatizing real estate and commercial enterprises to give it more exposure in the outdoor mediascape. The fact that there are relatively few messages and formats used on residential streets – as seen in the surveys both from Beijing and Shanghai – supports this conclusion. On these streets the local state would need to negotiate with private owners and work units. This may be difficult if residents view propaganda as intrusive and visually unappealing.

Second, local Party and state organs are preaching the sermon of spiritual civilization by directly privatizing propaganda organs and 'piggy-backing' on commercial advertisements. The same interview with a Shanghai municipal propaganda committee member revealed that municipal and district level officials responded to calls to downsize both Party and state propaganda organs by forming joint ventures with domestic advertising and marketing companies. As state budgets were cut, many propaganda workers began to seek part-time jobs, eventually forming cooperatives and joint ventures with foreign and domestic entrepreneurs. This 'cadre privatization' not only provided individual-level control over the emerging influence of private advertising and marketing companies, it introduced propaganda workers to new marketing strategies and advertising technologies.

One concrete product of this union was the establishment of a 'piggy-back' rule forcing advertisers to use at least ten percent of their durable holdings for a propaganda purpose. Advertising companies have responded by producing messages and formats that hybridize commercial and political appeals. The ubiquitous 'What Can I Do For Shanghai' postings also contain the names of the advertising company that created them, and how they may be contacted. A sign that advises pedestrians not to jump over jay-walking barriers also tries to sell them Beverly brand sports clothing. A bill-board selling Three Guns Underwear is mounted in a frame that has smaller side notices asking citizens to, 'Respect Traffic Safety Laws'.

As seen in Tables 4 and 5, such 'privatized' or 'piggy-backed' political ads are common across top issue areas in Beijing and Shanghai. Such a strategy is no doubt relatively easy to enforce if advertising companies contain downsized propaganda workers as employees or if they have formed joint ventures with privatized propaganda organs.

Finally, the same competition for the resources of investors and consumer/citizens forcing the local state to adopt the strategies of its neighbors is also driving it to experiment with messages containing new appeals to individual and collective identity formation. Here, as shown in the discussion of themes above, local authorities are not only selecting those spiritual civilization construction campaigns that directly benefit local development, they are doing so through ties to distinctly local identities

Table 12.4 Top issue areas and privatization for Shanghai 1998: 244 ads total

Issue Area	*Number of ads*	*Number privatized*
Afforestation and Protection of Environment	48	8
Citizen Conduct and Civilization	46	10
Public Health and Family Planning	35	7
Traffic Safety	23	3
Model Units	21	1
People and Army Support Campaign	19	9
Development and Modernization	12	2
Leader Thoughts (Deng Xiaoping, Jiang Zemin)	11	2
Features of Local Economy	10	2

Table 12.5 Top issue areas and privatization for Beijing 1998: 322 ads total

Issue Area	*Number of ads*	*Number privatized*
Citizen Conduct and Civilization	54	8
Afforestation and Protection of Environment	51	15
Political Events (Including NPC Elections)	42	0
Public Health and Family Planning	42	4
Crime Prevention and Legal Education	29	3
Features of Local Economy	27	13
Traffic Safety	26	4
Development and Modernization	19	6
Notice Boards and Newspaper Displays	14	3

Table 12.6 Top issue areas and reference to local or national in Shanghai 1998: 244 ads total

Issue Area	*Number ads*	*Local reference*	*National reference*
Afforestation and Protection of Environment	48	18	0
Citizen Conduct and Civilization	46	24	1
Public Health and Family Planning	35	11	4
Traffic Safety	23	2	0
Model Units	21	12	0
People and Army Support Campaign	19	2	0
Development and Modernization	12	1	5
Leader Thoughts (Deng Xiaoping, Jiang Zemin)	11	0	(0)
Features of Local Economy	10	3	0

As Tables 6 and 7 show, many of the top issue areas in political advertisements in Shanghai and Beijing in 1998 contain references to district and municipal government. Some of these references are in the text of the messages, as with the 'Ten Dos of Capital Citizen Behavior' in Beijing, and others are in subtext references to the Party or government authority that created the advertisement (usually the district or municipal Committee for the Construction of Socialist Spiritual Civilization).

Some make overt appeals to local identity through the use of symbols and visual imaginaries composed of historical figures and places. Images of Shanghai often juxtapose the skyscrapers of Pudong with the proud colonial structures of the Bund and a glittering art deco Shanghai style of architecture. Beijing's Xuanwu District, home to many cultural sites and traditional arts and crafts stores, has a series of 'spiritual civilization' billboards based on images of temples, palaces and Peking Opera characters.

Other ads make more subtle appeals, especially when seeking help in protecting the local economy. Beijing's Haidian District has a series of advertisements asking people to 'hammer down' (*daji daoban*) on technology piracy and report violations of intellectual property rights to a hotline.

Table 12.7 Top issue areas and reference to local or national in Beijing 1998: 332 ads total

Issue Area	*Number ads*	*Local reference*	*National reference*
Citizen Conduct and Civilization	54	26	10
Afforestation and Protection of Environment	51	20	1
Political Events (Including NPC Elections)	42	3	3
Public Health and Family Planning	42	24	2
Crime Prevention and Legal Education	29	8	0
Features of Local Economy	27	6	3
Traffic Safety	26	8	0
Development and Modernization	19	6	2
Notice Boards and Newspaper Displays	14	10	0

These ads are likely to resonate particularly strongly in this district, home of the workers, researchers and students of Zhongguancun, China's Silicon Valley and an important source of fiscal revenue for district and municipal governments.

China's local states are experimenters. Unexplored areas of research here include the impact of outdoor political advertising in general,[7] and the counter-intuitive hybridization of political and commercial messages in particular. Is anybody watching, and are they confused by these strategies? Further research also needs to be done on the constraints on adaptation imposed by the historical repertoire of symbols and language available to the local state.

Conclusion: consumer citizens and the local state in transition

The state is still preaching the sermon of China's socialist state authority, and yet now it is promoting individualist political identification and consumerist notions of citizenship. Surveys of outdoor political advertisements in China's urban districts demonstrate the Chinese state has adapted to marketization by selling a version of spiritual civilization that serves local development goals and needs. Decentralization of political authority has forced the local state to innovate and experiment with new messages that appeal to civic identities transcending transcend nation-state and yet grounding individuals in localities. 'What Can I Do For Shanghai?' may be the sermon of the future in China.

Notes

1 The field work necessary for this research was supported by the Transnational China Project of the Baker Institute for Public Policy at Rice University. The author would also like to acknowledge many helpful comments and suggestions from two presentations on different versions of this paper – at 'Maritime China:

Culture, Commerce and Society', the Annual Symposium of the Center for Chinese Studies, University of California Berkeley, March 13–14, 1998, and at 'Advertising Culture and the Formation of Transnational and Local Identities in Asia', the Transnational China Project, Rice University, and the Centre for the Study of Globalization and Cultures, University of Hong Kong, March 5–6, 2001 – and from the following scholars: Ackbar Abbas, Stephanie Hemelryk Donald, Evan Feigenbaum, Megan Ferry, Thomas Gold, William Kirby, Ping-Hui Liao, Benjamin Lee, David C. Lynch, Richard J. Smith, Frederic Wakeman, Wen-Hsin Yeh.

2 These are just the campaigns reported in central Party and government documents and media reports from 1997 and 1998, as compiled by the U.S. Government's Foreign Broadcast Information Service (FBIS).

3 For Shanghai in 1997 and 1998: Nanjing and Beijing Roads in Huangpu District; Nanjing, Beijing, Yuyuan and Julu in Jing'An District; Huaihai and Julu in Luwan District, Huaihai in Xuhui District; and Yuyuan and Dingxi in Changning District. For Beijing in 1998: Chongwenmenwai and Zhushikou Roads in Chongwen District; Andingmennei, Andingmenwai and Chaoyangmennei in Dongcheng District; Haidian and Zhichun in Haidian District; Xinjiekounei and Fuchengmennei in Xicheng District; Zhushikou, Niujie and Xuanwumenwai in Xuanwu District.

4 Durable signs included all electric postings, billboards,and signs on metal sheets; non-durable signs included cloth banners tied to walls, railings or between trees and posts, paper posters glued or taped to walls and windows, and signs drawn in chalk on blackboards.

5 The author was the sole coder, classifying signs by issue area according to the textual vocabulary: for example, a sign that contained the word development (*fazhan*) was classified as being in the 'development and modernization' category, etc. It is important to note that the survey did not record the number of political advertisements on the streets, which would be more prone to sampling error, but the number of different messages by theme, and not the number of times each message was repeated.

6 For a thorough and useful exploration of this literature see Lynch 1999, chapters 1 and 7.

7 For a pioneering study of public service announcements see Cheng and Chan 2001.

13

PROFESSIONAL SOCCER IN CHINA

A market report

Kenneth Lim

This chapter reviews the story of the marketing of professional soccer in China. As the author was very closely involved with this process I present the narrative as a report, listing the names of many people involved, some of whom are likely still to be working in the advertising industry when this book goes to press. I also present detailed descriptions of the campaigns: the strategies, the ad-placements, the public relations and the underlying themes which we linked to football in order to popularize it.

Professional soccer in China began in 1994 with the establishment of the Marlboro League in an inaugural partnership between the Chinese Football Association (CFA), the International Management Group (IMG) and Philip Morris Inc. In seven years, professional soccer has risen from a state-sponsored event with little revenue to an industry which annually rakes in over US$300 million in revenue.

The uptake of league soccer was immediate. The Marlboro League started in April 1994 with an average attendance of a few thousand per game. By the end of the season that November, certain venues were averaging 45,000 per game. The overall number of spectators for 1994 reached 2.3 million in the stadia, and a television audience of over 100 million. The Marlboro League had started out with twelve teams covering the cities of Nanjing, Guangzhou, Beijing, Taiyuan, Qingdao, Jinan, Shenyang, Dalian, Jilin, and Chengdu. This range gave it an equivalent geographical expanse to that of the European League.

This success notwithstanding, the marketing of soccer in 1994 was primitive. Some visionary sponsors such as the Far East Group sponsored their local teams (in Liaoning), but with little or no infrastructural safeguards or support. Neither the Liaoning Club nor the Liaoning Football Association could properly market the sponsorship or the team. The Philip Morris sponsorship deal with the Division A League in China was better developed, but signed only weeks before the kick-off game. There was again little scope for strategic manoeuvre. Therefore, to make sure that the event would be adequately covered by television, print news media, and that onsite advertising would be ready, a different sort of team had to be selected.

The Team; Division A

Chinese Football Association
Vice President, Xu Fang,
Vice President, Zhang Jilong,
Marketing Executive Fan Guangmin

Event Management – Leo Burnett Integrated Communications Team
Account Director (project head) Andrew Christy
Account Executive Kenneth Lim (project key liaison person)

Philip Morris Marketing Team
General Manager, Goddard Kwong,
Marketing Manager, Seraphina Wong
Marketing Executive Louis Soo.

International Management Group
Vice President, Richard Avory
Marketing Manager, John Fung.

Above-the-line advertising – Leo Burnett Philip Morris Team
(Supporting role)
The Brand Team which comprised:
Group Account Director, Benjamin Tsang (account head),
Associate Account Directors, Kenneth Chau and Tony Ip,
Account Managers Kenny Cheung, Belinda Wong and Doris Luey,
Creative Director Jet Lam and his team of designers.

The basic objectives of the core team were five-fold:

- To ensure the success of the Marlboro League in the drive towards FIFA World Cup qualification in the year 2002.
- To develop the football industry in China.
- To 'brand build' for Marlboro in association with China's most popular sport.
- To create ownership of the Marlboro League amongst the consumers in China?
- To create excitement and a sense of ownership of the Marlboro League amongst all citizens of China – even in the remote regions with no participating teams in the Marlboro League.

The team developed simple but fundamental strategies for the first phase, in 1994. These break down into five categories; event marketing, onsite marketing, television advertisement and coverage, print media news reportage, and public relations:

Event marketing

- A new Marlboro League logo was developed.
  This logo was from then on featured in every communication and document related to the Marlboro League These ranged from press conference backdrops to printed literature, posters, television backdrops and titling, press vests, press bags, letterheads, press releases and any other premium that we devised as additional incitement to customer interest and loyalty.

On-site (pitch-side) marketing

- (8) 1 metre × 6 metre advertising boards along the pitch
- (2) 1 metre × 12 metre Banners to be placed above the VIP stand and the grandstand opposite.
- 45,000 posters were distributed to soccer fans of each team during the season. (12 × 45,000 posters)
- 200,000 red Marlboro League baseball caps were distributed at random during matches with live CCTV coverage throughout the season.

Television

Television coverage is easier to obtain if the team provides the broadcasters with easy to use material. We provided the following variety of programmes, inserts and ads:

- Marlboro League titled opening sequence of live match broadcast on CCTV and provincial stations
- Thirty-second television commercials for the Marlboro League were placed through a comprehensive and extended media buying strategy.
- Production of documentaries covering the progress of the Marlboro League throughout major provincial stations.

Print

In order to use this medium wisely, we determined to seek news and feature coverage in the print media. We hoped that by fostering a discourse of both gossip and expert opinion around stars and coaches, we could attract column space from newspapers and from glossy magazines:

- Extensive Marlboro League branded reports and newspaper columns were placed throughout the country with in-depth reports on coaches and rising star players.

Public relations

- Press lunches were offered in selected cities to foster Philip Morris, CFA and Media relations.
- Marlboro League Press Passes were given out to accredited journalists.
- Marlboro League premiums were distributed randomly to all media, including Press vests, pens, watches, Marlboro League summer and winter jackets, Marlboro League tote bags, etc.

This suite of strategies became the industry standard for all soccer events in China. All seemed simple enough in planning. In reality, they were hard to manage because of the frail infrastructure and weak management support in all local markets for the Marlboro League. The media had to be paid for their reports, and the quality of sports-news journalism was in any case amateur.

Personalizing the Marlboro League

In order to make Marlboro League the sporting event for the nation, Philip Morris and Leo Burnett was quick to identify the need to personalize the 'Brand'. That is, a strategy had to be developed to give the 'Marlboro League' a life of his own. An exercise of brand transference was undertaken. Marlboro has classically been identified with the cowboy. This character personifies the Marlboro brand equities of 'Frontier, masculinity, individualism, independence, strength, naturalness, American-ness'. In order to personalize the Division 'A' League into 'Marlboro League', a campaign had to be created to adapt the Marlboro cowboy into a figure relevant to the sport of soccer in China. Through careful adaptation, the images of Marlboro League star players were groomed to communicate the following characteristics:

- Heroism
- Masculinity
- Strength
- Fortitude
- Determination
- Chinese-ness

In order to start the campaign, Philip Morris embarked on a star-making process for Marlboro League, which rewarded outstanding players for their sporting excellence. The Marlboro League awards were created, which included the categories of 'Player of the Year', 'Striker of the Year', 'Best Coach' and 'Best Referee'. The Player of the Year for 1994 was Li Bing. He was awarded a 24-carat gold football trophy that was made with over seven and a half teals of pure gold. Through extensive media coverage and support from the public, the Marlboro League awards were adopted by the nation's soccer fans as the bone fide award for sporting excellence in the field of soccer. This enabled subsequent winners of the awards to benefit from the honours. One player who benefited most from the Marlboro League awards was Shanghai Shen Hua Team's forward Fan Zhiyi. Fan Zhiyi is now the team captain for the Crystal Palace team in England, and is one of the key national players of Team China, the National Soccer Team of China, currently competing for qualification in the FIFA World Cup 2002.

The use of multiple-award-winning Fan Zhiyi in many of Marlboro League's promotion campaigns has given him national visibility. Fan's face could be seen on bus shelter posters, event posters, brochures, banners, newspapers articles, and magazine advertising, throughout the period of 1995 to 1998. As posterboy for the Marlboro League, Fan Zhiyi was transformed into the image of the new Marlboro man, with a close-up image of his chiselled face with his eyes staring deeply out towards the audience, epitomizing the brand qualities of 'determination, strength, fortitude, masculinity, heroism'. Fan became the hero of Chinese soccer. The process behind his fame was a protracted photo shoot. Capturing the Marlboro spirit in three prominent photographs took one full week of photography during the team's training camp in Kunming China, and cost more than US$50,000. The Marlboro League campaign spread out over China. At its peak, it had a budget of over US$15,million in a year. Most of its materials carried the image of Fan Zhiyi. Fan became an instant celebrity in China, and was mobbed and followed everywhere he went. The sports equipment manufacturer, Adidas, signed an endorsement contract with Fan to the value of RMB 1 million. It was an extraordinary amount for the period but it was echoed in top salaries across the league. With a television audience of over 100 million, some top players during the five year tenure of the Marlboro League saw their fortunes rise from a monthly income of about US$800 a month, to US$10,000. Fan reportedly earns 14,000 pounds sterling for each match he plays for Crystal Palace.

Due to a new global strategy, and the introduction of a new advertising law in China which prohibits tobacco sponsorship of sports in China, Pepsi took over the title sponsorship of the Division 'A' League in China in 1999. The first advertising move by Pepsi was to immediately sign up the leading the leading players from the Pepsi League, such as Hao Hai Dong (Dalian), Sen Si (Shanghai) and Li Jin Yu (Liaoning), to appear in their television campaign. Dressed in the Pepsi blue striped soccer gear, the players are featured in a series of television commercials cleverly adapted from existing international Pepsi storyboards from the West. A series of trading cards also followed and featured top players, as well as other top players from the European soccer market, such as David Beckham from Manchester United. Concurrently with the Pepsi campaign, Nike began to sign up individual players to endorse their products. This was in line with their global strategy of promoting star athletes, and also, a more cost-efficient method of being associated with the most popular sport in China. A contract to kit a soccer team costs about US$200,000 or more a year, whereas an individual contract with a star player may cost about US$30,000. Through athlete endorsements, Nike is able to personalize its brand with identifiable local sporting heroes and promote them creatively to the youth market.

New youth market

By 1999, the consumer profiles of China had changed dramatically. Youth make up 45 per cent of China's population, numbering up to 600 million. The youth market has risen from the ashes of the nouveau riche in China from the 1980s. Using grade 1 education as the benchmark, the first batch of post-cultural revolution consumers were, in 1999, between the ages of 18–21. Technically, they were the first batch of consumers who had benefited from the opening up of China's market economy, as well as social reforms. They were the first 'branded' generation who enjoyed the benefits of 'branded' goods and lifestyle choices. This generation of consumers also benefited from popular culture and the information explosion.

There was concurrently a new influx of foreign influences; American, European, Hong Kong , Taiwanese and Singaporean television, film and music products surged into the fashion scene, fads, subcultures and lifestyle activities within the larger cities of Beijing, Shanghai and Guangzhou. In an effort to manage the growth of influence in popular culture, the Central Government was quick to control the importation of foreign films and music, and imposed strict regulatory controls on Hong Kong and Taiwanese acts who were extremely popular in China in 1995. Hong Kong and Taiwanese concerts were rationed by an annual quota of about twenty concerts a year. Beijingers would consider themselves lucky if they attended two concerts by a Hong Kong or Taiwanese performer in any given year.

These rushes of consumer excitement were somewhat stifled by the Asian crisis in 1997 and 1998, The drive for the consumer dollar became extremely competitive as the regional economy nose-dived. China was anyway experiencing a difficult period of change through a series of privatization programmes, resulting in the unemployment of millions around the country. However, one direct effect of the recession in Hong Kong was the sudden rise of localization initiatives in many joint venture and private enterprises. As such, the gateway to white-collar jobs opened up to young Chinese executives, and in turn re-fuelled consumer spending power.

The Asian economic downturn also meant a sudden drop in investment into China. Brand managers had to justify their advertising and marketing expenditure with direct sales benefits. The number of mega-brand building campaigns in China shrunk as companies like Philip Morris, Nike, Motorola had to make significant cutbacks on their adspend in the region. To maximize their adspend, advertisers found an effective way of selling their products, through the use of celebrity endorsements. Celebrity endorsements allowed the brands to get instant recognition amongst the star struck public and allowed the public to live vicariously through the advertising image. Omega is now the top selling luxury watch in China, made possible by the media blitz caused by the Cindy Crawford tour to Shanghai and Beijing, which led the government to comment on the need for moderation in such events.

The general outdoor advertising environment in China shows a high concentration of Hong Kong and Taiwanese stars endorsing 'dot com' companies, beverages, mobile communication products and systems, and fashion. There is a sprinkling of Hollywood celebrity endorsements including Cindy Crawford's endorsement of Omega, and Arnold Schwarzenegger's endorsement of a local video CD system.

Why not sports celebrity endorsements?

With the success of soccer in China, and the high profile of soccer stars in the country, it seems odd that the current advertising environment in China does not feature many soccer or sports celebrities. This oddity is emphasized by the fact that China is one of the leading promoters of sporting excellence in the world, and that the government has traditionally promoted the goodwill and the spirit of sports throughout the country (Sun, this volume).

While the nation celebrates sporting excellence, the marketing of sports in the country remains unsophisticated. Despite the success of the Marlboro League and subsequently, the Pepsi League and the Hilton Basketball League, sports marketing has not grown beyond these umbrella events. Although sponsorship of clubs has risen sharply and the sport has grown to be an industry of significant size, there is still no proper structure within which to develop the athletes as a viable marketing entity. The market has not learnt from the Marlboro League that, in spite of a large marketing campaign promoting the brand of the event, the real equities of the sport are the athletes that play the game. Clubs were quick to learn from the success of J-League and the sophistication of the Manchester United Merchandising Store. They created their own mascots and created a whole line of merchandising programmes for the legion of fans. What they had overlooked was the human target the young girls were screaming for and the young lads were emulating.

The athletes from the soccer league are the symbols of success of modern China. They participate in the sport on their own merits and are on perpetual display for the consuming world to see. Fans live vicariously through their soccer heroes, who have now become fodder for national tabloid journalism. Some soccer players have even dated or married entertainment celebrities in the frenzy of media coverage (à la Beckham/Posh Spice). So, who made what mistakes? The problem rests with flaws in the management structure of the soccer industry put together by the Chinese Football Association, namely:

- There is no proper player representation. Clubs own the players 100 per cent.
- There is no proper marketing expertise within the federations and clubs.
- There is no proper management of the business within the clubs, with no welfare and career structure for individual athletes.
- Athletes are seen to be agents of the game, not as figures of society.

With their new-found celebrity, athletes have yet to find a social role for themselves. They do not have a voice with which consumers can identify in relation to their daily lives. The public sees the athletes as party animals with little to offer beyond their status as superior neighbourhood jocks.

Team China

In 1999, International Sports and Leisure (ISL), a Swiss-based sports marketing agent for FIFA signed a six year contract with the Chinese Football Association to market all China's national level soccer teams. 'Team China' was born. 'Team China' was created to secure ISL's dominance of global soccer by marketing the largest soccer nation in the world. This is a strategic move considering the 2002 FIFA World Cup will be held in Korea and Japan, which cover the most dominant areas of soccer in Asia. Team China is also a natural move up from the Pepsi League, as the national team forms the pinnacle of soccer in every nation. The basic structure of Team China is completely different from the Pepsi League in that it does not have a fixed match structure, but rather runs a schedule of friendly games, international tournaments and training camps. Team China is also the all star team comprising the best athletes from the nation, and the Pepsi League.

The objectives of the Team China project are:

- To harness the immense nationalistic interest in the national football teams into a positive unifying force behind the teams/players.

- To develop national sports icons to personify the Team China spirit.
- To create a promotional theme to support the national teams and their participating events.
- To attract and recognize commercial entities through the implementation of a Team China themed programme.
- To distinguish TC from all other sports properties in China.

ISL recognized that the success of Team China rests on its ability to mobilize the nation to support their national teams. In order to do so, the Team China brand had to be personalized and given an identity that is readily acceptable by the public.

Brand personality:

Like an elder brother – resilient, resourceful, persevering, dignified, proud of his nation

Advertising communication theme:

As our teams come of age, our nation can finally face a challenging world knowing we are united in our determination to succeed. For us, our family and for China, we will play hard with your unconditional support.

There are many considerations that will affect the success of Team China's communication strategy. The elder brother profile proposed by the strategy has to be developed and made convincing to the public. ISL's strategy has to create a group of strong profiles amongst the pool of athletes with sufficient clout within their social credibility and celebrity, to play the role of the elder brother to the nation of fans. The athletes have to be associated with all things good about the soccer lifestyle. The proponents of the soccer lifestyle will eventually build a credible soccer culture in China that is unique and convincing to the consumers.

Brand slogan:

My Team, My China, Our future

With this new brand personality and slogan on hand, ISL planned a series of campaigns that would communicate this new marketing platform to China. But as luck will have it, a series of events accelerated the process and added a new dimension to the Team China platform.

Women's soccer in China

Immediately after the dust had settled from the ISL – CFA contract signing ceremony, the Team China Women's Team qualified for the 1998 FIFA

Women's World Cup in Los Angeles. The qualification success shifted the focus of the nation to the sporting excellence of the women's soccer team. This was further compounded by FIFA President Dr Sepp Blatter's commitment to the 'Feminine' future of Soccer, which he made during his speech at the Symposium for Women's Soccer organized by FIFA during the 1998 FIFA Women's World Cup games in Los Angeles. Before Team China's Women's Squad left for the USA, ISL had organized a series of photo-sessions within their training camp in XiShan over three nights. The purpose of the shoot was variously to:

- Market the feminine nature of the athletes.
- Portray the ownership of the sport by the women athletes.
- Portray the marketability of the athletes to potential sponsors.
- Create a more media friendly image of the athletes.
- Modernize the image of the players for foreign markets.

Responses to the photo campaign were mixed. The public was not quite used to seeing the Chinese Women's Team in make-up nor arranged in relaxed poses around the goal. It was also the first time that anyone had shown a strong belief in the marketability of women's soccer in China. The photo shoot was a catalyst to the strong working relationship between ISL and the women athletes, but the public would take longer to be convinced.

When the Team China Women's Squad came back with the silver medals, however, having just lost at penalty shootout to the USA team, the goodwill and spirit of women soccer was globally celebrated by the Chinese community. Sun Wen and Gao Hong have become international celebrities of women's soccer, garnering recognition and accolades from around the world. Sun Wen was awarded the FIFA Player of the Century (Internet) award. With the celebration of Team China Women's Squad's national sporting excellence, came a realization that the soccer market for China had expanded to incorporate the women, children and young family sector. An influx of corporate sponsorship for women's soccer eventuated immediately after their return home. Team China had found a new group of ambassadors for the programme. In particular, the immediate celebrity status of many of the leading players; Sun Wen, Wen Lirong, Gao Hong and Liu Ailing; seemed to be a natural attraction for brands, but endorsement contracts have been minimal. Only time will tell whether the success of WUSA 2001 and the coming FIFA Women's World Cup 2003 in China will have lasting effects on women consumers and 'feminine' soccer.

Team China and UNICEF

In order to claim ownership of the sport, Team China had to develop the social profile of the women athletes. The maternal or sisterly role of the ambassadors needed to be identified and quickly created to strengthen their association with the community. An opportunity came up through a chance meeting with the Communications Officer of UNICEF, Mr Charles Rycroft, and then UNICEF volunteer Lai Wai Foon, who had expressed their desire in identifying a few public figures to develop and promote the UNICEF cause in China. The partnership of UNICEF and Team China was conceived at once. The most immediate project that UNICEF had for Team China was the 'Back to School' programme where rural girls were encouraged to return to school so as to improve their life skills. China's rural regions are notorious for their gender bias against girls, often reserving the basic rights of a child to their male offspring. Girls are often kept at home to tend to their farms and housework, and miss out on formal education.

Team China's goalkeeper, Gao Hong, herself coming from a farming family in Yangzhou, volunteered for a field trip in the region of Shaanxi to raise awareness for the plight of girls. In her two day field trip, Gao Hong visited three different villages in the region and discussed with the UNICEF education committee on strategies to solve the immediate problems of undernourished and undereducated girls in the region. Gao Hong's visit had generated sufficient media interest for UNICEF to award her the 'Special Envoy for Children' title. Leading on from Gao Hong's visit, a series of activities were generated from the Team China/UNICEF association:

- UNICEF's logo was printed in all of Team China's communication materials, including the onsite advertising board.
- A series of photographs with the Team China Women's Team wearing the UNICEF T-shirts was distributed amongst the media, further promoting the UNICEF message.
- FIFA's President, Dr Sepp Blatter made a 30 second TVC for Team China and UNICEF.
- UNICEF air their TVCs during Team China matches on television for free.

The Team China Women's Team had found a voice and a cause. Through UNICEF, the women athletes were able to create a role beyond the confines of the soccer. Their success in promoting the spirit and goodwill of the sport was testimony to their popularity even after failing to qualify for the top four in the Sydney Olympic Games 2000. Women's soccer has come to represent 'tenacity, dignity, strength, new feminism, family' and the athletes have been successful in attracting public interest in their personal development as social beings as well as in their professional careers.

The success of women athletes in China, especially after the Sydney Olympcis 2000, is now the subject of celebration amongst the people of China. Despite their failure to gain a medal, the President of the Ministry of Sports in China Mr Yuan Wei Min declared that 'the spirit of women's soccer must live on' and declared that the Chinese nation must celebrate the goodwill and spirit of women's soccer. For 2001, a series of 30 second TVCs, featuring the top women athletes of Team China and promoting equal opportunity for girls, will be released as part of the UNICEF campaign for the Rights of Girls in China.

Team China Men's Squad

Following the success of the Team China Women's Squad, ISL sought to do the same for the Men's Squad. The management of the Team China Men's Squad was more rigid than the women's. The early success of men's soccer implied that the CFA, the club teams and the player themselves were trapped by the expectations and demands of the sport. Although the operating procedures have improved significantly within the Chinese Football Association, the rapid growth of the sport has meant that the CFA has had difficulty keeping pace with it. There has been significant media coverage for the Team China Senior Men's squad because of the 2002 FIFA World Cup qualification matches. The hype over the chance that China may qualify for the World Cup was reinforced by their second place in the 2000 Asian Cup competition in Lebanon.

Coca Cola, in an effort to regain its sliding market share in China, and to capitalize on the forthcoming World Cup competition in Japan and Korea, jumped onto the bandwagon by sponsoring the Team China programme. Coca Cola's new strategy will pose a major threat to Pepsi Cola's stronghold on the soccer platform in China, as the Team China programme is effectively made up of the cream of the Pepsi League players. A strategy Coke may adopt to further reinforce their ownership of the sport is to utilize the player images in an extensive merchandising programme to promote their Team China sponsorship. Such maneouvres may cost Pepsi dearly, as Coke will thereby lay claim to the greatest assets of the Pepsi League as their own. 2001 and 2002 will see an intense cola war on the soccer platform in China. Whatever the outcome for Coke and Pepsi, the struggle will benefit the entire soccer industry in China.

Where do we go from here?

The major industry giants such as IMG, ISL, Octagon and even foreign clubs such as Manchester United (through their extensive merchandising programmes) are working hard at staking their claim to China, the largest sporting nation in the world. With such a short history of commercial sport, China still has a long way to go to reach the professional standards of other nations. Advertisers believe however that the rising standard of living amongst Chinese consumers, together with the maturing sports and consumer culture in China will speed its development.

FIFA is quick to recognize the significance of Asia in the development of the sport into a global pastime. Dr Sepp Blatter is committed to opening up new opportunities for the sport, lobbying for World Cup events to be held in Asia. All this helps the sport, but, whilst there are significant inroads being made to formalize the industry in China, athletes have yet to enjoy the full benefits of a professional soccer career. Their roles have to be redefined, and the CFA has to seek ways to provide protection and career opportunities for the athletes on and off the pitch.

The work that Pepsi, Coke, Marlboro, Legend and UNICEF have done just scratches the surface of a gold mine. Innovative marketing and creative development of soccer-based consumer culture has the potential to set new standards in global sports marketing in the future. All it takes is a brand with a vision.

SECTION 4

MEDIA, NEW MEDIA, AND CRISIS

14

SATELLITE AND CABLE PLATFORMS: DEVELOPMENT AND CONTENT[1]

Mark Harrison

Introduction

Television in China has undergone an extraordinary transformation since the early 1980s. It has been central in the realization of China's experiment in authoritarian market-driven modernization, both in policy terms and in the 'making visible' of often precarious efforts to balance breakneck economic development with the social conservatism and political dictatorship of the Chinese Communist Party (CCP). The most commercialized sector of the television industry, cable and satellite services has been the engine of China's modern media system. These technologies have been at the forefront of the commercial style of television that has created a mainland Chinese mode of consumerism and linked Chinese popular culture to Hong Kong, Taiwan, the Chinese diaspora and worldwide.

Cable and satellite television technologies powerfully represent the aspirations of the Chinese government for modernization on China's own terms. Media technology infrastructure is the clearest realization of the century-long Chinese national project of, 'Chinese learning for fundamental principles, Western learning for practical applications' (*zhongxue weiti, xixue weiyong*), of modern (read 'western') technology at the service of the Chinese language and culture (Laitinen 1990: 36). Equally, in common with any technology that facilitates the circulation of ideas, cable and satellite represent a profound challenge to the economy of power in China. The CCP sees the promise of sophisticated media technologies for national development. It also believes in the need to manage those technologies in its own interests, in accordance with the ideological sine qua non of the Party that its interests are coterminous to the interests of the Chinese nation. Therefore, there has been a consistent promotion of the importance of media technology for national development. Nonetheless, cable and satellite have been subject to policies that have often been chaotic and repressive, and manipulated by power struggles within the CCP and the government.

History: cable

Cable television in China has its origins in the 1970s. Along with housing, education and healthcare, cabled signal transmission systems were established initially to provide wired loudspeaker networks. Later, the same principle was applied to television signal distribution for members of collective factories and farms. These master access television (MATV) systems were simple cable relays for distributing free-to-air signal transmissions. MATV is different from CATV[2] (see below and also Shoesmith on ICTs, this volume) as MATV is a micro term referring to distribution through apartment buildings. They were received by single large rooftop antennae, thus avoiding clusters of antennae in high-density collective housing, and enabling good reception for all resident families (Schoenfeld 1994: 24). The first such system was set up in 1974 in the Beijing Grand Hotel (Zhu Zhu 2000). In this early phase of development master access television cable networks functioned only as an extension of the centralized free-to-air system, distributing Beijing (later China Central) Television and provincial broadcasts as they became available through the late 1970s.

As with all forms of communications technologies in China in this period, the development of cable television was severely impeded by the disastrous events of the early decades of the People's Republic of China. The Sino-Soviet split in 1959, the catastrophes of the Great Leap Forward and then the Cultural Revolution meant that by the mid-seventies China's economic conditions had scarcely developed from the level that prevailed prior to 'Liberation' in 1949 (Spence 1990: 639). Television broadcasts ceased completely in the early years of the Cultural Revolution and when limited services resumed were restricted to entirely doctrinaire broadcasts such as readings of quotations of Mao Zedong, model operas and occasional propagandistic war movies from other Communist countries (Albania and North Korea) (Hong 1998: 50). In 1975, only 1.9% of the population had access to television, and a fraction of that to cable (Hong 1998: 89). Nevertheless, the early master access cable systems provided a conceptual basis for the tremendous cabling undertakings that came in the following two decades. As the obvious solution to television reception in high-density housing, MATV gave a powerful policy impetus to the promotion of this type of television infrastructure.

The death of Mao Zedong in 1976 allowed for the ascendance of the right wing of the Chinese Communist Party, led by Deng Xiaoping. The CCP pragmatists who now controlled the government had a sharply a different philosophy of China's national development. Instead of utopian attempts to achieve a uniquely Chinese socialist form of development through harnessing the labour of China's 'masses', they wanted to achieve China's modernization in the more familiar terms of material wealth. This policy shift was pursued firstly through decentralization by permitting local and regional management and investment in industry, agriculture and infrastructure, and secondly through the selective importation of western technology under the 'Open Door' policy (Ladany 1988: 377).

Following de-collectivization, the government directed its reform measures at creating a modern economy that would build and satisfy the consumerist aspirations of the Chinese people, under the euphemism of 'socialism with Chinese characteristics'. For the television industry, those policies were formulated in 1983 at the 11th National Broadcasting Conference (Yu [Huang] 1998). The reforms of 1983 initiated a wide-ranging programme to create a modern national broadcasting infrastructure. Television was restructured into four geographical levels of administration with China Central Television (CCTV) (Yan [Liqun] 2000: 503), as the national broadcaster. Provinces, cities and counties had their own, subordinate broadcasting administration structures. Each of these other three levels was allowed relative autonomy to establish new broadcasting networks, and significantly, freedom to raise the necessary capital independently of the central government (Yan [Liqun] 2000: 504).

Decentralization allowed capital held by provincial and sub-provincial level organizations – party branches, municipal governments and state industries – to be directed at television infrastructure development. The predictable result was fantastic growth of the television system, particularly after Deng Xiaoping's 'Tour of the South' in 1992. While the state still owned all television in China in theory, in practice broadcasters became hybrids of state organizations and private businesses. Some broadcasters remained state-owned and -funded organizations, some broadcasters spun off new profit-making networks and some started from scratch as profit-making enterprises, although they too were nominally state-owned organizations.

For cable, the initial impetus from the 1983 reform period came from a State Council mandate to install MATV cable systems into all new apartment buildings, ostensibly to avoid antennae clusters. (Schoenfeld 1994: 24). However, the restructured regulatory framework greatly facilitated developing the MATV system into an integrated cable system. The basic cabling infrastructure is already in place, or being installed under the State Council mandate, and restrictions lifted on investment for profit in television. Many kinds of local and provincial organizations exercised the freedom they had been granted to invest in the link up of the MATV systems and construct true urban cable networks. Cable's cost-effectiveness and in-built subscriber revenue base made it especially viable for commercial operation. Although in this early period of establishment the cable system remained relatively small scale, with reception networks averaging only 400 subscribers (Schoenfeld 1994: 25), it became the basic technology of commercial television. Used by the majority of new stations as the major form of signal distribution, cable was the engine of the expansion of the television system. The Ministry of Radio, Film and Television (now SARFT) gives Shashi in Hubei province in 1985 as the location of the first cable television network in China (Qin [Lian] 2000: 1). The first cable network with over ten thousand household subscribers was at the Beijing Yanshan Petrochemical Corporation (Zhu Zhu 2000). Some existing free-to-air broadcasters spun off cable stations as their foray into commercial operations, and by 1990 there were 13 million household cable subscribers (Qin [Lian] 2000: 1). In 1997, China had over 2000 cable networks covering 60 million homes (China Television Broadcasting Yearbook 1998: 54). Estimates for 2000 put that figure at approximately 90 million homes, out of a total of 348 million households, making China the largest cable television market in the world. Annual growth rates for cable subscription of approximately 10 per cent give projections of approximately 150 million cable subscribers in 2005 and 250 million in 2010 (MFC Insight 2000). Cable's expansion in China was also made possible by its inexpensive subscription fees, among the lowest in the world at US$0.75-1.5 per month, with installation costs of US$20–30 per household, making cable an inexpensive entertainment choice for average Chinese, particularly those in urban centres (Yu Xu 1995: 56).

Regulation of cable television has undergone a number of changes under the influence of inter-governmental politics. Until the late 1990s, cable, like all forms of television, fell under the jurisdiction of the Ministry of Radio, Film and Television (MRFT). At that time the Ministry of Posts and Telecommunications regulated telephony. In the restructuring of media telecommunications in 1998, the MPT and a number of other ministries were amalgamated into the Ministry of Information Industries (MII) and MRFT was downgraded to the State Administration of Radio, Film and Television (SARFT) (China Online 2000a). However, in a typical expression of the internecine fighting within the government, the new regulatory institutions have overlapping areas of control. In theory, MII manages planning, administration and technical standards of broadcasting and telecommunications, which covers television, while SARFT regulates content, CCTV and the development of the cable system (China Online 2000b). SARFT regulations of cable content are an extension of the general television regulations, and are heavily focussed on the nation-building preoccupation of the CCP. They include prohibitions on endangering national unity, sovereignty and honour, endangering national peace, prosperity and interests, as well as disobeying national laws (China Television Broadcasting Yearbook 1998: 150).

The lack of clarity of administrative jurisdiction between SARFT and MII has generated confusion and competition for resources among the regulators. As a result, both MII and SARFT have competed over media infrastructure development. China Telecom, the state telephone provider within

MII has attempted to construct its own cable networks, while SARFT has planned to develop cable telephony services (China Online 2000b). It may be argued that the lack of administrative clarity has stimulated rather than hindered the development of cable and other media and telecommunications infrastructure. The on-going power struggle between MII and SARFT has encouraged them both to exploit regulatory grey areas, and to develop services in ways that deliberately intrude on each other's jurisdiction. SARFT's most ambitious undertaking has been to build fibre-optic cable connections between the more than 2000 cable networks over China (He [Sheng] 1999). SARFT has flagged the possibility of creating a national cable network that can compete with the various national telecommunications providers, and CCTV (He [Sheng] 1999).

History: satellite

Satellite television has had a more problematic history during China's reform period. Like cable, impetus for its development came as part of the 1983 reforms. In that year, as part of the government's overall project of providing television services to the entire nation, China Telecommunications Broadcast Satellite Corporation (ChinaSat) was formed under the then Ministry of Radio, Film and Television. In 1993, interdepartmental rivalry saw ChinaSat switch allegiances to the (then) Ministry of Posts and Telecommunications (ChinaSat 2000). Satellite television technology is a potent expression of the post-Mao nation-building and modernization ideology of the government and the CCP. Its capacity to bring television signals to the most remote and most impoverished regions, and its use of extremely costly and sophisticated military-derived technologies of rocketry, telecommunications and computing make satellite an internationally visible demonstration of China's emergence as a world power. The CCP government's preoccupation with promoting this particular view of China's nationhood and also maintaining its position as the Chinese nation's only legitimate representative, gave it a strong ideological motivation to invest heavily in satellite technology in the 1980s. ChinaSat began in 1985 by leasing transponders on IntelSat, and purchased the aging Spacenet 1 in 1992. In 1988 China used its own rockets to launch two American-built *Dongfang hong* (The East is Red) satellites, so that by the early 1990s, China had begun to acquire significant satellite telecommunications capability (ChinaSat 2000).

The finance available for developing and implementing satellite technologies encouraged other Chinese ventures. In 1994, SinoSat was formed by China Aerospace; the Defence, Science and Technology Commission; the People's Bank of China and the Government of Shanghai. The venture challenged ChinaSat's domination of the Chinese satellite communications market. SinoSat has used European satellite technology rather than

American hardware and is heavily backed by German industrial interests, notably Daimler Benz and Dornier. It transmits the Xinhua News Agency's Global Satellite Data Broadcasting System, Shanghai TV, and a rural television service to remote areas (SinoSat 2000).

Hong Kong-based telecommunications enterprises were also active in this period, beginning with AsiaSat, a consortium of Chinese, Hong Kong and European telecommunications companies, including the China International Trust and Investment Corporation, Hutchison Whampoa, and Britain's Cable and Wireless (AsiaSat 2000). AsiaSat 1, a second-hand satellite launched by the group in 1990, was the first Chinese commercial satellite launch (AsiaSat 2000).

In the late 1980s, the availability of the equipment needed to receive satellite television signals was largely unrestricted by the Chinese government, although it remained too expensive and complex for most individual Chinese to obtain and use. From the beginning of satellite television in China the primary reception method has been Satellite Master Access Television (SMATV). This works along the same principles as terrestrial MATV, with signals received by a large dish, typically up to 5m in diameter, and distributed into homes through a cable network mixed with channels of local, provincial and national programming. The original providers of this system were CCTV, in accordance with their brief of being a truly national broadcaster, and some of the larger provincial networks. Therefore, for most home viewers, the satellite television system was and continues to be integrated into the cable system. In the 1990s, SMATV transmission has proved popular with large provincial free-to-air broadcasters such as Heilongjiang Television and Jiangsu television for whom uplinking to satellites hugely expands their audience base across China and overseas, and generates more advertising revenue (Jiangsu Cable Television 2000a). Heilongjiang Television began a satellite service at the end of 1997 on AsiaSat 1, and claims access to fifty countries in Asia and the Pacific (Heilongjiang Television 2000).

The alternative technology of satellite broadcasting, Direct to Home (DTH) has taken Chinese television to the steps of the Open Door, and proves a more challenging field of broadcasting for both regulators and potential participants. The simpler reception equipment, including a much smaller dish, down to as small as 30 cm, means that DTH satellite television enabled new players to bypass China's technically and organizationally tangled cable infrastructure and access the home viewer directly. Its commercial possibilities attracted the attention of both international media organizations and China's nascent space industry. AsiaSat 1 was originally conceived of as a DTH satellite provider, with its primary contractor originally being Star TV, which started as a Hong Kong-based, mainly English-language service covering China, South East and South Asia (Yu Xu 1995: 50).

The government has encouraged the development of national satellite services through SMATV and DTH systems. In the 1990s, ChinaSat, SinoSat, AsiaSat and its Hong Kong-based competitor ApStar all launched new communications satellites covering China, so that by 1998 there were an estimated 170 transponders available to Chinese media organizations. In 1996 there were ten provincial television stations providing their programming over satellites, but by the end of 2000 there were thirty-one, with provincial-level television broadcasters from Sichuan, Guizhou and Guangdong each able to access over 400m people, while CCTV reaches as many as 1bn people through satellites. Sixty-one per cent of this viewership was receiving the signals though SMATV systems, with 39 per cent using DTH (People's Daily 2000).

Despite this growth, the government vision for satellite television as a nation-building medium conflicts with its technical and commercial possibilities. The efficiency with which satellite broadcasting can cover such large areas of territory and which makes it the ultimate mass medium is inconsistent with an ideology requiring that coverage follow the territorial boundaries of nations. The government believes in the positive political and social effects on national unity of CCTV and regional broadcasters having satellite access to the whole nation in Mandarin (*putonghua*). At the same time, the Government is hostile to the provision of satellite television in China by foreign companies.

The best known disagreement between the Chinese government and a global media player occurred in the early 1990s over Star TV. Although there were approximately 100,000 individual satellite dishes in China at the time, Star TV's attempt to create a pan-Asia television service was a commercial failure. Its take-over by News Corporation in 1993 began an aggressive and high-profile global involvement in the Chinese television market. Following the News Corp acquisition, its CEO Rupert Murdoch made a well-publicized statement of his belief in the anti-totalitarian potential of global media, shortly after which the State Council issued a circular banning unauthorized satellite reception under threat of fines and jail terms (Karp 1994: 69). Under the restrictions, reception of foreign satellite services was permitted only in hotels rated at three stars and above, residences approved for foreigners and certain approved organizations. To enforce this regulation, the government banned the private ownership of dishes and required that foreign television signals available through SMATV cable networks be encrypted with decoders incorporated into cable set-top boxes, which were supplied under the same limitations as the DTH services (Karp 1994: 69). The foreign satellite ban was followed by a broader movement against westernization, or 'bourgeois liberalization', a periodic occurrence in China in accordance with the government's often clumsy management of the social effects of creating a market economy (Xi [Mi] 1994).

Measures against foreign satellite services have continued periodically though the 1990s. In 1999 the Government launched a major campaign against illegal foreign television reception, including the seizure of satellite receiving dishes and decoder-equipped set-top boxes for viewing restricted programme signals relayed over cable networks, the majority of which equipment is smuggled from Taiwan. The government also started a telephone hotline and encouraged citizens to report individuals and organizations receiving illegal broadcasts (Beijing Scene 1999). These periodic crackdowns do little to control the availability of the equipment required to receive the restricted programming, especially along the eastern seaboard.

Operation

The technical infrastructure of cable and satellite television in China means that a typical cable service provides a selection of a dozen or more cable, free-to-air and satellite feeds from local and provincial stations, CCTV and occasionally international services. Therefore the problems of regulation and management of the system become extremely convoluted. With international satellite as well as free-to-air feeds available through many larger cable providers, services are theoretically under the jurisdiction of the full range of television regulations.

One such small operator (DDTV) is in the city of Dandong in Liaoning province close to the border with North Korea. Starting first as a free-to-air television station in 1960 and then as a cable station in 1992, the two combined into a single television provider in 1994. The free-to-air service covers 1.4 million people in the Dandong City area, while the cable service has 80,000 household subscribers (Dandong Television and Dandong Cable Television 2000a). The two delivery systems provide complementary services, with one free-to-air channel broadcasting news and current affairs as well as government announcements, and the cable channels broadcasting lifestyle and drama series respectively. Even at the county level, DDTV is producing a local news bulletin, a current affairs programme called 'Investigative Journalist', as well as its own sports and arts programmes which are cross-broadcast on the free-to-air and cable services.

From the coverage figures offered by DDTV, an estimated one-third to one-half of viewers in Dandong City would have a cable service. Those without receive a limited number of free-to-air channels: DDTV1, the two Liaoning Province free-to-air channels and some relayed free-to-air CCTV broadcasts. Those with cable subscriptions receive a total of eighteen channels. Three are from DDTV as well as seven of the eight CCTV channels, plus four provincial channels – two each from Liaoning Cable TV and Liaoning TV – as well as various feeds from other provincial broadcasters, including Guangdong Provincial Television (Dandong Television and

Dandong Cable Television 2000b). The services offered illustrate the combination of satellite, free-to-air and cable technologies utilized in what is essentially a very sophisticated MATV system. The case also illustrates a social hierarchy of availability between those with and without a cable service. Households with cable have access to more television signals, particularly from outside of their home province.

Suzhou is a picturesque and historic city west of Shanghai in Jiangsu Province. Suzhou Cable Television is owned and run by the Suzhou Broadcast and Television Bureau of the Suzhou city government, which also runs the Suzhou People's Radio Station and the city's free-to-air television station. Suzhou Cable TV provides thirty nine channels. These comprise eight domestic CCTV channels, Jiangsu Province free-to-air and cable, Shanghai TV and its commercial start-up competitor Shanghai Oriental, plus a number of other major provincial feeds, and fifteen foreign services provided in an encrypted format, including CNN, HBO Asia, Deutschewelle, French TV-5 Asia, NHK, the Korean Broadcasting Service and Phoenix Television from Hong Kong. Suzhou CTV even produces a nightly English language news programme read by two charismatic young English graduates from Suzhou University, Jin Lei and Zhao Xia (Suzhou Cable Television News 2001).

At the provincial level is Jiangsu Cable Television, which, while not releasing total viewer figures, claims peaks of 42 per cent of available sets in Jiangsu province for its most popular programme *Super Weekend* (*Feichang Zhoumo*) (Jiangsu Cable Television 2000b). The company runs two channels with the familiar mix of serial dramas, news (including government announcements) and sport, and is part of a media company that includes a monthly current affairs magazine *The East* (*Dongfang*), a daily newspaper, and an internet site (Jiangsu Cable Television 2000c). Jiangsu Cable Television also produces its own programming, notably a television spin-off of its print magazine. It sells advertising on its television networks for up to 13,000 yuan for a thirty-second spot during its peak viewing periods (Jiangsu Cable Television 2000d).

Another significant provider is Phoenix Television, a Hong Kong-based television company part-owned by New Corporation. After the restrictions on foreign DTH satellite reception were put in place in 1993, News looked for alternative ways into the television market. Its response was to access the SMATV system through its investment in the Phoenix TV network, which started in 1996 as a joint venture with two mainland media companies, Asia Today and China Wise. Phoenix is distributed via satellite to cable networks and is available to an estimated 45 million households mostly in the relatively affluent east and south (Rothman and Barker 1999). It runs two channels: one of movies, and the other light entertainment, including Taiwanese and Japanese soap operas, talk shows, and a hugely popular Taiwanese dating game show (Kuhn 1999; Keane, this volume). Although

Phoenix incurred heavy losses in its start-up period, it soon saw large increases in advertising revenue, and was highly profitable by the end of 2000 (Phoenix Television 2000).

Content

Despite the variety of cable and satellite services available across cities and counties in China, there is a surprising uniformity to programming content. Most cable and satellite television providers supply a familiar variety of mainland Chinese, Hong Kong, Taiwanese, and Japanese serial dramas, movies, game shows, news programmes and sport. Those who generate the most income from subscriptions and advertising revenue, the broadcasters using cable and satellite television distribution, are the most audience-responsive providers. Their profiles epitomize the reconfiguration of Chinese television from an ideologically driven system operating top-down from *Zhongnanhai* (politically centralized in Beijing) into a system that creates and regenerates Chinese consumer cultures. The stylistic model for this transformation has been the populist and fashion-driven commercial media from Taiwan, Hong Kong and the Chinese diaspora, and, through them, Japan. This mode of programming encourages audience loyalty by using character-driven drama serials, populist current affairs, and a star system. Stars tend to be young and cheery, such as Yong Cheng and Bai Mei, the attractive hosts of the popular Shanghai Cable Television relationship programme *We Are Family* (*Wo xiang you ge jia*). These strategies also inscribe aspirational consumerism (Fung and Ma, this volume) through global and local brand-exposure and through the representation of desirable lifestyles.

The television system's burgeoning demand for this kind of programming has proved a rich field for commercial producers in Hong Kong and Taiwan. It has inspired ingenious solutions to the general chaos of the cable distribution system and the problem of copyright infringement. Programme exchange business models, in which programmes are bartered for advertising time which is then on-sold, have been in operation by foreign and Hong Kong media companies since the mid-1980s. More sophisticated yet have been the forays into programme production by companies such as the Hong Kong-based advertising agency United Media in partnership with McCann Erickson, which has produced hit contemporary serials for the cable market funded by multinational corporations. In the series *Love Talks* (*Zhenqing gaobai*) and *Home* (*Yuanlai yijiaren*), global consumer product manufacturers pay for extremely high levels of product placement, sometimes even with plot lines that revolve around their particular consumer products (United Media 1999). Motorola and Unilever have both taken up such opportunities to develop brand identity in China. Firmly targeted at a growing urban audience with disposable income, these highly commercialized productions are slick, contemporary, and entertaining. In this way, cable and satellite television systems are central to consumption-based configurations of power in post-Mao Chinese society. The Chinese government has been concerned to manage this language of power, and the media which carry it, in the interests of the state, and its promotion of a consumer culture has sat relatively easily with this reactionary political exercise.

Despite the government's repeated admonitions on the dangers of 'bourgeois liberalization', the practices of cable and satellite television in China have proved to be readily incorporated into the interests of the state, through discourses of nationhood. The expansion of cable and satellite television from local MATV systems into a national infrastructure is the result of direct government regulation and investment, and it is also the function of an ideology, maintained both within China and internationally, which imagines the Chinese nation as a single unified television market. The commercial decisions by broadcasters from Heilongjiang to Guangdong to relay their programming by satellites across the whole of China and into the diaspora is contingent on an ideological belief that 'China' is a viable national and transnational experience. Content produced and traded within the Chinese television market reproduces the historically-specific and evolving ideologies of what constitutes the experience of being nationally Chinese. Therefore, even the very large urban centres of Shanghai and Guangzhou do not produce a sufficient amount of local and regional programming to compete with the political and cultural hegemony that nationalist ideology exercises over the rest of China.

Future

The development of the cable and satellite systems continues apace. Unquestionably the most interesting development is the advent of Internet services in China using the cable infrastructure. For the Chinese government, the Internet holds both promise and threat. The Internet provides an opportunity to create a technologized and media-rich society that will leapfrog China into a post-industrial economy. It is a technology that circumvents China's historical industrial weakness relative to the West; its failure to produce the 'mechanical articles' which powered Western global hegemony in the 19th and 20th centuries. The Internet creates a technological foundation for China's historical strength, a cultural tradition of unparalleled richness.

The development of the Internet has been the subject of intense inter-authority rivalry between SARFT and MII. Under regulations promulgated in 1998, the Internet has been classified as a telecommunications technology, and therefore falls under the province of MII and China Telecom (China Online 2000a). This has failed to stop SARFT going ahead with ambitious plans to use the cable infrastructure it controls to create a national broadband Internet service with various joint ventures. It set up the

China Network Communications Corp. (China NetCom) as a joint venture with the Chinese Academy of Sciences, the Ministry of Railways and the Shanghai Municipal Government (He Sheng 1999). China Netcom is constructing a fibre-optic backbone across fifteen cities in which local cable operators provide the 'last mile' connection into individual households. SARFT aims to provide a range of internet-type services under common network technical standards that it has created for this purpose. Century Vision Network, a joint venture between SARFT and American-owned China Broadband Corporation, aims to establish broadband internet services using the SARFT national fibre optic cable network and city and provincial level cable infrastructure. The test sites are in Fuzhou in Fujian Province, Yunnan Province and Wuxi in Jiangsu Province. The Century Vision Network is making its services available through set-top box technology that its promoters claim will give subscribers access to broadband content, communications and e-commerce with personal computing delivered through household television sets (ISPWorld 2000). The set-top box concept presents a cheaper alternative to stand-alone computers in the home, which have low penetration levels in China, although the costs of the service, at US$15–20 per month is significantly higher than simple cable TV services (ISPWorld 2000).

These developments suggest that the status of television may change over the next several years. The extended capability of cable technology into Internet based media practice requires new Government mechanisms of self-protection and self-advertisement. With a government that stakes so much of its legitimacy on being the best representative of that nation, television, even in its most commercial forms, has become highly consonant with the interests of the CCP and the Chinese government. It will not be lightly set aside.

Notes

1 Much of the material for this chapter was gathered by the author while working on the project, 'The Globalization of the Television Industries and Markets of Asia: The Cases of India and Greater China', funded by an Australian Research Council Small Grant, awarded to Professor John Sinclair at Victoria University of Technology.

2 CATV also known as CCTV-closed circuit television, ie the entire closed access system of cabling, programming and subscription. However, as CCTV is also the name of the major broadcaster (Chinese Central television) we use CATV to avoid confusion. Also note, ICTs are a form of closed circuit TV, distinct from both broadcasting and narrow casting.

15

NETWORKS AND INDUSTRIAL COMMUNITY TELEVISION IN CHINA

Precursors to a revolution

Brian Shoesmith and Wang Handong

Introduction

China is arguably the most networked nation in the world. When people refer to Chinese networks, however, they usually refer to *guanxi*, that complex set of relations and obligations that governs so much personal as well as official interaction in China (Yang [Mayfair Mei-hui] 1994) and which has flowed on into the new economic conditions that may be called *guanxi* capitalism. At the same time the concept of the network applies equally well to the classic system of governance based on the four formal levels of government or the 'four capabilities', the central (*zhongyang*), provincial and autonomous regions (*sheng*), prefectural cities (*shi*) and county-level cities (*xian*), where each level is charged with the responsibility of enacting the authority of the centre. Further, the term network describes equally well the formal system of mass communication introduced in the 1950s and 1960s with minimum technology and expanded during the 1970s, 1980s and 1990s to include satellite and cable television and the World Wide Web. In short, networking is one of the defining characteristics of Chinese social, political and communicative organization.

This paper explores a hitherto ignored aspect of the contemporary Chinese communication network: the closed circuit television network system established in the 1970s in the industrial work units. We discuss the origins of the system, its functions, and influence on audience formation and expectations of the role of television in post-Mao China. The preliminary general discussion of the system is illuminated by three case studies of work unit television in which we demonstrate the significance of Industrial Community Television (ICTs) to the evolving Chinese mediascape. Our argument is that ICTs developed in unexpected directions and in effect were the precursors of the cable revolution that emerged in Chinese television in the 1990s. Moreover, their success at the grass roots level was an important factor in convincing the Chinese authorities that cable was a viable option for a national television network when it was confronted by the spectre of a foreign-dominated transborder satellite broadcasting system that has threatened to erode the sovereignty of China's domestic media.

The *shenghuo qu* and the *shengchan qu*

After the founding of the People's Republic of China in 1949, many new types of factories and industrial companies were established. A factory's zone consisted of a production area (*shengchan qu*) and a living area (*shenghuo qu*). Managers and workers were allocated housing in the living area according to seniority and their families were provided with everyday services commensurate with their position. A factory in China was similar in its composition and activities to a small society. This remains the case throughout China today. A factory may own a school, department store, hospital, and even a police station. Because the Chinese employment system restricts mobility, a Chinese worker, like most of his/her neighbours, may be born, educated, married, pleasured and buried within a *shenghuo qu*, and the road from the *shenghuo qu* to *shengchan qu* becomes a metaphor for his/her life.

We propose to use the term 'community' as an analytic tool rather than the more common term 'work unit' (*danwei*). There are two reasons for this. First, a community, broadly speaking, consists of persons who have common ties in social interaction and who live within a geographic area; this establishes the ground for thinking of the *shenghuo qu* as a community. Second, and more importantly for us, the period we are discussing is a transitional phase. While the industrial communities retain many of the characteristics of the older-style work unit they are also undergoing quite fundamental changes, for example, in the manner in which information is distributed within the community and also in the relations between management and the workers. From our perspective the significance of the *shenghuo qu* and the role of the ICT within its boundaries must be acknowledged.

The history of the ICT

The Industrial Community Television (ICT) concept was introduced into China in the 1970s. ICTs subsequently became an important part of the Chinese mediascape as a bridge between the mass media and Chinese industrial workers. They were also instrumental in establishing a cable infrastructure in China that was crucial to the unfolding television culture that now saturates Chinese everyday life, both in the cities and the rural areas. Initially the ICTs were highly localized and parasitical in that they relayed rather than originated content, but as television became the prime form of domestic entertainment during the 1980s and 1990s, and gradually moved away from its ideological function as an arm of the propaganda apparatus, ICTs became more ambitious in their scope. To all intents and purposes they became mini-broadcast stations that helped create the appetite for television that now characterizes Chinese domestic life. As such, they helped foster a sense of the local and the regional that now lies at the heart of the problems confronting the administration of television in China.

The rationale for the introduction of ICTs was to extend and supplement the national television network in the 1970s, a time when the Chinese government set up microwave relay trunks to broadcast CCTV (China Central Television) nationwide. Many industrial communities, especially those in marginal urban areas, opened TV relay stations that provided an amplified TV signal for domestic consumption. By the beginning of the 1980s, following the initial social reforms, the national relay system broke down in the face of competition from the cable, or circuit TV, which the industrial communities set up to provide programming for their communities. This service was frequently little more than extended video movie programming, used to 'season' CCTV's single channel broadcasts with some form of entertainment. In 1984 the central government prompted local levels of government to establish television stations using their own funds (Huang [Yu] 1994). Many industrial communities joined this wave of activity in the belief they would either gain financial support from the authorities or gain some form of technical advantage compared to their neighbours. The communities expanded their television capacity installing complex cable systems and in some cases their own broadcast standard studios.

The slogan 'Own channel and own programme' (*ziban pindao, ziban jiemu*) represents the changing status of the ICTs within the Chinese system. From the 1980s to the present this system has matured to include satellite TV reception in its programming repertoire. ICTs now relay four satellite channels of CCTV as a minimum, plus locally produced programmes and regional programmes distributed by satellite into the homes of the Chinese worker. Most Chinese viewers were accessing at least twenty television channels by the mid-1990s (Huang and Green 2000: 282). Until October 1993, when the new rules relating to access to satellite broadcasting were introduced, they also programmed STAR TV into their repertoire.

The structure of ICTs

An ICT is operated by staff members who are employees of the industrial community, either the industry itself or members of the community. Their number may vary according to the size of the industrial complex. In most cases the ICT is either an independent department within the community or it is attached to another section of the complex such as professional education, information, propaganda or the trade union of the factory. Further, the name may vary from community to community. They may be described as 'factory zone TV station', 'electronic education labour unit' or 'video office'. In essence, each of these units, irrespective of its nomenclature, fulfils a similar function within the industrial community.

The property of the ICT, including facilities and plant, belongs to the industrial community. The manager of the community has ultimate power over the ICTs operations. Whether this model will persist as the economic reforms take hold is difficult to predict. Nevertheless it is clear that the transition from state ownership of the means of production to a modified system of worker control of these means within the Chinese industrial system will affect the economic organization and functioning of the ICTs.

ICTs often work under the direction of CCTV and/or local TV stations especially in the areas of professional training, technology provision and programme production. The State Administration of Radio, Film and Television (SARFT) and the local bureaux effectively administer ICTs through policy implementation, although the actual implementation of central policy is often subject to interpretation that favours the locality (Redl and Simons, this volume). In fact, there is an assumption on the part of many ICT operatives that grass-roots operations should be the principal determinant of control. These views reflect the growing professionalization of the television industry in China across the board. The larger ICTs, who resist takeover by the commercial cable operators in the respective cities, have professionalized their staff profile.

The function of ICTs

The shift from community-based distribution systems towards leisure consumption and video exhibition poses serious questions about the role of ICTs in the *shenghuo qu*. Their primary role as public broadcaster, providing and producing community news, talk shows, documentaries and discussion programmes must now be questioned. On the surface ICTs now appear to function as conduits for the commodification of Chinese culture. However, ICTs retain the potential to fulfil a public function: due to their relatively small size ICTs can be a real interactive medium that encourages a participatory communication process. The contradiction between the leisure/entertainment nexus on one hand, and the public/participatory on the other remains to be solved. The audience and its desires will be the key to this issue.

Education is another major factor to be considered. Many ICTs were established under the rubrics of 'electronic education labour' or 'television education studio'. Generally, ICTs collaborate with the professional training department of the factory and have close relationships with educational units outside of the community. Some ICTs have joined a network for the exchange and distribution of educational programmes. Increasingly the interaction between education and audience desires is seen as the major determinant of the ICT's future.

We now propose to provide detailed description of three actual ICTs we visited in the late 1990s. The case studies are a textile factory located in a small provincial city where management withdrew the station subsidy thereby forcing it to become 'commercial' in order to survive; a major electricity generating plan on the outskirts of Wuhan that remains wedded to the classical administrative model; and a major iron and steel unit in which the ICT was acquiring all of the trappings of an independent television station. In selecting these three examples we wish to substantiate our general characterization of the ICT and at the same time show that despite the tendencies within the Chinese system to standardize, at the grass roots level actual organizations evolve in ways that challenge the strongly held views about the centralized control of the media that prevail in much of the scholarship of the Chinese media.

Case study 1

Qingshan Power Plant is part of the Central and Southern China Electric Network and is located on the eastern-most boundary of Wuhan in Honggang *cheng* (Red Steel City). Red Steel City is an industrial area created in the 1950s as part of the 'Great Leap Forward'. Qingshan Power Plant has operated continuously since its foundation in 1953 as an integral part of Wuhan's power generation system. However, it is now clearly run down and in need of rejuvenation.

Qingshan represents an exemplary work unit in the manner in which it functions but is atypical in its spatial organization. The 2,400 families comprising the unit live 7 kilometres away from the generating plant and the shifts are bussed in at the appropriate times. The separation of the *shengchan qu* from the *shenghuo qu* affects both the manner in which the unit is organized and functions and the manner in which television is distributed within the unit. For example the separation of production from the community means that the unit has to supply social facilities in both areas. In respect to the ICT, programmes are made in the studio located in the production area and the tapes are then sent to the community area where they are circulated via CATV. The distribution point, comprising a bank of VCRs, is heavily secured.

Institutionally the ICT is under the authority of the local Director of the Chinese Communist Party's Propaganda Department, while operational responsibility is divested to the Station Manager. In discussions about the station both agreed that television had three principal functions in the work unit; namely propaganda, education and entertainment, although each suggested a different emphasis. The day before we interviewed the Director of Propaganda and Station Manger a new Plant Director had assumed control of the work unit with a brief to improve its productive capacity as well the conditions of the workers. There was more than a hint that the changes outlined by the Plant Director would flow on to the ICT with a greater emphasis being placed on propaganda which appeared to make the Propaganda Department official and the Station Manager uneasy as they had both grasped that despite the official ideological emphasis of broadcasting the popularity of the station lay in its entertainment content. The tensions between managers at this level, we would argue, replicate the tensions between various state apparatuses involved in the administration of television in the 1990s at the national level.

The three functions of television translated into two types of programming. The first type of programming is common to all ICTs and involves the relay of central, provincial and metropolitan programming to the community. To a degree, all ICTs have the autonomy to programme how they like so long as they carry CCTV Channel 1 News at 7.30 p.m. The relay function is important to the national broadcaster because the ICT has in practice become the principal means of distribution of CCTV in China, especially in the remoter regions. Virtually all ICTs follow a similar format with the only difference being the actual provincial or metropolitan stations relayed. Qingshan ICT provided fourteen channels to its viewers from the sources shown in the table below.

The 'imported' channels duplicate schedules but at the same time provide a range of drama, news and propaganda to the community viewers. By far the most interesting channels is Channel 6 the community channel produced *in situ* to meet the perceived needs of the unit directorate in terms of propaganda and the community audience in terms of information and entertainment.

Channel 6 programmes consist of two broad categories: propaganda and entertainment. The propaganda programmes may be divided into other important categories; news programmes, special topic programmes and educational programmes. Entertainment comprises drama and request programmes.

Table 15.1 Television channels

Station	*Source*	*Channels*
CCTV	National	4
Hubei Television	Provincial	2
Wuhan City TV	Metropolitan	2
Huanxi TV	Metropolitan	1
Xiaogan TV	Metropolitan	1
Shandong TV	Provincial	1
Zhejiang TV	Provincial	1
Yunnan/Guizhan TV	Provincial	1
Channel 6	Local Community	1

The news programmes, which last ten minutes a day, tend to consist of news about:

- unit workers and their output
- production quotas
- lecture by the Director of Propaganda at special times or on pressing issues
- future entertainment.

Special Topic programmes, which last fifteen to twenty minutes a day, focus on work unit matters deemed to be significant by management and include

- 'Love Qingshan'
- the feats of industrious workers.

Educational programmes, which last thirty minutes a day, provide essential propaganda on 'how to behave' correctly in the work unit and the need to study. Titles screened under the heading of education included

- 'Fight Against Corruption'
- 'Hong Kong Today'
- 'History of China'
- 'History of the Chinese Revolution'.

Clearly each of these categories is a form of propaganda and collectively constitutes the most important function of the ICT according to management. However, we were unable to meet with the 'consumers' to judge how effective these programmes were in mediating between the desires of the unit management and the expectations of the workers. In discussing the programmes with the Director of Propaganda it was clear that he saw programmes like 'Towards Success' as significant because they helped the workers to 'love the factory and make a greater contribution'. In short the public function of an ICT was to engender a socialist spiritual civilization (*jingshen wenming*) or 'industrial socialist culture' in the work force (see Lewis, this volume). Because the ICT is part of the community it was felt that it was more effective in achieving this aim than the national broadcaster CCTV. However, no matter how hard the Director of Propaganda sought to justify allocating the bulk of the RMB 80,000 budget (US$9,650)(not including salaries) towards propaganda and directing the six staff towards prioritizing propaganda content, the management kept returning to the issue of entertainment.

An analysis of a day's scheduled programmes revealed that 70 per cent of programme time was devoted to entertainment and only 30 per cent to news and propaganda. Moreover, both the Director of Propaganda and the

Station Manager admitted that the entertainment programmes were the most popular with workers, especially the 'Request Programmes'. Essentially these are music request programmes normally found on radio translated to closed circuit television where workers request particular song clips for particular purposes such as commemorating a teacher or to 'soften community tensions'. This was mentioned several times with reference to mother/daughter-in-law relations. Frequently the lyrics of songs are modified to reflect personal feeling and at times workers write and record their own songs. In short, the request programmes replicate karaoke on a broader, more public scale. Other popular entertainment programmes that we noted included imported Peruvian soap operas.

Qingshan is a typical ICT. It exists and operates through direct subsidy from the directorate of the work unit. In return for this subsidy the ICT is expected to articulate the desires of management in respect to production, behaviour and human resources. The ICT is viewed almost exclusively as an instrument of propaganda by management whereas consumers (the workers in Qingshan) choose to see the broadcaster in terms of entertainment. The dichotomy between propaganda and entertainment causes tension between the broadcasters and management and between management and the workers. Thus even the request programmes are part of the management function insofar as they are deliberately used to resolve social tensions. Finally, the Qingshan ICT is little more than a relay station for other broadcasters. Despite their best efforts the minimal staff attached to the ICT cannot produce sufficient product to satisfy local demand and as such the ICT remains an essentially parasitical broadcast form.

Case study 2

Puqi is a small city in Hubei Province located 150 kilometres south-west of Wuhan. The city is well served by the road and rail network, which has seen the city develop a considerable industrial base. Part of this base is the China Puqi General Textile Mill situated approximately 20 kilometres west of the city in a picturesque wooded hilly area. The Mill was established by the People's Liberation Army in 1969 and transferred to Hubei provincial administration in 1975. It claims to be one of the élite group of 500 largest industrial enterprises in China and exports US$10 million worth of goods annually. In short the Puqi General Textile Mill is a substantial organization with over 30,000 residents, 16,000 of whom work in the Mill. The ICT serving this community was established in 1984, reaching 8 000 homes. In 1994 its subsidy was withdrawn by the Mill management with central government authority. This event significantly altered the functions, operations, status and importance of the ICT in the Puqi community.

In order to stay operational the ICT had to charge its viewers for service. In the case of Puqi this was 4 RMB per month. These charges fundamentally alter the relationship of the ICT to its audience. The Director of Propaganda continued to emphasize the propaganda function of the station especially in spreading 'industrial culture' but admitted that the Mill Director no longer used the station to address the workers on important matters. Nevertheless the ICT continued to report government and party policy in detail. However, a significant new item of news had crept into the agenda: the ICT also reported leisure activities available to workers as part of its news. Moreover, the local union had taken an active interest in the station's functions and in one instance had exercised considerable muscle. In 1995, in line with central policy, the Mill management began charging rents for worker accommodation and indeed encouraged workers to buy their apartments. This became a matter of wide community concern, even discontent according to the station manager, so the station covered the story and with the encouragement of the union also covered related issues. To the surprise of management the workers seized the opportunity to articulate their concerns forcing management to modify its policy on housing. In the grand scheme of things this may seem a very minor issue but within the context of the work unit this was perceived to be an event of enormous significance – if only for the fact that management actually appeared to have listened to workers' demands.

Operationally the station manager and his thirteen staff had to concentrate on raising sufficient funds to maintain a twenty-four hour a day, seven days a week service. Their solution has been to turn the Puqi ICT channel into an intensely local news and entertainment channel and leave CCTV news to the relay broadcast. The intensity of the local production is apparent from an analysis of the weekly schedule. There is a daily fifteen-minute news programme that is devoted exclusively to local issues. A further three hours per day is devoted to local entertainment programmes. The station manager was embarrassed at the quality of the programmes but justified them because they raised revenue. The local programmes included a local talent show (*The Big Show*), special performances from the Mill and local sports. However, the most popular form of local programming are the workers' requests programmes where workers pay 10 RMB for a song and 100 RMB for their favourite movie to be screened. The community is surprisingly well endowed with telephones (over 2000 in 1996), which leads to a form of interactive TV on weekends when the station devotes up nine hours to workers' requests.

The decision of the Mill management to end the ICT's subsidy in 1994 fundamentally changed the status of the broadcaster. In effect it moved more towards being a cable station in own right rather than a closed circuit relay operation. Further, it is clear that the workers had changed their position vis-à-vis the station seeing it more as a community based organization than something that solely articulated the management line. This view is borne out by the pressure for the station to become involved in the housing issue and the manner in which they use it for service requests. The station manager claimed that up to one third of the ICTs had lost their work unit subsidy and had followed similar strategies in order to stay operational. If this is the case then we have witnessed a significant change to the Chinese mediascape at the grass roots level. At the same time we have witnessed a situation whereby the ICT movement has been seriously weakened with significant numbers of stations vulnerable to takeover by the commercial cable operators. In part it is the takeover of the ICTs that has boosted the numbers of subscribers to cable television in a number of regions in China. For example, while this research was being conducted, the Wuhan University ICT entered into negotiations with Wuhan Cable TV discussing the conditions under which Wuhan Cable would assume control of the university's ICT. The irony is that as television become more important for Chinese economic reform, fulfilling a propaganda function of a totally different order, many work units seek to divest themselves of the broadcasters in order to save money.

Case study 3

Wuhan Iron and Steel Company (WISCO) is a major industrial unit overlooking the Yangze River, and has a population of 55,000. The work unit has its own publishing house in addition to the ICT, a metallurgical university of note, a technical school, high schools and primary schools, as well as hospitals and other services. In short WISCO comes closest to the ideal of the community we referred to earlier in terms of its size while functioning as a prototype Chinese work unit in the scope of services offered.

WISCO TV was founded in 1980, emerging out of the company's technical television section. It is totally funded by the company and twenty-one staff are organized into four divisions: the news department, the special issues department, advertising, and general editing department. Like all ICTs the station comes under the aegis of the Propaganda Department of the unit although the station manager, who is also Vice-Director of Propaganda, claimed that propaganda was the third most important function of the station. Of greater importance were information and entertainment. Talking to the staff over an extended period time we gained the impression that increased professionalism of production had become the principal aim of the broadcasters rather than propaganda. In fact compared to the other ICTs we visited, we were struck by the general affluence of the station. The equipment was new, the production spaces adequate and the general conditions pleasant, suggesting the claim that the ICT was regarded as equal to a municipal broadcast station was accurate. In fact, the WISCO operation was much better equipped than the municipal station at Yueying, a small city in the southwest of Hubei. The degree of sophistication exhibited by the station in all aspects of its operations meant that it was better placed than Wuhan University when negotiating with Wuhan Cable TV.

The scale of operations and its capacity to meet audience expectations is ultimately what differentiates WISCO ICT from its counterparts. It broadcasts on two dedicated channels as well as fourteen relay channels and captures 80% of the community audience. This scale of operation also provided the management with a degree of confidence about their future that was absent elsewhere. This self-reliance seemingly allowed the management to give us the opportunity to actually meet members of the audience to discuss their perceptions of television. It is to this that we now wish to turn.

In the time-honoured Chinese way, it took several banquets to arrange a meeting with workers within the community. Originally we had wanted to knock on doors and introduce ourselves and ask questions. We were quickly disabused on the idea as being entirely impractical. It would also be greeted with intense suspicion by the very people we wished to meet. Consequently we agreed to the management of the ICT arranging the meeting with a 'representative sample of workers' in the WISCO Workers' Club, a large seven-storey building that also housed the ICT.

The dynamics of the meeting were interesting. The management team, which included the Director of Propaganda and Head of Publishing, sat at the front of the room with the research team, which included the translator. The workers sat around the perimeter of the meeting room, pretty much segregated by gender. The Station Manager introduced us and explained the purpose of the meeting. He was followed by the Director of Propaganda, who stressed the importance of the work we doing and invited participants to talk freely about their respective experiences of television. Then Wang Handong explained in more detail the project and Shoesmith spoke in English (which was translated) about how grateful the team was to have the opportunity to meet the workers from WISCO. The participants then introduced themselves (there were twenty-eight: sixteen men and twelve women) and it was immediately apparent that the 'representative sample' was composed of middle and junior management augmented by some junior cadres. After the introductions participants were invited to speak. There was an extended period of silence that did not seem to faze the Chinese participants. Finally one of the oldest men in the room cleared his throat and embarked on 'a severe criticism' of the ICT management.

The crux of criticism revolved around a recently introduced service fee of 6 RMB per month for all families within the work unit. He pointed out that if community members were to pay for television services for the first time they were entitled to a decent service. Community based programmes should be more timely and relevant and a better range of relayed programmes was called for. All of this was delivered in a quiet measured tone. Immediately he had finished other participants leapt to support him. The translator was quite shocked at what transpired, claiming it was the first time he had ever experienced such forthright criticism in a public venue. The intensity of the criticism compelled the Station Manager to reply. His argument was that it was all the fault of senior management who were progressively withdrawing the station production subsidy. Moreover, community members had indicated that they did not wish the ICT to be subsumed by Wuhan Cable TV and that for it to continue as a community broadcaster it had to raise funds in other ways. The community was too large to run music request programmes and there was insufficient support for advertising. Consequently a fee-for-service was the only equitable way to proceed. However, the station management took note of the discontent and promised to perform better in future, meeting the demands of the workers. This exchange took up virtually all of the time allocated for the discussion.

The benefit of the exchange was that it opened the ground for people to express themselves freely, as urged to, about television. The results were uncanny, almost as if there is a universal set of concerns about the perceived influence of television in society among the 'middle classes'. Mothers expressed their concerns about their children watching too much television at the expense of homework. They were also concerned about youth watching violent martial art programmes and their husbands allowing sport to dominate family viewing time. The men expressed contempt for the soap operas their wives seemed to favour and saw control of the 'remote' as a masculine right. In short, from this brief session, it seems television in the domestic setting is a gendered activity. The single point of agreement between the men and women was around violence on television and children. The Japanese cartoons were singled out for condemnation (see Donald, this volume). Similar views were expressed elsewhere in different contexts in respect to the *manga* and *animé* widely screened throughout China that were felt to be too violent. This may be an expression of the latent anti-Japanese feelings one hears expressed in China or it may be a genuine concern.

The WISCO ICT is atypical of the stations we visited as part of this research. It is larger, commanding much greater resources, better organized, more professional in its approach to broadcasting than the usual ICT and yet it remains vulnerable to takeover by the commercial cable operator. It is also open to criticism from its consumers. What was set up as a showpiece, we presume, on the part of management became a vehicle for the 'workers' to voice their discontent about the nature and content of programmes viewed. Taken in conjunction with the union activity over housing at the General Puqi Textile Mill, the concerns articulated at the research meeting are suggestive of a deeper social malaise within the work units. There is considerable material arguing that the work unit's days are numbered but there is little research showing how the workers themselves are responding to the uncertainty the economic reforms are generating. We think these examples are symptomatic. They also demonstrate how important television has become to the social fabric of the work unit.

Conclusion

Despite the expansion in commercial cable operations in major Chinese urban centres, frequently involving the unacknowledged acquisition of community stations, the ICT remains a fundamental unit of the contemporary Chinese mediascape. In significant ways ICTs have become more central to television than before because their function has developed beyond that of relay. As we have demonstrated, ICTs have national and provincial organizations to protect their interests, although a tenuous relationship exists between central policy-making and the actual implementation of such policies at the local region. Moreover, it is in the interest of the Central Propaganda Department to maintain the ICT as a counterbalance to the commercial cable stations as they can be mobilized more quickly and efficiently to the cause. Within this context ICTs have evolved. Many continue to produce their own programmes; especially community news and entertainment programmes. Others have begun to actually lease their facilities to the commercial producers in order to improve their programme offerings to the community. The larger and better-equipped units have begun to co-produce with the commercial cable operators. Irrespective of their level of imbrication in the commercialization of Chinese television all the ICTs have retained one significant feature; they are grass-root organizations. As such they have acquired a significant social function insofar as they constitute the basic level in the network.

16

THE SURFER-IN-CHIEF AND THE WOULD-BE KINGS OF CONTENT

A short study of Sina.com and Netease.com

Hu Xin[1]

The Chinese language is rich with metaphorical allusions to describe all kinds of political scenarios. However, perhaps the best allusion to describe the Internet in China is the English phase: 'an irresistible force confronts an immovable object'. In this case the immovable object is the Chinese Communist Party's media policy. In China policies are often decided by the opinion of a paramount leader. The 'Great Helmsman' Mao Zedong and the 'Architect of Reform' Deng Xiaoping both published collected volumes covering every aspect of their works. These became the theoretical foundations guiding government policy and administration during their time at paramount leaders of the Chinese Communist Party.

The Internet is no exception. President Jiang Zemin, regarded as China's Surfer-in-Chief' has expounded his opinions on the Internet on several occasions (Ramo 1998). In an interview with the American magazine *Science*, Jiang noted that the development of the Internet has given people a wealth of information. 'I'd like to point out that the added value of information is reflected by the fact that it is open to all and shared by all', he said. Then he added that he hoped all young people, Chinese and foreign, and scientists and scholars around the world would make the best use of the Internet, but remain on guard against its negative impacts *(Xinhua News Agency*, 9 June 2000). In his speech on 22 August 2000 to the 16th World Computer Congress in Beijing, China's paramount leader warned that the Internet could deliver 'an overflow of trash information' that could be 'unhealthy to the point of being downright harmful'. He called for an international treaty to prevent unhealthy information on the net.

Chinese Internet policy represents a detailed interpretation of the thoughts of China's Surfer-in-Chief. The Internet has been encouraged as an information technology and hailed as a business model for new media, but no real preferential treatment is extended. After 20 years economic reform and liberalization, media policy remains relatively unchanged in China. The *Chinese Journalist Code* (1991), which sets out the role of the print media states that:

> The Chinese media is one of the important parts in the socialist society under the leadership of the Chinese Communist Party. All journalists should propagate Marxism and Mao Zedong thought, and the policies by the Party and government, report news and distribute information, reflect and direct public opinion, in order to enhance the socialist culture both materially and spiritually, the socialist democracy and the legal system, as well as fulfil its role of an organ of the Party and the people.
>
> (Zhang Wei 1997: 126)

As many chapters in this book have demonstrated, media organizations in China are in the process of becoming commercially run enterprises. However market competition has succeeded in promoting diversity of content without offering a challenge to official ideology. In fact, the influence of the market can limit the potential for public debate and reinforce dominant ideologies. Eric Ma argues that the development of the market – with the blessing of the Chinese leadership – is constructing a hybrid system of overt conflict that embodies structural coexistence. In this state-market complex the Chinese state-Party apparatus is not weakening its control but exerting power over the media either directly by political means or by the rule of the market. Ma cites the example of STAR TV (part owned by Rupert Murdoch) who yielded to the Chinese government by dropping its BBC news service. The *BBC World Service* had earlier fallen foul of the Chinese Government for its critical reports (Ma [Eric] 2000: 25–8). This so-called 'Chinese state-market nexus' can also apply to today's online media.

Rather than taking political risks to make their fortune on-line, news companies have resorted to more tabloid forms of content including stories featuring violence and sex, as well as sports programmes to attract eyeballs and clicks. This strategy is considered pragmatic due to the limited advertiser base, the intensive competition, and the vulnerability of the market. *The Asian Wall Street Journal* has said that China is brandishing a subtle carrot-and-stick approach towards the private sector of the Internet industry. It has made its homegrown Internet élite dependent on nurturing close ties with government in order to get their businesses off the ground. The bottom-line is that 'portal operators take pains to tread carefully, neatly side-stepping the publication of news that might get their licenses revoked' (Kalathil 2000).

As for China's future engagement with world information flows, Frederick S. Tipson has suggested that China would adapt a strategy somewhere between Singapore and Taiwan approaches by preserving the formal impression of political supervision at the same time as promoting the rapid application of information technologies (Tipson 1999, 232–4). This is a view held also by Cartledge and Lovelock (1999) who argue that the Internet is a means of advancing China's stake in the new information economy while utilizing the architecture of the Net as a means to reassert central surveillance and administration.

Compared with e-commerce or other Internet services, China's on-line media have developed more rapidly and with a greater degree of sophistication.There are some important reasons: First, business enterprises have realized that e-commerce requires an effective electronic payment and goods delivery system. This is not available in China. However delivering news on-line is relatively simple. Moreover, on-line news has to some extent satisfied people's appetite for more diverse news and information.

Second, media industries in China exhibit different degrees of openness. The traditional media outlets in China are effectively state-owned enterprises and although most are in various stages of becoming commercial enterprises, they still suffer from over-bureaucratization and poor performance. Also, they are restricted by propaganda policy and censorship regulations. On-line media have been seen as an alternative, bringing fresh views and more diverse information to the public sphere.

Moreover, the Internet provides an opportunity to expedite the commercialization process and enlarge market share for the traditional media. The Chinese media market remains extremely decentralized due to the existing organizational and distribution system: there are more than a thousand newspapers, a thousand radio broadcasting stations, and more than 800 terrestrial TV stations in China, but no large commercial media conglomerate. Local media dominate; and some of the more ambitious are now pursuing the commercial benefits of the national market through the Internet. On March 9, 2000 nine newspapers in Beijing co-established a news web site, *21 Dragon News Network*. Two months later in Shanghai, *eastday.com* began operation. This was a commercial alliance established by *Jiefang Daily*, *Wenhui Daily*, *Xinmin Evening Daily*, *Shanghai Television* and more than ten of the largest traditional media in Shanghai.

Make money, not war

Sina.com and Netease.com are the two most popular portal web sites in China. Both organizations have emerged from technology and software companies. Their success has been founded largely on news and information content services in spite of their proprietors having no background in traditional media provision. Sina.com was created in 1999 in a merger between a Chinese software company Stone Rich Sight Information Technology Company Ltd. (SRS) of Beijing and a US web site company –

SINANET.com of Sunnyvale, California. It quickly became popular and has been voted most visited web site in the last three surveys conducted by the China Internet Network Information Centre (CNNIC). Sina.com claims to be the largest Chinese-language Web site in the world. According to its own report it had over 34 million average daily page-views and 7 million registered users as of June 2000 (*www.sina.com/corp/about/index.html*).

From the very beginning Sina aimed to provide on-line news services. In early 1999 before major traditional media had established their web sites, Sina was re-publishing news from local newspaper partners and Internet sources. This strategy proved to be very successful. The web site published hundreds of news items in rotation. Soon after it was established Sina was able to take advantage of the NATO bombing of the Chinese embassy in Belgrade by providing fast, continuous and comprehensive reporting on the event. This established its reputation and at the same time it achieved huge popularity. Two months later in a survey conducted by CNNIC, Sina.com overtook Sohu.com as China's number one site for the first time.

Sina's heavy reliance on on-line news makes it very cautious. To avoid sensitive political topics, Sina provides a lot of feature news related to crime, entertainment, sport, and society gossip. Celebrity news, dramatic events or breaking news events from overseas often become the focus of the lead story or the main photo. Domestic political news on the other hand is sourced from *The People's Daily* or *Xinhua News Agency*. Although its 'overnight success' has been attributed to its news content, Sina has been wary of becoming a target of regulation or periodic crackdowns. In an interview the CEO of Sina, Wang Zhidong, was evasive about his company's role as a news provider. He claimed Sina was 'only a platform for news articles from the traditional media' and would never employ journalists. In spite of the fact that Sina's advertising revenues for the web-site have exceeded its e-commerce and software revenues, when asked if Sina was a media company or software company Wang replied 'I would rather you call it a new style software company' (Fang [Xiangmin] et al. 2000). Sina's chief manager, Jiang Fengnian was also quoted in the same interviews as saying they were concentrating on entertainment and sports and endeavouring to avoid sensitive topics. 'We hope the government understands our motives and effort,' he said.

Sina has two affiliated sites in the United States and Taiwan. Although membership agreements are almost identical, there is an extra clause attached to Beijing membership that warns members not to disseminate or download anti-Government literature. The agreement further states: 'If members disseminate or transfer any counter-revolutionary, pornographic or other illegal information the trace record in Sina's system may be used as evidence in court.' (*www.sina.com/corp/about/index.html*)

Their efforts have paid off. Despite being established later than Sohu and Netease, Sina was the first to be approved for listing on the Nasdaq index in April 2000. This competitive advantage enabled it to raise US$68,000,000 before the collapse of the Nasdaq in May 2000. In July 2000 Sina was selected by the government and the Chinese Olympic committee as the official web site for on-line coverage of the 2000 Summer Olympics in Sydney.

Netease

Netease is another provider of Chinese-language online content services in China. According to the results released by the Hong Kong-based Interactive Audience Measurement Asia (IAMAsia), it topped a survey of China's top domain names in terms of total number of unique visitors, pulling in approximately 4.9 million people, or 67.3 per cent of all Internet users who logged on at home in October. (*www.iamasia.com*)

Netease was founded by Ding Lei in Guangzhou in mid-1997. At the age of 26 Ding Lei had established the company to develop software products to facilitate Internet use. He successfully launched a bilingual (English and Chinese) Web-based message distribution system on its site that was adopted by many Internet sites offering e-mail accounts to the public. At that time approximately 50 per cent of China's netizens used the free e-mail accounts supported by Netease's software (*www.chinaonline.com*). Netease has developed a number of popular Web-based products, including personalized home pages, virtual communities, chat rooms, games, and entertainment channels. It soon became a leading on-line service provider in China. In June 2000 Netease commenced its initial public offering (IPO) on the Nasdaq.

At the time of writing Netease had 16 Chinese-language content channels including domestic and international news, finance, sports, entertainment, leisure, culture, science, IT, games, real estate, women's issues, health care, careers, fashion, and education. What makes it noticeable is that it presents very upfront comment and opinions in its board bulletin service 'The third eye'. Most topics focus on current public or social affairs. In contrast to Sina its users needn't register and there is no formal agreement between provider and user. It simply reminds users to comply with laws, indicating that any responsibility and risks are taken by the presenters themselves.

In September 2000, during the 50th anniversary of the Korean War, the bulletin introduced a topic, 'Thinking of the Korean War' that attracted many comments questioning China's participation in that historic conflict. From September 6 to September 28, twenty-one long articles were published on the bulletin – more than half expressing negative views on this issue. Claims were made that the Chinese government had hidden the fact that it was North Korea who had initiated the war, not South Korea as in Chinese history textbooks. They complained that the war had brought disastrous consequences for the country. At the same time all the official media were celebrating the anniversary of 'victory' and commemorating the war heroes. Incidentally, Sina.com also had a column dedicated to the anniversary in which most articles were stories written by veterans and their relatives. In contrast with Netease all the contributions justified China's participation in the war.

Shortly after this event in October, and following in the wake of China's success in the Sydney Olympic (see Sun, this volume), Beijing was pulling out all stops to bid for the 2008 Olympic Games. The bulletin started a discussion. Many of the comments opposed the bid and criticized the government's intention to bid for the Olympics. One conscientious objector opined 'I abstain from the bid for the Olympic Games', saying that the government never consulted with people about bidding for the Olympic Games and that there was no democratic process in such decision-making. Another contribution, entitled 'lying in name of the Olympics', retorted that the Olympics movement is intended by the government to distract people from serious social problems like unemployment, corruption, and economic recession. Such articles had never appeared in the traditional media, all of which were intent on glorifying the Olympic spirit and the benefits of hosting the Games.

In October 2000 the expatriate Chinese writer Gao Xingjian was awarded Nobel Prize for Literature. Although he is the first Chinese recipient of the prestigious award, the Nobel Literature Prize Commitee was accused of 'ulterior political motives'. All official media played down this event. Surprisingly, I came across an article 'Gao Xingian, a strange name' in Netease.com written by another overseas Chinese writer. This article introduced the literary value of Gao Xingjian's work, condemned the Chinese Communist Party's despotism over culture directly, and called Jiang Zemin 'the dictator' (Hu Ping 2000). It is debatable as to what made Netease so adventurous in publishing such material. Perhaps it is due to the fact that it operates from the more open southern part of China or that it is a more individual company (Ding Lei hold 58 per cent of the company's share).

Sina and Netease currently represent the mainstream commercial on-line media in China. They have the advantage of new technology to attract users and compete with traditional media; however, they have to appease officials and please regulators in order to negotiate their living space. There has been a certain degree of friction evident between the Chinese leadership and such popular web sites. Sohu.com, for example, has been suspended once when it was linked to porn web sites in its search section. But there has been no major clash or legal action. Those commercial online media companies tend to complain about the restrictions but never try to challenge them.

When new regulations were imposed by the State Council on November 7, 2000 that forced commercial web sites to publish only 'news' that had been vetted by traditional media, Wang Zhidong, the president of Sina, said 'Actually, Sina has been constantly adjusting itself in accordance with the ideas over the past year'. Wang Juntao, chairman of 8848.com. another popular web site, said that the regulations have been released in a timely fashion and would play a positive role in regulating the Internet. (*www.china-online.com* 9 Nov, 2000)

Although online media have enjoyed greater freedom during the past few years compared with the old traditional media, the new international companies and young Dot Com millionaires who run them have little intention of becoming political revolutionaries. They simply do not want to destroy their relationship with the government. With intense competition among providers and a market for unofficial information, some have tried to challenge convention and present free opinion and hot topics on bulletin board where it is difficult to be caught and easy to pass the buck. Others have charted a more conservative course: instead of covering controversial political topics they resort to entertainment and sports to attract 'eyeballs and clicks.'

New regulations on online news are likely to further the trend towards the conservative option of entertainment content. The effect on on-line media will be dramatic. First, online media will lose its cutting edge in news reporting in its competition with traditional media. Required to originate content from government media sources, they will have no chance to be quicker than traditional media. At the same time, the new policy lacks a concrete definition of news, suggesting that sports, entertainment and business information would be untouched. More offerings of 'neutral' fare like sports and entertainment are expected.

The Internet is unlike any of the traditional media, and this is what makes it so disruptive and troublesome. When one considers its origins (it was created as a way of transmitting information even after a nuclear attack), and its disregard of national boundaries, it is an extremely difficult, if not impossible, medium to control. The case of Falun Gong illustrates this well.

In 1999 the Chinese government launched a crackdown campaign against Falun Gong, an unauthorized spiritual group led by Li Hongzhi. Unlike other groups and movements, Falun Gong used the Internet successfully to organize, and disseminate information to members. It has Websites based all over the world, including Asia, the United States, United Kingdom, Canada, Israel, and Australia. When the CCP's propaganda arm denounced the sect, its US-based leader, Li Hongzhi, was on the Internet within hours giving his side of the story. In response, the Chinese government blocked all the Falun Gong web-sites from China. If you search for Falun Gong in the Chinese search engine *www.sohu.com* you find only highly critical official web-sites. If you search in Sina.com it will give you nothing but a message warning that you are searching for something inappropriate. Falun Gong have also claimed that their overseas web-site has been hacked into by hackers employed by the Chinese government.

Conclusion: the meet market or DIY citizenship?

While Chinese domestic on-line media like Sina.com and Netease.com appear not to have delivered any serious political challenge, the true impact of the web could be its capacity to disseminate alternative views and diverse opinions on formerly taboo subjects. The most obvious change is that there are now many Chinese language sites for gay people, and for people of different religions. In early 2001, there was a gay forum within Netease's 'culture' channel under the title of 'comrade' (Gay people are often addressed as comrade in China today). In Sina's chat room http://yuan2.sina.com.cn:9000/party/ there are rooms called 'intimate contact', 'adult topic', 'Loving a stranger', 'Cohabitation', all of which are the hot topics among young Chinese.

In a love poll on 12 Jan. 2001 (http://yuan2.sina.com.cn:9000/quiz/) questions included: Do you mind that your girlfriend is not a virgin? Do you accept sexual activity before marriage? What do you think about extramarital affairs? How do you deal with your ex-lover, if she or he contacts you when you already have a partner? In 'man and woman' discussion groups (http://living.sina.com.cn/) there are columns about 'sexual harassment in the office', 'extramarital affairs, and 'we are cohabiting'. Most postings are from users. In the past these kinds of stories had only been seen in foreign movies, although some discussion did also appear in women's and youth magazines. Now, the fact that an even wider cross-section of Chinese people can use this technology to develop alternative forms of cultural identity is in itself a great leap forward.

It is not enough, however, to just look at the potential changes brought by online media. We need to bear in mind how the Internet – and on-line media organizations – are compromised by relationships with power. The Chinese Communist Party's attempts to manipulate the new information technology for propaganda purposes is only one of a number of factors determining the future of the Internet in China. The future of on-line media companies will for some time depend on cultivating relationships with government bodies responsible for regulating the Internet industry. In this market, only those who are skilful both in business and politics will survive. The Internet may not be able to play a role of a liberator or revolutionary as the mass media did in China in the past. Rather, its capacity to act as educator or motivator will be most important to the Old Middle Kingdom.

Note

1 Translation Michael Keane.

17

RESPONSES TO CRISIS

Convergence, content industries and media governance

Michael Keane and Stephanie Hemelryk Donald

In this final chapter we look at some possible futures for the communications media in China in the context of rapid technological change and the internationalization of regulations governing media markets. We re-examine issues raised in the previous chapters in the light of changes occurring within the Chinese media environment and link these to the development of the knowledge economy and the Chinese National Information Infrastructure (CNNI). The forces driving change are complex and are more influenced by global events, political processes, and multilateral trade agreements than at any time in the past. They include technological change, the re-socializing of social expectations during two decades of economic reform, liberalization of broadcasting and telecommunications markets, and the realization by the government that political repression and the construction of a Chinese knowledge economy are mutually inconsistent.

The communication media are fundamentally about change and continuity, a fact that has been demonstrated by the active role of journalists and film-makers in the greatest social revolution in modern history – the formation of the People's Republic of China and the maintenance of the hegemony of the Chinese Communist Party. However, the media that served China's revolutionary cause to great effect were the 'traditional' media of print, cinema, and broadcasting. These 'traditional' media were able to operate with great efficiency due to several factors. First, there was an absence of major structural change or disruptive technologies during the early period of media expansion (1930s–1990s). Second, resistance to change was reinforced by excessive vertical integration and bureaucratic control over who was allowed to 'belong' to the media and the content that was subsequently allowed to be disseminated, and the form it was allowed to take. Third, media industry scope was domestic, directed at an imagined national community, identified as 'the people' (*renmin*) or the 'masses' (*renmin qunzhong*).

These traditional structural elements have had a diminishing influence on China's media institutions since deregulation and market diversification took effect in the mid-1980s. While there is still a strong case to be made for ideological control as a central distinguishing feature of Chinese media systems, there is an equally strong argument to be made for crisis as a metaphor to understand China's media environment in the first decade of the new millennium. As Hu Xin has demonstrated in the previous chapter 'disruptive' technologies such as the Internet challenge the inflexibility of bureaucratic administration and allow information to be set free (although there are regulatory measures to limit such freedoms). With the convergence of broadcasting, telecommunications and computing, content that was formerly confined to one media platform (television) is now capable of being accessed over multiple platforms (Internet, WAP). Significantly, the more innovative media production units in China are seeking to establish themselves as independent profit seeking institutions that can draw on foreign partnerships: this is more so in new media industries such as Internet service providers (ISPs). In addition, the illusion of the mass audience so central to control metaphors has begun to fragment into many pieces. To understand the nature of this crisis, we therefore require new analytical tools that bring into play the combined effects of new media and new information technologies.

Networks, knowledge and innovation

China has long been regarded as having a highly networked form of social organization. In an eloquent study of the beginnings of mass culture in China Leo Lee and Andrew Nathan note that the Ming and Qing dynasties were typified by 'active local and long-distance trade, cosmopolitan cities, frequent travel, and extensive communication across regions and among social groups' (Lee and Nathan 1985: 360). With modern communications systems now allowing rapid interconnectivity, the capacity to network is greater than ever before. Governments in Mainland China and Taiwan have sought to exploit the economic potential of overseas networks to encourage investment. It is also well documented that people of Chinese heritage frequently draw upon networking practices in adopted homelands.[1] In China networks have historically served both as a means of information transmission (referred to as *xuanchuan* [lit. 'dissemination']) and social integration.

The electronic network infrastructure that is vital to securing a place in the global knowledge economy brings with it the risks and benefits of cultural exchange. We note that China was once an open trading nation whose influences and famous inventions shaped humankind's progress. Chinese culture – particularly by virtue of its Confucian and Buddhist foundations – influenced the native cultural traditions of Korea, Japan, and Vietnam. The 'middle kingdom' (*Zhongguo*) was a 'sending culture' (Lotman 1990) during the imperial period but became a 'receiving culture' in the late nineteenth and early twentieth century when a succession of foreign occupations gradually introduced new philosophies, fashions, fads, music, literature, and technologies. This flow of foreign culture ended abruptly in 1949 as heavy regulation of the cultural sector prohibited cultural imports and foreign ideas for the following three decades.

China is now once again 'receiving' as globally promiscuous flows of information, finance, and philosophies take root. According to some accounts, 'authentic' Chinese culture is in danger of being eroded by content cloned from foreign 'mass culture' formats, propagated through the mass media of television, and the new interactive media of Internet, computer software applications, and CD-Rom. The familiar argument here is that contemporary popular culture is vulgar, unoriginal, and cheap to produce and distribute. At stake are not just aesthetics, but rather 'consumer satisfaction' or cultural artefacts. The issue is cultural quality within a shift towards a new kind of networked society – one in which users have greater choice. The quality control issue was raised by none other than Wang Meng, the former Minister of Culture during the 1980s, who signalled that the widespread perception of Chinese goods as being inferior to foreign product was gradually infiltrating into the cultural sphere. Meanwhile the fear of cultural stagnation is countered by civic educational programmes that aim to raise the ethical quality (*suzhi*) of the population at the same time as raising the production quality (*zhiliang*) of products (see Lewis, this volume).

Described in government policy as the construction of a socialist 'spiritual civilization' (*jingshen wenming*) (translated by Xinhua as 'ethical and cultural progress'), this discourse will be pivotal in the re-imagining of the role of China's cultural and media industries in the coming decade. Central to the issue of *jingshen wenming* and *suzhi* improvement is the vision of a global knowledge economy in which China can participate with confidence and national pride. The knowledge economy is currently at the core of national development strategies in China and draws upon a vision of enhanced quality, technological capacity and innovation. A number of major studies of the benefits and challenges of the knowledge economy have been published in China in recent years (Gan 1998; He 1999; Zhou 1999; Cui 1999; Wu 1998; Jin 1999). One of the contentions is that Chinese society is well-placed to take advantage of the knowledge economy, being traditionally a networked society (that is, if one discounts the attempts of the Communist government to organize organic networks into politicized bureaucracies). The knowledge economy, if allowed to develop, can therefore be 'rewired' on to the traditional network society of China.

The optimism inherent in this vision is tempered by the fact that China has a large population of unskilled workers and a relatively small pool of knowledge workers. However, this is precisely the rationale of cultural policy in China: to raise the education level of its citizens. As government sponsored information technology initiatives in the U.K, Europe, Singapore and Malaysia have demonstrated, the promotion of knowledge-based applications and the development of the economy have a number of points of intersection. The knowledge economy is premised on innovation while cultural regeneration is linked to aspirations of creativity. With both the knowledge economy and the media increasingly evolving towards service industry models rather than 'mass' broadcasting models, flexibility and skills upgrading have become central elements of economic development.

The relationship between audiovisual industries and national development strategies are currently receiving increasing attention in all countries, and in all political systems. Terms such as innovation, technology transfer, skills upgrading, incubation, and market creation, which were formerly applied to knowledge-based, high-value-added industries such as the computer and multimedia industries, are now entering into the language of cultural and media policy. During the past decade there has been increasingly open national debate within China concerning the role of information and communication technologies in enabling China's 'four modernizations' resulting in a revision of emphasis with science and technology taking on the defacto mantle of the leading modernization. As China looks towards cities like Taipei, Singapore, and Hong Kong, the realization is clear that 'clean' information and service industries are displacing labour-intensive industries. As for all countries undergoing expansion and liberalization of content systems, however, the techno-utopia that is heralded as the 'cultural right' of future generations faces a more immediate problem. With satellite wireless and broadband cable technology promising greater multi-channel capacity, there is currently a demand for content.

Meanwhile WTO entry stipulates that China must open its markets to foreign media interests and telecommunications companies. This is where foreign media interests and new content providers sense a window of opportunity. As the Chinese government contemplates the impacts of WTO accession, the once stable and heavily regulated Chinese cultural sector is in a state of crisis, beset by problems of piracy, format duplication, turf battles among regulatory bureaus, and uneven profitability. As we have seen in a number of the chapters in this book there are a number of reasons for this sense of crisis. First, the past two decades of incremental social and economic liberalization have created a demand for cultural and leisure products. Second, the decentralization of media industry administration has led to capitalization by the back door and investment by non-media interests. Third, emerging audiovisual technologies such as the Internet, DVDs, CD-ROM, and MP3 software now enable rapid duplication of ideas and cultural artifacts. Fourth, path dependent ways of networking along with innovative and semi-legal business practices (sometimes referred to within media circles as *cabianqiu* or 'edge-ball') make the implementation of media law extremely problematic. The flow-on results of these changes are anti-competitive market structures that encourage systematic duplication of product at the expense of innovation and experimentation, and rampant piracy of copyright material.

It is a shift from thinking about media industries as dispensing one kind of product (say, television programmes) to thinking about 'platforms' that distribute a mix of information and entertainment content that underlies the challenges facing China's regulators. The challenge confronting producers is how to be innovative: this in turn requires a well-functioning and regulated market that encourages and rewards innovation. As Keane (this volume) has discussed in relation to Chinese television format cloning, the prognosis for a healthy industry is dependent on enabling diversity of programming rather than duplication. This can only be achieved by an appropriate mix of regulation and competition. In the past two decades the lack of real competition and diversity among Chinese media industries, combined with the domestic restrictions on the nature of content has produced a media environment lacking vitality and innovation.

Access

As many of the contributions to this volume have suggested, it is access to information – and the capacity to use that information – that is re-configuring power relations in China. While the rapid pace of change is disconcerting for many, particularly those older demographics unfamiliar with new technology, the new media are embraced by those sections of the population with the political and intellectual capital to take advantage of the changing communications landscape. Despite China's aging population, however, there is reason to be optimistic about the benefits of technological change for the greater consuming public.[2] The convergence of broadcasting, telecommunications and computing technologies, and the fact that consumers in China – as elsewhere – are becoming more media savvy, indicates that the content the public gets more closely resembles what the public wants and needs. This is an important point. As interactivity and user customization of media services increasingly penetrate the 'imagined community' of consumers, they in turn obtain more leverage in influencing the nature of content. To use a biological metaphor, greater participation through new media contributes to the diversity of content circulating in the mediasphere.

This gain is achieved at a cost. Consumers must be made visible to the marketing strategies of subscription-based media providers. The relationship between producers and consumers therefore evolves, not so much in the sense of Marx's classic understanding of production and consumption being inseparable, but rather in a mutually dependent fashion. Producers of media content are able to use new technologies to know their audiences, their users; conversely, patterns of use alter as consumers are able to take part in producing the content they desire. The distance between production and consumption disappears as do the 'old media' models of passive consumers and hypodermic syringe effects. Whereas the old media of 'pre-formed' content (finished programmes, films) were dispensed through a limited number of pipelines, new media are increasingly dispensed through multiple platforms. Being primarily interactive, they allow the consumer to modify content (digital TV), choose from a buffet of content (video-on-demand, pay TV), and to time-shift (view content at their own leisure).

However, the relationship between the availability of new media technology and its uptake is not as clear-cut as it is in developed countries, such as Singapore, that have embarked on systematic re-education and re-skilling of the population. Seventy per cent of China's population are still categorized as peasants with low education and incomes (although this figure is projected to drop to 45 per cent by 2025),[3] fifty-six per cent of Internet users were under the age of 24 and two-thirds were unmarried (SMCP 19 February 2001). The predominant consuming public of new media is primarily young – university students who have yet to become conspicuous consumers (ibid.). A similar conundrum exists for the development of e-commerce. Despite the number of computer users now totally 22.5 million, most use the Internet for sending email and accessing chat rooms. E-commerce has temporarily stalled due to the realization by investors of patterns of usage and the problem of lack of trust within Chinese society. This latter point is crucial. Social stratification combined with endemic piracy has made Chinese people reluctant to trust e-commerce.

The conundrum of crisis is therefore captured in the supply–demand equation where the 'push' of new technological systems confronts the 'pull' of consumer demand (Hukill et al. 2000: 302). In the case of China it is the push of broadband cable technology that promises to leapfrog China into the information age. Despite the economic gap between the new urban middle-classes and the large rural demographic, the emerging digital divide between the university educated and the aging population, the 'advantage' that China has is that people of all ages and incomes have unprecedented exposure to cable TV (see Harrison; Shoesmith and Wang, this volume). This bodes well for future uptake of media systems and content. Moreover, with services and content no longer tied to specific delivery platforms, it is possible to conceive of the cable network becoming the dominant platform for delivery of customized content including video-on-demand, games, interactive data services, as well as the traditional 'pre-formed' media fare of television dramas, news, and talk shows.

These changes herald a new way of thinking about the role of the media both in the way that the media are governed and in the uses people make of the media. Developments in delivery platforms – in satellite, broad-band cable, in digitalization and in the growth of the Internet – have destroyed the easiest and most obvious rationale for state control of broadcasting, namely technologically-defined scarcity of resources. These technological developments have coincided with increasing political pressure for privatization and/or de-regulation – in the name of micro-economic reform, or, increasing consumer choice. New regulatory challenges emerge as the distinctions between broadcasting and telecommunications become more difficult to sustain and as the unbundling of service/market platforms allows more players – often non-media interests – into a reinvigorated mediasphere. In the face of the IT/convergence revolution broadcasters have adopted three principal strategies. First, the diversification of content on to all available delivery platforms; second, mergers and acquisitions; and third, the introduction of innovative services (Lim 2001). From the perspective of the consumer of media products there is the realization that the rush to develop an information infrastructure has outpaced the provision of quality content. While it is fine to have multi-channel capacity, the Chinese consumer is unlikely to be stimulated by constantly revolving repeats of last years tele-dramas, variety concerts and blatantly cannibalized formats from Taiwan. Ultimately the acceptance of new media technologies will depend on the attractiveness of the content on offer.

Convergence

The term convergence has been used regularly to refer to the increasing inter-operability of systems, in particular the rapid change in the ways that voice, data, images and video can be transmitted and stored. When converted to digital form the distinction between types of information effectively becomes blurred as each becomes a stream of bits or multimedia information. However the term has a broader usage. In Asian countries the term embodies three interrelated forms (Ono et al. 2000). First, cross-sector convergence evidenced by the increasing liberalization of telecommunications and broadcasting sectors, leading in turn to improved efficiency and the spread of new services such as video-on-demand through telephone networks and audio streaming capacity on the internet. Second, the development of the Internet itself is embedded within the China National Information Infrastructure (CNII). This was developed partly as a response to the international regulatory architecture of the Global Information Infrastructure (GII), and partly as a mechanism to extend the administrative and surveillance capacities of the central state into the evolving information economy (Cartledge and Lovelock 1999). In comparison, the GII was devised as means of serving as a policy instrument for the coordination of formal agreements such as the General Agreement on Trade in Services (GATS) incubated through the WTO. The third form of convergence is administrative convergence whereby the regulatory functions attached to electronic communications come under the bureaucratic scrutiny of a central body. In China this overarching body is the Ministry of Information Industry (MII) formed in 1998 by bringing together the former

Ministry of Radio, Film and Television (MRFT), the Ministry of Electronic Industries (MEI) and the Ministry of Posts and Telecommunications (MPT) (see Ure and Liang 2000; Lynch 1999).

The capacity of the MII and the SARFT to regulate China's audiovisual industries now comes under increased global pressure, adding to the regulatory turf battles that have been breaking out across different provinces and between ministries in recent years (See Harrison, this volume; Redl and Simons, this volume). The 'new media' environment is fundamentally propelled by technological developments. Convergence, globalization and digitization create new technological and business models and practices, many of which are international rather than domestic, they utilize digital transmission systems, and they spawn multi-channel marketplaces. There are additional factors: competition between delivery platforms, fragmented audiences, and pressures to form business alliances to share content. Put together, these are forcing a new model of operations to emerge. The new media environment in China as elsewhere is challenging industry practice as much as the Chinese government's cultural and social rationales of regulation. With cross-sector convergence the traditional audiovisual sectors (television, cinema) are now placed alongside telecommunications, e-commerce, banking and financial services, and education.

WTO and the demise of the nation state?

We made the suggestion at the beginning of this chapter that a combination of unprecedented forces has seriously diminished the capacity of the Chinese nation-state to manage its media sector. These forces include flows of disruptive technology and ideas, unruly transnational capital, and international governance of the WTO (GATS), and the flow-on effects of social and political liberalizations.

By way of concluding this study, we propose a few open-ended scenarios based on the potential effects of such transformations over the next decade or so. We suggest that the development of good content and viable content industries ultimately depends on creating an environment in which both innovation and regulation are complementary. As Chinese consumers increasingly become the arbiters of success and failure of cultural products, and industries increasingly seek to differentiate their products to gain the attention of consumers, we will observe some degree of market integration.

As we mentioned in the opening chapter of this volume, since China's economic reforms began in 1978, Western political commentators have attempted to characterize China's transition from planned economy to market economy under various formulations. While the idea of 'post-socialism' is an appealing one given the domino effect of Communism's crisis in the Soviet bloc, we need to bear in mind that China still remains a socialist state. China is arguably post-socialist in the way that it is managing its economic reforms – and if one were to be pedantic China is probably less socialist than a number of Scandinavian countries in relation to social welfare. However, we argue that to illustrate China's conversion to free market principles as 'plan to market' is fundamentally flawed. Cultural production in China occurs within market structures, but had done so long before the economic reforms took place. However unproductive, inefficient and dependent on government subvention these may have been they were still market structures.

As we have argued previously, the Asian authoritarian model (Donald and Keane, this volume) fits well in China, which has long operated a pragmatic politics of communication. Further, we suggest that the notion of governmentality, allied with what we might call the promotional state, holds a certain explanatory potential. The idea of governmentality presupposes a shift in the art of government from an interventionist model (social engineering, bio-power) to a more liberal mode of allowing people to self-regulate. In terms of cultural policy in China, this is expressed in a shift from an 'engineer state model' to a model where the state remains the architect of cultural administration but retreats from its overt interventionist role. The premise is that engineer state-type intervention requires constant policing and is inconsistent with a well-functioning media industry environment. This leaves the state to play a different role, one that we characterize as a promotional role, trumpeting the benefits of technology, progress, and Chinese nationalism. China's accession to the WTO provides a vehicle for its global self-promotion as an open trading nation. At the same time there is a fall-back position that allows for blatant nationalism should the new Western incursions into its markets undermine cultural sovereignty and the cherished social values of its imagined citizenship.

However, to illustrate the difficulty of applying such models across all media systems, we reiterate Redl and Simons' argument in Chapter 2: 'In many ways, the development of media, as all new industries in China, has progressed in a circular manner. Each full revolution (spurred on a combination of political

Table 17.1 Media beyond 2000

	2000–
Economic system	State capitalism/authoritarian liberalism
Media regulation	Architect state model (state facilitates regulatory guidelines for investment in infrastructure); state facilitates and promotes
Social stratification	Emerging digital divide; increasing economic stratification
Function of media	Informational/provision of repertoire of cultural choices
Types of media	Broadband cable; digital TV, WAPs; new media
Media characteristic	Convergence/internationalization of content
Crisis	The high cost of upgrading technological infrastructure. The threats of foreign content and the impact of WTO accession. Controlling the technology of the internet.

and commercial factors) results in a larger and more advanced circle, but one that still inherits the imperfections of the previous one.'

'Best practice' is the sole criterion of truth

The story we have told in this book has been one of rapid change, undertaken in crisis mode. Inevitably, serious problems are inherent in the pace and intensity of recent media developments. Best practice, the mantra of ethical, workable, sustainable, profitable high quality production, is not likely to be immediately invented in such conditions. China's rush to develop large-scale broadband infrastructure without due consideration to content and markets represents one considerable area of 'best practice' shortfall. As audience demographic fragmentation continues, and as lower and upper income consumers diverge in taste and usage patterns, Chinese media producers will have to take account of content scarcity. The animation sector (Donald, this volume) is just one case where regulatory broadcast stipulations, local demand, and domestic industry provision do not coincide. China, as a huge and internationally active market, urgently needs to allow more innovative activity in content development and service entrepreneurship.

The national mega-enterprises are unlikely to push the envelope for fear of losing their patronage with the leadership. This suggests that much of the true innovation will come from small scale players. Interesting co-productions with technologically advanced international partners, cross-organizational promotion strategies and idea-exchange, *imaginative* format developments, local issue reportage and documentary, are all desirable, and are happening in some quarters. Further a regeneration of the e-commerce and e-tourism potential that is almost dormant at the time of writing, would ideally spark new collaborations across platforms, and attract new revenue sources for drama, youth programming and other high cost innovations.

Internationalism, as opposed to generic paranoia around the spectre of globalization, is also an important thematic in predicting China's media future. There is a large diasporic population of potential consumers of Chinese language media product, whose influence may be significant in years to come. Currently, however, the shift from domestic markets to international markets promised by WTO accession is unlikely to be China's strong suit in the audiovisual sector. China's television, cinema, and web-based content have yet to gain credibility in world markets. The occasional prize-winning cinema of Zhang Yimou and Chen Kaige, and touring, palatable film-seasons (Silk Screen Season 2000) do not add up to quotidien content and a reliable market source. China will need to develop consistency, and also to control is endemic of copyright violation, if it is to stake a claim for itself as an exporter of content.

For a viable audiovisual sector players need to gain return on investment. Market efficiency is not a luxury in an economy that can no longer wholly rely on state support and subsidy. Subsidy does continue, but only in return for highly politicized (and internationally unsaleable) content (Chu, this volume). This is doubly unhelpful if regulation advantages are also slanted in this direction. If monopoly control remains vested in the hands of bureaucratic entrepreneurs, those who are part of the Chinese Communist Party, the will of the CCP is likely to be expressed as more mainstream melody productions with limited audience appeal and next to no export potential.

Despite the inevitability of measuring China's media transformation in the contexts of global media and telecommunications industries, the inevitability of economic liberalization is far from certain. It is in any case a moot point whether commercialization necessarily engenders real diversity in media content. Celebrations of pluralism may be a little premature – and that comment echoes many who warn against the early demise of the national communicative space (Schlesinger 2000: 100–2).

The content available to the Chinese media consumer is likely to develop as a regional buffet rather than an international banquet. Regional diversity is desirable on its own account, and Chinese companies are best placed to provide it. From the perspective of internationalization, regional diversity can be mobilized to explore specific, located, experiences in a larger 'human' context. In practice, then, limitations on foreign content and a preference for local stories mean that if Western media interests are to capture Chinese markets they will need to 'glocalize'. This term has referred to the assimilation of global practices and content in a local situation (Sreberny 2000). Here, we suggest that foreign content providers need to engage in 'active glocalization'. They, together with their domestic co-producers, must take China's social, cultural and political mores, memories, and aesthetic currencies seriously, if they are to achieve deep purchase and a lasting profile in the markets.

In conclusion, we suggest that the current relationship between governance, convergence and the content industries requires re-configuration in order to produce 'best practice' for media in China. Convergence is a classic 'challenge and opportunity' moment for the industry. It should regenerate the creative imagination of producers, as technical possibilities, divergent and increasingly 'active' audiences and international linkages demand innovatory responses. Old media will not disappear, but they will eventually need to re-invent their self-expectations, as their consumers try other ways of accessing information, entertainment and, indoctritainment (Sun, this volume). None of these observations are new, they apply to most national media industries, and to global media empires. Media governance is, similarly, a potent question worldwide, as Internet-led boundary crossers, tax-shy film enterprises, and the US Department of Commerce work hard to reduce national controls on media delivery. In China, we argue, the issue is of a different order of priority. There is a gross imbalance between the audience potential and the legal flexibility of the industries that serve them. The Government treads an uncomfortable line between Party-demands for continued ideological leadership, and the State imperative to grow the home industries as a protection against post-WTO foreign invasions of content and ownership. Defining and maintaining a balance between multiple and not entirely commensurate national interests, is the large task ahead for media governance in the PRC.

Notes

1 See for example Cunningham and Sinclair (2000).

2 Despite the growth in the number of Internet users, 56 per cent of users are under the age of 24. Students are major users, accounting for 20 per cent of the total. About two-thirds of users are unmarried, and 41 per cent earn between 500 and 1000 yuan per month. Users making more than 1500 yuan a month made up only 20 per cent of the total. Overall, the majority of China's Internet users were from the middle- or lower-income classes (SCMP, Friday 199 February 2001)

3 Sources: UN Centre for Human Settlements: *An Urbanizing World: Global Report on Human Settlements, 1996*, China State Statistical Yearbook, 1998.

NOTES ON CONTRIBUTORS

Yingchi Chu is Lecturer in Chinese and media studies at Murdoch University. Her publications include *Hong Kong Cinema and National Cinema: Coloniser, Motherland and Self* (working title, forthcoming Curzon, 2002).

Anthony Y.H. Fung is Assistant Professor at the School of Journalism and Communication at the Chinese University of Hong Kong. His Ph.D. concerned theories of political economy of mass media in Hong Kong (University of Minnesota). Edited books include *Cultural Feeling: In the Voices of Their Own* and *The Special Administrative Region (SAR), Public Policy and Ethics.*

Stephanie Hemelryk Donald is Senior Lecturer in media and communication at the University of Melbourne, and fellow of the Asia Research Centre, Murdoch University. Publications include *Public Secrets, Public Spaces: Cinema and Civility in China, The Global Media Atlas* (BFI), and *Picturing Power in the People's Republic of China.*

Mark Harrison completed his doctorate at Monash University School of Asian Languages and Studies, Melbourne. He is now Postdoctoral Research Fellow at the Centre for the Study of Democracy at the University of Westminster.

Hu Xin obtained a Master of Digital Media from the Queensland University of Technology where he was a visiting scholar in 2000. He now works in the Internet industry in China.

Huang Yingfen is Doctoral Candidate in Communication at Simon Fraser University, Canada. She has an MA in Film and Television at UCLA. Her research interests include the spectacle and ideology of late capitalism the Third World criticism and the critique of modernity, and cultural geography.

Michael Keane is Research Fellow at the Creative Industries Research and Applications Centre at Queensland (CIRAC) University of Technology. His Ph.D. dissertation (1999) discussed policy and Chinese domestic television drama development in the 1990s. Research interests are media governance, and television format trade and creative industry developments in East Asia.

Jeroen de Kloet completed his Ph.D. at the Amsterdam School for Social Science Research (University of Amsterdam) on popular music and youth cultures in China, focussing on Beijing rock culture. He is affiliated to the Institute of Infonomics, University of Maastricht, conducting research on Internet use in Asia.

Tain Dow Lee is Professor of film/ television aesthetics and criticism in the Department of Mass Communications, Hsuan Chuang University. He founded the Communication Arts Research Institute, Taipei. His publications include *Taiwanese Cinemas, Society and History* (1998); *Beyond Tokyo Rainbow Bridge: The Imaginary Appropriation of Japanese Television Trendy Drama in Taiwan* (1999); and *The Globalization of Transnational Media: Imaginary Spheres and Identity Incorporation* (2000).

Steven W. Lewis is Senior Researcher in Asian Politics and Economics, Baker Institute for Public Policy, and Lecturer, Department of Political Science, at Rice University in Houston, Texas, USA. His research critiques theories, and conducts original empirical work on transitions in China and other former central planned economies.

Kenneth Lim graduated with honours in Media and Communication Studies from Murdoch University. He has been at the forefront of developments in the advertising industry in the Greater China region over the past four years.

Eric K.W. Ma is Associate Professor at the School of Journalism and Communication of the Chinese University of Hong Kong. He is the author of *Culture, Politics and Television in Hong Kong* (Routledge, 1999).

Laikwan Pang received her Ph.D. at Washington University in Comparative Literature. She is now a Lecturer of the General Education Center at the Hong Kong Polytechnic University. Publications include *Vision and Nation: Building a New China in Cinema, The Chinese Left-wing Cinema, 1932–1937.*

Anke Redl is an industry analyst working in Beijing.

Brian Shoesmith is Associate Professor at Edith Cowan University. He wrote a Ph.D. on the film policy in India during the Raj (1913–1947). His other major research interest is cable and satellite television in Asia. Publications include *Rethinking Pop Music in Asia: Cosmopolitan Flows, Political Tempos and Aesthetic Industries* (2001) and a volume on Indian national cinema (forthcoming, CUP).

Rowan Simons is an industry analyst working in Beijing.

Wanning Sun is Lecturer in Media and Information at Curtin University. Her research interests include Chinese media, diasporic Chinese media, and media, mobility and Chinese transnationalism. She is currently writing a book *Leaving China: Media, Mobility and Transnational Imagination.*

Wang Handong is Associate Professor and Head of Television Studies in the School of Journalism and Communication at Wuhan University, P.R. China, and Visiting Fellow in Edith Cowan University and Wilhelms University of Muenster. Research interests are Chinese television policy, media criticism, and comparative, linguistic communications in ancient China.

Yin Hong is Vice-chairman and Professor of the Department of Communications at Tsinghua University in China. Publications include *World Films: A Historical Reading* (2000), *The Reading of Mirror Image: On Chinese Film and TV Culture in the '90s* (1998), *The Study of Contemporary Popular Culture in China* (1998). Yin Hong is an executive member of the Association of Film Critics in China and the University and College Association of Film and TV in China.

BIBLIOGRAPHY

Althusser, Louis and Étienne Balibar (1970) *Reading Capital.* Trans. Ben Brewster. London: New Left Books.

Anagnost, Ann (1997) 'Children and national transcendence in China' in Kenneth G. Lieberthal, Shuen-fu Lin, Ernest P. Young (eds) *Constructing China: The interaction of culture and economics,* Ann Arbor: University of Michigan Press.

Anderson, Benedict (1983) *Imagined Communities: Reflections on the origin and spread of nationalism,* London: Verso.

Appadurai, Arjun, (1996) *Modernity at large: cultural dimensions of globalization,* Minneapolis: University of Minnesota Press.

AsiaSat (2000) http://www.asiasat.com.hk, accessed 19 January 2001.

Barmé, Géremie. R. (1999) *In the Red – on contemporary chinese culture.* New York: Columbia University Press.

Beijing Scene (1999) 'Dirty Dishes', http://www.beijingscene.com/V05I009/inshort/inshort.htm, accessed 27 January 2001.

Benewick, Robert and Stephanie Donald (1999) *The State of China Atlas,* New York: Penguin Books.

Birch, David (1998a) 'Communication policy in Asia: limited democracy and the public sphere', *Media International Australia incorporating Culture and Policy,* 86, February 1998, pp. 87–102.

— (1998b) 'Public Cultures: 'Asian' and 'Australian' Spaces', *Southern Review,* special issue on Culture and Citizenship, 31(1), pp. 64–73.

— (1999) 'Reading State Communication as Public Culture, Some Issues of Critical Discourse Analysis in Singapore', in Phyllis Chew and Annalise Kramer-Dahl eds *Reading Culture: Textual Practice in Singapore,* Singapore: Times Academic Press, pp. 19–36.

— (2000) 'Civic or Civil Contingencies? Regulating Media and Society in Singapore', forthcoming in Philip Kitley and Stuart Cunningham (eds) *Television, Regulation and Civil Society in Asia,* Centre for Cultural and Media Policy, Brisbane.

Blair, Helen and Al Rainnie (2000) 'Flexible Films?' *Media Culture and Society,* 22, 2, pp: 187–204.

Brugger, Bill and David Kelly (1990) *Chinese Marxism in the Post-Mao Era,* Stanford: Stanford University Press.

Buckley, Christopher (1999) 'How a revolution becomes a dinner party: stratification, mobility and the new rich in urban China' in M. Pinches (ed.) *Culture and Privilege in Capitalist Asia*, London: Routledge.

Burns, John (1994), 'Strengthening Control of China's Leadership Selection: The 1990 Nomenklatura' *China Quarterly*, No. 138, pp. 458–91.

Cai, Xiang (1993) '1981–1992: Looking at the past, and looking to the future of Chinese popular television drama' (1981–1992: woguo tongsu dianshiju de huigu yu qianzhan, pp. 2–7 in *Television Research* (*Dianshi yanjiu*), 4.

Cartledge, Simon and Peter Lovelock (1999) 'China promotes the Internet', pp. 12–13 in *The China Business Review*, 26, 3.

Castells, Manuel (1997), *The Power of Identity, The Information Age: Economy, Society and Culture*, Volume II, Oxford: Blackwell

Caves, Richard E. (2000) *Creative Industries: Contracts between Art and Commerce*, Cambridge: Harvard University Press.

Chan, Anita (1985) *Children of Mao: Personality Development and Political Activism in the Red Guard Generation*, Seattle: University of Washington Press.

Chan, Joseph [Man] (1993) 'Commercialization without independence: trends and tensions of media development in China', in Maurice Brosseau, Hsin-Chi Kuan (eds) *China Review (1993)* Hong Kong: Chinese University of Hong Kong.

— (1994) 'Media internationalization in China: processes and tensions', *Journal of Communications* Vol. 44, No. 3, pp. 70–88.

— (1995) 'Calling the piper without paying the tune: the reassertion of media controls in China' in Lo Chi Kin, Suzanne Pepper and Tsui Kai Yuen (eds) *China Review (1995)*, Hong Kong: Chinese University of Hong Kong.

— (1996) 'Television development in Greater China: structure, export, and market formation' in John Sinclair et al. (eds) *New Patterns in Global Television: Peripheral vision*, Oxford: Oxford University Press.

— (2000) 'When capitalist and socialist TV clash: the impact of Hong Kong TV on Guangzhou residents' in C.C. Lee (ed.) *Money, Power and Media*, Evanston, Ill.: Northwestern University Press.

Chang, Julian (1997) 'The mechanics of state propaganda in the People's Republic of China and the Soviet Union in the 1950s', in T. Cheek and T. Saitch (eds) *New Perspectives on State Socialism in China*, New York: M.E. Sharpe.

Chen, Gang (1996) *Mass Culture and Utopia (Dazhong wenhua yu wutuobang)*, Beijing, Zuojia chubanshe.

Cheng, Huailin and Chan, Joseph Man (1998) 'Bird-caged press freedom in China', in Joseph Y.S. Cheng (ed.) *China in the Post-Deng Era*, Hong Kong: The Chinese University Press.

Chen, Kuan-Hsing (2000) 'The formation and consumption of KTV in Taiwan' in Chua Beng Huat (ed.) *Consumption in Asia: Lifestyles and Identities*, London: Routledge.

Chen, Xiaomei (1999) 'Growing up with posters in the Maoist era', in Harriet Evans and Stephanie Donald (eds), *Picturing Power in the People's Republic of China*. Lanham: Rowman and Littlefield.

Cheng, Hong and Kara Chan (2001) 'Public Service Advertising in China: Social Marketing in the Making', American Academy of Advertising Special 2001 Asia-Pacific Conference, Kisarazu, Japan, 31 May–June 2001.

Chih, Yu-shih (1999) *Collective Democracy: Political and Legal Reform in China*, Hong Kong, Chinese University Press.

China Broadcasting Year Book (1996–1998) State Statistical Publishing House, Beijing.

China Online (2000a) 'Ministry of Information Industry (MII)': http://65.161.182.23.80/refer/ministry_profiles/MII.asp, accessed 1 February 2001.

China Online (2000b) 'State Administration of Radio, Film and Television': http://65.161.182.23.80/refer/ministry_profiles/SARFTI.asp, accessed 1 February 2001.

ChinaSat (2000) 'Chinasat – China and Communication Satellite Systems': http://www.fas.org/spp/guide/china/comm/chinasat.htm, accessed 19 January 2001.

China State Statistical Yearbooks (1998–2000) State Statistical Publishing House, Beijing.

China Television Broadcasting Yearbook (1998) Beijing Broadcasting Institute, Beijing.

Chow, Rey (1995) *Primitive Passions*, New York: Columbia University Press.

Chu, Yingchi and Stephanie Hemelryk Donald and Andrea Witcomb (in press), 'Children and Publicness in the Media-sphere', in Gary Rawnsley and Ming-yeh Rawnsley (eds) *Media and Politics in Greater China*, London: Curzon Press.

Chua, Beng-huat (1999) 'Bodies in shopping centres: displays, shapes and intimacies', in *UTS Review* 5/2, pp. 114–28.

Clark, Paul (1987) *Chinese Cinema: Cultural and Politics Since 1949*, Cambridge: Cambridge University Press.

Cohen, Myron L. (1993). 'Cultural and Political Inventions in Modern China: The Case of the Chinese "Peasant"', *Daedalus* 122:2.

Cui, Baoguo (1999a) *Media Evolution and Social Development* (*meijie gaibian yu shehui fazhan*) Beijing: Beijing Normal University Press.

— (1999b) *Information Society Theory and Models*, Beijing: Higher Education Press.

Cunningham, Stuart and John Sinclair (eds) (2000) *Floating Lives: The media and Asian diasporas: negotiating cultural identity through media*, Brisbane: University of Queensland Press.

Curran, James and Myung-Jin Park (2000) 'Beyond globalization theory', in James Curran and Myung-Jin Park (eds) *De-Westernizing Media Studies*, London: Routledge.

Dai, Degang (1999) 'A survey on the cinema-going habits of Beijing audiences' ['*Dui Beijing dianying guangzhong guangying qingkuan de tiaocha baogao*'] *The Journal of Beijing Film Academy*, Vol. 2, pp. 92–7.

Dandong Television and Dandong Cable Television (2000a) http://202.96.94.14/ddtv/jj.htm, accessed 28 July 2000.

Dandong Television and Dandong Cable Television (2000b) http://202.96.94.14/ddtv/yx.htm, accessed 2 June 2000.

Davies, Derek (1999) 'The Press', in Michael Haas (ed) *The Singapore Puzzle*, Westport: Praeger, pp. 77–106.

Dianying tongxu (1989) 'Dianying congheng tan: dianyingju juzhang Teng Jinxian dajize wen' (An interview with Chief Director of Film Bureau, Teng Jinxian), *Dianying tongxu*, issue 124, pp. 1–2.

'Dianying ju: yunxu jinkou 20 bu dengyu bixu jinkou 20 bu' (Film Bureau: Allow 20 imported films in the (WTO) agreement does not mean China has to import 20 films) 29 December 2000, Http://www.filmsea.com/focus/xlp/sf00101.htm

'Dianying: piruan riyi jiu, heri chong feiyang' (Film: when it will return to its golden time), *Yangcheng wanbao*, 17 December 2000.

Dirlik, Arif (1989) 'Postsocialism? Reflections on 'socialism with Chinese characteristics" in Arif Dirlik and M. Meisner (eds) *Marxism and the Chinese Experience: Issues in Contemporary Chinese Socialism*, New York: M.E. Sharpe.

Donald, James and Stephanie Hemelryk Donald (2000) 'The Publicness of Cinema', in Gledhill and Williams (eds) *Reinventing Film Studies*, London: Edward Arnold, pp. 114129.

Donald, Stephanie (Hemelryk) (1999) 'Children as Political Messengers: Art, Childhood, and Continuity', in Harriet Evans and Stephanie Donald (eds).

— (2000) *Public Secrets: Public Spaces: Cinema and Civility in China*, Lanham: Rowman and Littlefield.

— (2001) (in press) 'Children's Day: The fashionable performance of modern citizenship in China', in Wendy Parkins (ed) *Fashioning the Body Politic: Dress, Gender, Citizenship*, Oxford: Berg.

Dong, Fang (1996) '*Establishing new exhibition lines: the development of the Oriental Film Company with fierce competition*' ['*Dongfang gongsi zujian yuanxian, zai jinzhen zhong qiu fazhen*], *Zhongguo dianying nianjian* [*China Film Yearbook* 1996], pp. 214–16.

Downing, John D.H. (1996) *Internationalizing Media Theory: Transition, Power, Culture, Reflections on Media in Russia, Poland and Hungary 1980–1995*, Thousand Oaks, Calif.: Sage.

Duara, Prasenjit (1988) *Culture, Power and the State: Rural North China, 1900–1942*, Stanford: Stanford University Press.

Elias, Norbert and Eric Dunning (1986) *Quest for Excitement: Sport and Leisure in the Civilising Process*, Oxford: Basil Blackwell.

Evans, Harriet and Stephanie Donald (1999a) 'Introducing Posters of China's Cultural Revolution', in Harriet Evans and Stephanie Donald (eds) pp. 1–26.

— (eds) (1999b) *Picturing Power in the People's Republic of China: Posters of the Cultural Revolution*, Lanham: Rowman and Littlefield.

Fan, Chengze Simon (2000) 'Economic development and the changing patterns of consumption in urban China' in Chua Beng-huat (ed.) *Consumption in Asia: Lifestyles and Identities*, London: Routledge.

Fang, Xiangmin, Li Peng and Wang Xin (2000) 'Scrutinising Sina' [in Chinese] *Sanlian Life Weekly* [in Chinese], March 2000.

Farquhar, Mary Ann (1999) *Children's Literature in China: From Lu Xun to Mao Zedong*, Armonk: M.E. Sharpe.

Fincher, Ruth and Jane Jacobs (eds) (1998) *Cities of Difference*, New York: Guilford Press.

Fitzgerald, John (1995) 'The Nationless State: The Search for a Nation in Modern Chinese Nationalism' *Australian Journal of Chinese Affairs*, 33.

— (1996) *Awakening China: Politics, Culture and Class in the Nationalist Revolution*, Stanford: Stanford University Press.

Fung, Anthony, 'Guangzhou People Reading Hong Kong Television,' *Mass Communication Research*, (National Chengzhi University, Taiwan), 2000, 61, pp. 259–75.

— (2000) 'Critical Ideology, Local Resistance and Incomplete Globalization: Guangzhou people decoding Hong Kong television soap operas', *Second International Conference on Chinese Cinema, Year 2000 and Beyond: History, Technology and Future of Transnational Chinese Film and Television*, Hong Kong Baptist University, 19–21 April 2000. Forthcoming as 'Guangzhou People Reading Hong Kong Television' *Mass Communication Research*, 2000, 61, pp. 259–75.

Fung, Anthony and Chin-chuan Lee (forthcoming) 'Market and Politics: Hong Kong press during sovereignty transfer', in Wensha Jia, Ray Heisey and Lucy Lu (eds) *Chinese Communication Studies: Contexts and Comparisons*, Greenwood Press.

Gan, De'an (1998) *Creativity of Knowledge Economy*, Wuhan: Huanzhong (Central China) University of Science and Technology.

Garnham, Nicholas (1990) *Capitalism and Communication*, London: Sage.

— (2000) *Emancipation, the Media, and Modernity: Arguments about the Media and Social Theory*, Oxford: Oxford University Press.

Gibson, Mark (2000) 'The Powers of Pokémon: Histories of Television, Histories of Concepts of Power' (seen in draft).

Giddens, Anthony (1990) *The Consequences of Modernity*, Stanford, Calif: Stanford University Press.

— (1991) *Modernity and Self-identity: Self and society in the late modern age*' Cambridge: Polity.

Goban-Klas, Tomasz (1994) *The Orchestration of the Media: The Politics of Mass Communications in Communist Poland and the Afermath*, Boulder: Westview Press.

Gold, Thomas B. (1993) 'Go With Your Feelings: Hong Kong and Taiwan Popular Culture in Greater China', *The China Quarterly*, No. 136: 907–25.

Goodman, David (1996) 'The People's Republic of China: the party-state, capitalist revolution and new entrepreneurs', in R. Robison and D.G. Goodman, *The New Rich in Asia: Mobile Phones, McDonalds and Middle-class Revolution*, London and New York: Routledge.

Goodman, David and Beverly Hooper (1994) *China's Quiet Revolution: New Interactions Between State and Society*, New York: Longman Cheshire.

Guback, Thomas (1987) 'Government financial support to the film industry in the United States', in A. Austin (ed.) *Current Research in Film: Audiences, Economics, and Law*, Vol. 3, Norwood: Ablex Publishing Corporations.

Gunaratne, Shelton A. (2000) *Handbook of the Media in Asia*, New Delhi: Sage.

Gurevitch, Michael (1986) 'The Globalisation of Electronic Journalism', *Mass Media and Society* (eds) J. Curran and M. Gurevitch, London: Arnold.

Hall, Stuart (1992) 'The question of identity', in *Modernity and Its Futures*, ed. S. Hall, D. Held and T. McGrew, Cambridge: Polity Press, pp. 273–326.

Hamlin, Michael Alan (2000) *The New Asian Corporation – Managing For the Future in Post-Crisis Asia*, San Francisco: Jossey-Bass Publishers.

Hao, X. and Chen, Y. (2000) 'Film and Social Change: The Chinese cinema in the Reform Era', *Journal of Popular Film and Television*, Vol. 28, pp. 36–45.

Harding, Harry (1995) 'The Concept of 'Greater China': Themes, Variations and Reservations', in *Greater China: The Next Superpower?* ed. David Shambaugh, Oxford: Oxford University Press, pp. 8–34.

Hartley, John (1992) *Tele-ology: Studies in Television*, London: Routledge.

— (1999) *Uses of Television*, London: Routledge.

Hartley, John and Alan McKee (2000) *The Indigenous Public Sphere*, London: Oxford University Press.

He, Sheng (1999) 'China to build IP network', *China Daily*, 30 April 1999.

He, Xiaobing (1994) 'Who is the god of television: television's cultural stratification' (*Shei shi dianshi de shangdi? Dianshi de jieceng wenhua dingwei*), *Beijing Broadcasting Institute Journal* (now *Modern Communication*), No. 2, pp. 9–17.

He, Yuchang (1999) *Knowledge is Power: The Emerging Knowledge Economy*, Guangzhou: Guangdong Tourism Publisher.

Heilongjiang Television (2000) http://www.hljtv.com/weixing.htm, accessed 28 July 2000.

Hong, Junhao (1998) *The Internationalization of Television in China: The Evolution of Ideology, Society, and Media Since the Reform*, Westport, Conn: Praeger.

Hooper, Beverly (2000) 'Globalisation and Resistance in Post-Mao China: the Case of Foreign Consumer Products' *Asian Studies Review*, 24, 4.

Howkins, J. (1982) *Mass Communication in China*, New York: Longman.

Hu, Jubing (1995) *Xin zhongguo dianying yishi xingtai shi* (*History of New China's Film Ideology*), Beijing: Zhongguo guangbo dianshi chuban she.

Hu Ping (2000) 'Gao Xingjian, a strange name', 13 October 2000: *http://news.163.com/viewpoint.html*, accessed 19 October 2000.

Huang, Shengmin and Ding Junjie (1998), *Media Management and Industry Research* (*meijie jingying yu chanyehua yanjiu*), Beijing: Qiye guanli chubanse.

— (1999) *Perspectives on Chinese Media Industries in the Context of Internationalisation* (*Guoji beijingxia de zhongguo meijie chanyehua toushi*), Beijing: Qiye guanli chubanse.

Huang, Yu (1994) 'Peaceful evolution: the case of television reform in Post-Mao China', in *Media Culture & Society*, 16, pp. 217–41.

Huang, Yu and Andrew Green (2000) 'From Mao to the millennium: 40 years of television in China (1958–98)', in David French and Michael Richards (eds) *Television in Contemporary Asia*, New Delhi: Sage.

Hukill, Mark, Ryoto Ono, and Chandrasekhar Vallath (eds) (2000) *Electronic Communication Convergence: Policy Challenges in Asia*, New Delhi: Sage.

Huot, Claire (2000) *China's New Cultural Scene – A Handbook of Changes*, Durham: Duke University Press.

IAMAsia (2000) 'China's most-visited web domain names and web properties for home Internet users, November 2000': *http://www.iamasia.com/presscentre/pressrel/pressrel_news.cfm?content_id=363*, accessed 20 December 2000.

IFPI (2000) *IFPI Music Piracy Report 2000*. IFPI, June 2000.

— (1999) *The Recording Industry in Numbers 1999*. London: IFPI.

— (2000) *The Recording Industry in Numbers 2000*. London: IFPI.

ISPWorld (2000) 'China Climbs On Broadband Bandwagon': http://www.isp-world.com/bs/BS_102500b.htm, accessed 27 January 2001.

Jayasuriya, Kanishka (2001) 'The rule of law and governance in East Asia', in Mark Beeson (ed.) *Reconfiguring East Asia: Regional Institutions and Organisations after the Crisis*, London: Curzon.

Ji, Bingxuan (2000) 'Proclaim the mainstream melody, produce more quality dramas, (changxiang zhuxuanlü,duochu jingpinju), speech to the 2000 Television Drama Topic Advisory Meeting, in *Chinese Television* (*Zhongguo dianshi*) 7, p. 3.

Jia, Honglin (1999) Dianying yingxiao [Guide to Film Market], Beijing: Zhongguo guangbo.

Jiangsu Cable Television (2000a) http://www.100hope.com/tvadv1.htm, accessed 2 June 2000.

Jiangsu Cable Television (2000b) http://www.100hope.com/weekend.htm, accessed 2 June 2000.

Jiangsu Cable Television (2000c) http://www.100hope.com/aboutus.htm, accessed 2 June 2000.

Jiangsu Cable Television (2000d) http://www.100hope.com/tvadv1.htm, accessed 2 June 2000.

Jin, Wulun (1999) *Informatisation and the Knowledge Economy*, Beijing: Chinese Academy of Social Science.

Jones, Andrew F. (1992) *Like a Knife – Ideology and Genre in Contemporary Chinese Popular Music*. Cornell East Asia Series. Cornell University.

— (1994) 'The Politics of Popular Music in Post-Tiananmen China', In *Popular Protest & Political Culture in Modern China* (eds) Elizabeth J. Perry and Jeffrey N. Wasserstrom, Second edn, Oxford: Westview Press, pp. 148–65.

Kalathil, Shanthi (2000) 'Cyber Censors: A Thousand Web Sites Almost Bloom', *The Asian Wall Street Journal*, 29 August 2000.

Karp, Johnathan (1994) 'Do It Our Way', *Far Eastern Economic Review*, 21 April: pp 68–70.

Keane, Michael (1999) 'Television and civilisation: the unity of opposites?', *International Journal of Cultural Studies*, vol. 2, no. 2, pp. 246–59.

_____(2001a) 'Broadcasting policy, creative compliance, and the myth of civil society in China', *Media, Culture & Society* (forthcoming).

— (2001b) 'The Chinese pie and the imported crust: an examination of new television diets in the People's Republic of China', *Hybridity*, 2/1 (in press).

— (2001c) 'Redefining Chinese Citizenship', *Economy & Society*, 30.1, pp. 1-17.

— (2001d) 'TV drama in China: Engineering Souls for the Market', in Tim Craig and Richard King (eds) *Global Goes Local: Popular Culture in Asia*, University of British Colombia Press, pp. 176–202.

Kelliher, Daniel (1992) *Peasant Power and China: The Era of Rural Reform, 1979–1989*, New Haven: Yale University Press.

Kinder, Marsha (1991) *Playing with Power in Movies, Television, and Video Games: From Muppet Babies to Teenage Mutant Turtles*, Los Angeles: University of California Press.

King, Susan Edward and Donald P. Cushman (eds) (1992) *Political Communication: Engineering Visions of Order in the Socialist World*, Albany, NY: SUNY Press.

Kloet, Jeroen de (1998) 'Living in Confusion, Remembering Clearly: Rock in China', in *Popular Music: Intercultural Interpretations*, ed. Toru Mitsui, Kanazawa: Kanazawa University, pp. 38–50.

— (2000) 'Let Him Fuckin' See the Green Smoke beneath My Groin – the Mythology of Chinese Rock', in *Postmodernism and China* (eds) Arif Dirlik and Xudong Zhang, Durham: Duke University Press.

Kraus, Richard (1995) 'China's artists between plan and market', in Deborah Davis et al., *Urban Spaces in Contemporary China: the Potential for Autonomy and Community in Post-Mao China*, Cambridge: Cambridge University Press.

Kuhn, Anthony (1999) 'China Phoenix Rises: 'Illegal' Murdoch Station Wins Viewers ... and Leaders, too', International Press Institute: http://www.freemedia.at/IPIReport4.99/ipirep4.99_china.htm, accessed 6 August 2000.

Kwok, Reginald and Alvin So (eds) (1995) *The Hong Kong–Guangdong Link: partnership in flux*, Hong Kong: Hong Kong University Press.

Ladany, Lazlo (1988) 'The Communist Party of China and Marxism: 1921–1985 A Self Portrait', Hoover Institution Press, Stanford, California

Laing, Dave (1993) 'Copyright and the International Music Industry', in *Music and Copyright*, ed. Simon Frith, Edinburgh: Edinburgh University Press, pp. 22–39.

— (1998) 'Knockin' on China's Door', in *Popular Music: Intercultural Interpretations*, ed. Toru Mitsui, Kanazawa: Kanazawa University, pp. 337–42.

Laitinen, Kauko (1990) *Chinese Nationalism in the Late Qing Dynasty: Zhang Binglin as an Anti-Manchu propagandist*, London: Curzon Press.

Lam, Willy Wo-Lap (2000) 'State power versus the Internet', in Roland Rich and Louise Williams, *Losing Control: Freedom of the Press in Asia*, Canberra: Asia Pacific Press.

Lash, Scott (1999) *Another Modernity: A different rationality,* Oxford: Blackwell.

Law, Kar (ed.) (2000), *Border Crossing in Hong Kong Cinema: The Twenty Fourth Hong Kong International Film Festival*, Hong Kong: Leisure and Cultural Services Department.

Lee, Chin-chuan (2000a) 'Chinese communication: prisms, trajectories, and modes of understanding' in C.C. Lee (ed.) *Power, Money and Media: Communication patterns and bureaucratic control in cultural China.* Evanston, Ill.: Northwestern University Press.

Lee, Leo O. and Andrew J. Nathan (1985) 'The beginnings of mass culture: journalism and fiction in the late Ch'ing and beyond', in David Johnson, Andrew J. Nathan and Evelyn S. Rawski (eds) *Popular Culture in Late Imperial China*, Los Angeles: University of California Press.

Lee, Tain-Dow (1997a) 'Transnational communication conglomerates and Chinese popular music', paper presented at the conference on Localism, Globalism and Cultural Modernity of East Asia, Chinese University of Hong Kong. April 1997.

— (1997b) 'The myths of Asia–Pacific media globalization', paper presented at the fifth International Symposium of Cinema, Television and Video, Communication Arts Research Institute, Taipei, Taiwan. May 1997.

— (1997) *Taiwan Cinema, Society and History*, Taipei: Asia-Pacific Publishing Co.

Lee, Terence and David Birch (2001) 'Internet Regulation in Singapore: A Policy/ing Discourse'. (Seen in manuscript.)

Leung, Grace and Joseph Chan (1997) 'The Hong Kong cinema and its overseas market: A historical review, 1950-1995', in *Fifty Years of Electric Shadows: The 21st Hong Kong International Film Festival*, Hong Kong: Urban Council.

Lewis, Steven W. (1996) 'Testing general theories of change in property rights: privatization experiments and economic development zones in China', unpublished dissertation manuscript, Washington University in St Louis.

— (1997) 'Marketization and government credibility in shanghai: federalist and local corporatist explanations' in David Weimer (ed) *The Political*

Economy of Property Rights, Cambridge: Cambridge University Press, pp. 259–87.

Li, Lianjiang, and Kevin J. O'Brien (1996) 'Villagers and popular resistance in contemporary China' *Modern China*, Vol. 22, pp. 28–61.

Li, Ding-Tzann (1998) 'A colonized empire: reflections on the expansion of Hong Kong films in Asian countries', in K.H. Chen (ed.) *Trajectories: Inter-Asia Cultural Studies*, London and New York: Routledge.

Li, Kangsheng (2000) 'Shenceng wenti zaiyu shichang' ('Buried problems in the market'), *Dianying yishu* [*Film Art*] 272 (2000.3), 10–11.

Li, Shi (2000) 'Dianying gongzuo ze libing moma: quanguo dianying gongzuo huiyi zongshu' (A Brief Summary of National Film Conference), *Wenyi bao*, 30 March 2000.

Lim, Hock Chuan (2001) 'IT revolution: demanding new vision and management strategies', paper presented at *10th JAMCO International Symposium*, 26 February 2001, Kuala Lumpur, Malaysia.

Lin, Lisheng (1993) 'Jiushi niandai zhongguo dianying de jingji biangen he yishu fengye' (Economic Changes and Art Divisions in the 1990s Chinese Cinema), Issue 248, *Film Art*, May 1993, p. 37.

Liu, Jianzhong (2000), Director of Film Department, PRC. Press conference, November 2000, http:// www.filmsea.com/focus/xlp/sf00101.htm

Liu, Kang (1998) 'Is there an alternative to (capitalism) globalization? The debate about modernity in China', in F. Jameson and M. Miyoshi (eds) *The Cultures of Globalization*, Durham and London: Duke University Press.

Liu, Huizhong (2000) 'Adventures of chinese children's film in the hi-tech market', *Journal of Audio-visual Techniques*, Vol. 4.

Liu, Alan P.L. (1971) *Communications and National Integration in Communist China*. Los Angeles: University of California Press.

Litzinger, Ralph (2000) 'The privacy rage: discourse of intimacy and suffering in 1990s China', paper presented at the *Crossroad Cultural Studies Conference*, 21–5 June, Birmingham, England.

Lotman, Yuri M. (1990) *The Universe of the Mind: A Semiotic Theory of Culture*. Translated by Ann Shukman. Bloomington and Indianapolis: Indiana University Press.

Lu, Shaoyang (2000) 'Renzhen duidai dianying' (Be Serious About Film), *Wenyi Bao*, 17 February 2000.

Lull, James (1991) *China Turned on: Television, Reform and Resistance*, London: Routledge.

Luo, Min (2000) 'Under Cupid's altar' (*Zou xia shentan de qiupide*), Unpublished Master's thesis, Beijing Normal University Research Institute.

Lynch, Daniel C. (1999) *After the Propaganda State: Media, Politics and 'Thought Work' in Reformed China*, Stanford: Stanford University Press.

Ma, Eric (1999). *Culture, Politics and Television in Hong Kong*, London: Routledge.

— (2000) 'Rethinking media studies: the case of China', in James Curran and Myung-Jin Park (eds) *De-westernizing Media Studies*, London: Routledge.

— (2001) 'Mapping transborder imagination', in J. Chan and B. McIntyre (eds) *In Search of Boundaries: Communication, Nation-States and Cultural Identities*, Westport, Conn.: Greenwood.

— (2001) (forthcoming), 'Consuming satellite modernities', *Cultural Studies.*

Ma, Ning (1999) '2000 nian: xin zhuliu dianying zhenzheng de qidian' (2000-The Starting Point of New Mainstream Film), *Dangdai dianying*, Vol. 91, 15 July 1999.

— (2000) 'Xin zhuliu dianying: dui guocan dianying de yige jianyi' [A suggestion for National Films], *Dangdai dianying*, vol. 94, 15 January 2000.

Manion, Melanie (1993) *Retirement of Revolutionaries in China: Public Choices, Social Norms, Private Interests*, Princeton, New Jersey: Princeton University Press.

Mao, Yu (1999) '1998: Zouguo dianying de siji' [A General Review of Films of 1998], *Dangdai dianying*, Vol. 94, 15 January 1999.

— (2000) 'Dianying jie quanwei renshi dui dangqian dianying shichang de sikao' (Experts' Views on Chinese Film Market), *Zhongguo dianying bao*, 29 December 2000.

Mathews, Gordon (2000) *Global Culture/Individual Identity: Searching for home in the cultural supermarket*, London: Routledge.

McCraken, Grant (1988) *Culture and Consumption: New approaches to the symbolic character of consumer goods and activities*, Bloomington: Indiana University Press.

MFC Insight (2000) 'The China cable and broadcast market': http://www.mfcinsight.com/article/001116/oped4.html, November 16, accessed 19 January 2001.

Ming, Anxiang (1999), *The Information Superhighway and Mass Broadcasting (Xinxi gaosu gonglu yu dazhong chuanbo)*, Beijing: Huaxia Publishing.

Montinola, Gabriella, Yingyi Qian and Barry Weingast (1995) 'Federalism, Chinese Style: The Political Basis for Economic Success in China', *World Politics*, Vol. 48, pp. 50–81.

Moran, Albert (1998) *Copycat TV: Globalisation, Program Formats and Cultural Identity*, Luton, England: University of Luton Press.

Morley, David and Kevin Robins (1995) *Spaces of Identity*, London: Routledge.

Naughton, Barry (1992) 'Hierarchy and the bargaining economy: government and enterprise in the reform process', in Kenneth G. Lieberthal and David M. Lampton (eds) *Bureaucracy, Politics and Decision Making in Post-Mao China*, Berkeley, Calif: University of California Press, pp. 245–79.

Negus, Keith (1992) *Producing Pop – Culture and Conflict in the Popular Music Industry*. London: Edward Arnold.

— (1998) 'Cultural production and the corporation: musical genres and the strategic management of creativity in the US recording industry', *Media, Culture & Society*, 20 (1998): 359–79.

Ni, Zhen (1993b) *Guanyu jiaqiang dianying zhipianchan xiang shehui chouzi paishe gushi yingpian guanli de guiding (Regulations on Film Studios Seeking outside Investment on Feature Film Productions).*

— (1994) *Gaige yu zhongguo dianying*, Beijing: Zhongguo dianying chuban che.

Ni, Zhen – as author of SARFT and MFRT documents cited:

— (1994) *Guanyu zhongwai hezuo shezhi dianying de guangli guiding (Regulations on Co-operative Film Productions).*

— (1995) *Guanyu gaige gushi yingpian shezhi guanli gongzuo de guiding (Regulations on Reform in Feature Film Productions).*

— (1996a) *Dianying guangli tiaoli (Film Regulations).*

— (1996b) *Guanyu jinyibu jiaqiang gushi pian zhipian shengchan guangli de tongzhi* (*Announcement on Further Strengthening Feature Film Productions*).

— (1996c) *Guanyu guochan pian, hepai pian zhuchuang renyuan gouchen de guiding* (*Regulations on the Formation of Crew Members in Domestic and Co-operative Film Productions*).

— (1996d) *Guanyu sheli zhichi dianying jinping '9550' gongcheng zhuanxiang zijin youguan guiding de tongzi* (*Announcement on Establishing Funds for 9550 Project*)

O'Brien, Kevin and Lianjiang Li (2000) 'Accommodating democracy in a one-party state: introducing village elections in China' *China Quarterly*, No. 162, pp. 465–89.

Oi, Jean C. (1992) 'Fiscal reform and the economic foundations of local state corporatism in China', *World Politics*, 45: 99–126.

Ong, Aihua (1999) *Flexible Citizenship: The cultural logics of transnationality*, Durham: Duke University Press.

Ono, Ryoto, Mark Hukill and Chandrasekhar Vallath (2000) 'Convergence policy challenges in Asia', in Mark Hukill, Ryoto Ono, and Chandrasekhar Vallath, *Electronic Communication Convergence: Policy Challenges in Asia*, New Delhi: Sage.

Osterhammel, Jurgen (1989) *China Und Die Weltgesellschaft Vom 18. Jahrhundert Bis Im Unsere Zeit*, Munchen: Beck.

Pan, Zhongdang and Joseph Man Chan (2000). 'Building a market-based party organ: television and national integration in China', in David French and Michael Richards (eds.) *Television in Contemporary Asia*, New Delhi: Sage.

Pang, Laikwan (2001) *Vision and Nation: Building a New China in Cinema. The Chinese Left-wing Cinema Movement, 1932–37*, Lanham, Boulder, New York, Oxford: Rowman and Littlefield Publishers.

People's Daily (2000) 'China's satellite TV having wider coverage': http://www.peopledaily.co.jp/english/200011/09/print20001109_54778.html, accessed 19 January 2001.

Phoenix Television (2000) 'Phoenix ... still smokin'!': http://www.techbuddha.com/hearsay/phoenixsmokinhearsay.html, accessed 27 January 2001

Preston, P.W. (1997) *Political/Culture Identity*, London: Sage.

Pu, Renren (2000) 'Aoyu tupian, jiewang gaofei' (Olympic Images Flying Across the Net) *Chinese Journalist*, No. 10: 37.

Qin, Lian (2000) 'Wired China's television: challenge and opportunity', paper presented at Television: Past, Present and Futures, University of Queensland, 1–3 December 2000.

Ramo, Joshua Cooper (1998) 'China gets wired', *Time*, Vol. 151 No. 1.

Robertson, Roland (1995) 'Globalization: time–space homogeneity–heterogeneity', in M. Featherstone, S. Lash and R. Robertson (eds) *Global Modernities* London: Sage, pp. 25–44.

Rodan, Garry (1998a) 'Asia and the international press: the political significance of expanding markets', *Democratization*, 5 (Summer 1998): 125–54.

— (1998b) 'The Internet and political control in Singapore', *Political Science Weekly*, 113 (Spring 1998), pp. 63–89.

Rodrigue, Michael (2000) 'What is a format': http://www.tvformats.com/f01.htm, accessed 26 September 2000.

Rosen, Stanley (1995) 'Women and reform in China', in Gerard A. Postiglione and Lee Wing On (eds) *Social Change and Educational Development: Mainland China, Taiwan and Hong Kong*, Centre of Asian Studies: University of Hong Kong.

Rothman, Warren H. and Jonathan B. Barker (1999) 'Cable Connections', *The China Business Review*: http://www.rothmanbarker.com/Cable%20 Connections.htm, accessed 6 August 2000.

Rowe, David (1999) *Sport, Culture and the Media*, Buckingham: Open University Press.

— (2000) 'Global media events and the positioning of presence', *Media International Australia*, No. 97: 11–22.

Sanders, Robert (1992) ''The Role of Mass Communication Processes in Producing Upheavals in the Soviet Union, Eastern Europe and China' in Susan Edward King and Donald P. Cushman (eds) *Political Communication: Engineering Visions of Order in the Socialist World*, Albany, NY: SUNY Press, pp. 143–62.

Sargeson, Sally (2001) 'Building the family future: attitudes towards housing construction in four Zhejiang villages', proceedings of the conference on *Managing Housing and Social Change,* City University of Hong Kong, 16–18 April 2001.

Sassen, Saskia (1999) 'Servicing the global economy: reconfigured states and private agents', in K. Olds, P. Dickens, P. Kelly, L. Kong, and H. Yeung (eds) *Globalisation and the Asia-Pacific*, London and New York: Routledge.

Sauvé, Pierre and Robert M. Stern (2000) *GATS 2000: New Directions in Services Trade Liberalization*, Washington D.C.: The Brookings Institute Press.

Saywell, T. (1999) 'On The Edge', *Far Eastern Economic Review*, 25 February 1999, pp. 46–8.

Schein, Louisa (1997) 'Gender and internal orientalism', *Modern China*, Vol. 23, No. 1: pp. 69–98.

Schell, Orville (1995) *Mandate of Heaven: A New Generation of Entrepreneurs, Dissidents, Bohemians and Technocrats Lays Claim to China's Future*, New York: Simon & Schuster.

Schlesinger, Philip (2000) 'The nation and communicative space' in Howard Tumber (ed) *Media Power, Professionals and Policy*, London: Routledge, pp. 99–115.

Schoenfeld, Susan (1994) 'Cable Ready', *The China Business Review*, September–October 1994: 24–8.

Schurmann, Franz (1968) *Ideology and Organization in Communist China*, Los Angeles: University of California Press.

Shi, Jinghuan (1995) 'China's cultural tradition and women's participation in education', in Gerard A. Postiglione et al.

Shirk, Susan L. (1984) 'The decline of virtuocracy in China', in James L. Watson (ed.) *Class and Social Stratification in Post-revolutionary China*, Cambridge: Cambridge University Press.

Siebert, F.T., Peterson and W. Schramm (1956) *Four Theories of the Press*, Urbana: University of Illinois Press.

Sinclair, John (1996) 'Culture and trade: some theoretical and practical considerations', in Emile McAnany and Kenton Wilkinson (eds) *Mass Media and Free Trade: NAFTA and the Cultural Industries*, Austin: University of Texas.

— (2000) 'More than an old flame: national symbolism and the media in the torch ceremony of the Olympics', *Media International Australia*, No. 97, pp. 35–46.

SinoSat (2000) 'SinoSat–China and communication satellite systems': http://www.fas.org/spp/guide/china/comm/sinosat.htm, accessed 19 January 2001.

Smart, Josephine (1998) 'Transnationalism and modernity in the South China region: reflections on future research agendas in anthropology' in S. Cheung (ed) *On the South China Track*. Hong Kong: Hong Kong Institute of Asia-Pacific Studies.

Smith, Anthony (1990) 'Towards global culture?' *Global Culture: Nationalism, Globalisation and Modernity*, M. Featherstone (ed) London: Sage Publications.

So, Alvin Y. and W.K. Stephen Chiu (2000) 'Modern East Asia in world-systems analysis', in T.D. Hall (ed.) *A World-System Reader*, Lanham, Boulder, New York, Oxford: Rowman and Littlefield Publishers.

Solinger, Dorothy (1999) *Contesting Citizenship in Urban China: Peasant Migrants, the State and the Logic of the Market*. Berkeley: University of California Press.

Sparks, Colin (1997) 'Post-communist media in transition', in John Corner, Philip Schlesinger and Roger Silverstone (eds) (1997) *International Media Research: A Critical Survey* London: Routledge. pp. 96–122.

— (2000) 'Media theory after the fall of European communism: Why the old models from East and West won't do anymore', in Curran and Parks (eds) pp. 35–49.

Spence, Johnathan (1990) *The Search For Modern China*, New York, W.W Norton.

Sreberny, Annabelle (2000) 'The global and the local in international communications', in James Curran and Michael Gurevitch (eds). *Mass Media and Society*, London: Edward Arnold, pp. 93–119.

State Administrative Radio Film and Television (1993a) *Dianying hangye jizhi gaige fangan shishi xize* (*Details in Carrying Out the Reform in the Film Industry*).

Steen, Andreas (1996) *Der Lange Marsch Des Rock'n'Roll – Pop Und Rockmusik in Der Volksrepublik China*. Berliner China-Studien, No. 32. Hamburg: LIT Verlag.

— (2000) 'Sound, protest and business – Modern Sky Co. and the new ideology of Chinese rock.' *Berliner China Hefte* 19 (October), pp. 40–64.

Su, Shaozhi (1994) 'Chinese Communist ideology and media control', in Chin-Chuan Lee (ed) *China's Media, Media's China*, Boulder: Westview Press.

Su, Sijin (1994) 'Hybrid organizational forms in South China: 'One firm, two systems' in Thomas P. Lyons and Victor Nee (eds) *The Economic Transformation of South China: Reform and Development in the Post-Mao Era*, Ithaca, New York: Cornell University Press, pp. 199–214.

Sun, Wanning (1996) 'In search of new frameworks: issues in the study of Chinese media', *Media International Australia*, No. 79 (February), pp. 40–8.

— (1998) 'Love your country in your own way: Chinese nationalism, media and public culture', *Social Semiotics*, Volume 8, no. 1, pp. 297–308.

— (2000) 'Internet, memory and the Chinese diaspora – The case of the Nanjing massacre', *New Formations*, 40, 30–48.

— (2001) 'Media events or media stories? time, space and Chinese (trans)nationalism', *International Journal of Cultural Studies*, (in press).

Suzhou Cable Television News (2001): http://scnews.2500sz.com/about_szradio_tv.htm, accessed 21 February 2001.

Tang, Tsou (1986) *The Cultural Revolution and Post-Mao Reforms: A Historical Perspective*, The University of Chicago Press, Chicago, p. 263.

Tang, Xiaobing (1996) *Global Space and the Nationalist Discourse of Modernity: The Historical Thinking of Liang Qichao*, Stanford: Stanford University Press.

Tao, Dongfeng (1996) 'Reviewing and reflecting on the 1990s cultural debates' (jiushi niandai wenhua lunzheng de huigu yu fansi), in Zhang Qian (ed) *The Blue Book of Chinese Culture 1995–1996 (Zhongguo wenhua lanpi shu)*, Guangxi: Lijiang chubanshe.

Teng, Jinxian (1989) 'Shenhua gaige, hongguan tiaokong, jiaqiang guanli, wenchan gaozi' (Deepening Reform, Macro Regulating, Strengthening Management, and Steadily Producing High Qualities), *Dianying tongxun*, issue 116, February, pp. 1–5.

Tipson, Frederick S. (1999) 'China and the information revolution', in Elizabeth and Michel Oskenbery (eds) *China Joins the World, Progress and Prospects,* New York: Council of Foreign Relations.

Tomlinson, John (1999), *Globalization and Culture*, Cambridge: Polity Press.

Tse, David (2001) 'Singular characteristics of the China market', presentation at Advertising Culture in Asia seminar, Hong Kong University, 5–6 March 2001.

Unger, Jonathan (ed) (1996) *Chinese Nationalism* Armonk: M.E. Sharpe.

United Media (1999) 'United Media announces high ratings, wide acceptance and success of its highly acclaimed television drama 'Love Talks' and the creation of new website ChineseE.com/lovetalks': http://www.umhl.com/pr112999.html, accessed 2 June 2000.

Ure, John and Xiong-jian Liang (2000) 'Convergence and China's national information infrastructure, in Mark Hukill, Ryoto Ono, and Chandrasekhar Vallath (eds) *Electronic Communication Convergence: Policy Challenges in Asia*', New Delhi: Sage.

Van Manen, J. (1994) *Televisie Formats: En-iden nar Nederlands Recht*, Amsterdam: Otto Cranwinckle Uitgever.

Virant, Christiaan (1999) 'Mandapop' *That's Shanghai*, 12.

Walder, Andrew (1995) 'Local governments as industrial firms: an organizational analysis of China's transitional economy', *American Journal of Sociology*, Vol. 101, No. 2, pp. 263–301.

Wang, Bingwen (1999) 'Guanyu "Kuaile da benying" de qingkuang huibao' (A report on the TV programme 'The Citadel of Happiness'), *Hunan Television Correspondence*.

Wang, Christine, Christopher Heady, and Wing T. Woo (1996) *Fiscal Management and Economic Reform in the People's Republic of China*, Hong Kong: Oxford University Press.

Wang, Gengnian (1999) 'Bawo shiji, zhenfeng jingshen, zaichuang jiaji, yingjie xin shijiüjiu dangqian guochan dianying taishi da dangdai jize wen' (Be Ready to Make Greater Achievementüa dialogue with Contemporary China Cinema), Vol. 88, 15 January 1999.?

— (2000) 'Yinian haojing junxu ji, zuishi chenghuang julü shiüjiu dangqian zhongguo dianying fazhan taishi da *dangdai jize* wen' (About Chinese Film: Answering Reporter), *Dangdai dianying*, Vol. 94, 15 January 2000.

Wang, Hongyou (1996) 'A broad view on Shanghai's film market in 1995' ['*Jiuwu Shanghai dianying shichang mianmianguan*'] *Zhonguo dianying nianjian 1996* [*China Film Yearbook 1996*], pp. 212–14.

Wang, Jing (1996) *High Culture Fever: Politics, Aesthetics and Ideology in Deng's China,* Los Angeles: University of California Press.

Wang, Shaoguang (1995) 'The politics of private time', in Deborah Davis et al. *Urban Spaces in Contemporary China: The Potential for Autonomy and Community in Post-Mao China*, Cambridge: Cambridge University Press.

Waters, Malcolm (2001) *Globalization*, 2nd ed., New York: Routledge.

Wittrock Bjorn (2000) 'Modernity: one, none, or many?' *Daedalus*, 129, pp. 1–29.

Wu, Kuangwen (2000) 'Ju minzu pinpai zhi qi' [Raising the brand name of ethnicity], Dianying yishu [Film Art] 272 (2000.3), 20–21.

Wu, Xuanong (ed.) (1999) Shanghai dianying zhi [An account of Shanghai's cinema]. Shanghai: Shanghai shehui kexue yuan.

www. chinaonline.com (2000) 'William Ding, Founder and Co-CTO of Nctease. comInc.':http://www.chinaonline.com/refer/biographies/business/C00021371.asp, accessed 6 August 2000.

www.chinaonline.com (2000) 'Heads of online news services react to new regs': http://www.chinaonline.com/topstories/001109/1/C00110803.asp, accessed 30 December 2000.

www.sina.com (2000) 'About Sina.com': http://www.sina.com/corp/about/index. html, accessed 26 June 2000.

Xi, Mi (1994) 'Old ideas losing appeal for headstrong youth', China Daily, 7 April 1994.

Xie, Xizhang (1996) 'Dazhong kuaican yu yishi xingtai shenhua' (Fast food for the masses and the myth of ideology), in Zhang Qian (ed.) *Zhongguo wenhua lanpi shu 1995–1996. [The Blue Book of Chinese Culture 1995-1996]*, Guilin: Lijiang Publishing.

Xinhua Domestic News Service (1997) 'Spiritual Civilization Committee Formed' (translated in FBIS-CHI-97-101), 26 May 1997.

Xinhua Domestic News Service (2000) 'Ding Guangen, Li Tieying Speak at PRC Spiritual Civilization Meeting' (translated in FBIS-CHI-2000-1225), 25 December 2000.

Xinhua Foreign News Service (2001a) 'Premier Zhu Calls For Ethics in Line With Socialist Market Economy' (transcribed in FBIS-CHI-2001-0305), 5 March 2001.

Xinhua Foreign News Service (2001b) 'Text of Zhu Rongji's Report on Outline of 10th Five-Year Plan' (transcribed in FBIS-CHI-2001-0316), 16 March 2001.

Xinhua news agency (2000) 'Jiang on better use of Internet', 19, June.

Xu, Jiren (2000) 'Yong chuang xin siwei baodao aoyun'(Innovative Ways of Reporting Olympic Games', Chinese Journalist, No. 10, pp. 34–5.

Yan, Jun (1999) *Beijing Xinsheng (New Sound of Beijing)*. Hunan: Wenyi Publishing.

Yan, Liqun (2000) 'China', in Shelton Gunaratne (ed) *Handbook of the Media in Asia*, New Delhi: Sage, pp. 497–526.

Yang, Bin (2000) *Bamai jiabin (Feeling the pulse of the contestant)* Beijing: Zhongguo guoji guangbo chubanshe.

Yang, Jun (1999) *Dialogues With 12 Media Persons*, Beijing: Beijing University Press.

Yang, Mayfair Mei-hui (1994) *Gifts, Favors and Banquets: The Arts of Social Relationships in China*, Ithaca, NY: Cornell University Press.

Yang, Taoyuan (2000) 'Zuei hao de sheng ao xuan chuan zai ling jiang dan shang' (The best propaganda for Beijing 2008 lies on the medal podium), *Liangwang Magazine*, No. 40, pp. 4–6.

Ye, Zhe (2000) 'Cong 'jiaoyou' kan wenhua' (Looking at culture from a relationships perspective)', in *Southern Television Academic Journal* (*Nanfang dianshi xuekan*) 2, pp. 4–5.

Yin, Hong (1999) '1998 Zhongguo dianying beiwang' (A General Review of China Films in 1998), *Dangdai dianying*, Vol. 88, 15 January 1999.

— (2000) '1999 zhongguo dianying beiwang' (1999: the Diplomacy of Chinese Film), *Dangdai dianying*, Vol. 94, 15 January 2000.

Yu, F.T.C. (1964) *Mass Persuasion in Communist China*, London: Pall Mall Press Ltd.

Yu, Hang and Anthony Green (2000) 'From Mao to the Millennium: 40 Years of Television in China', in David French and Michael Richards (eds) *Television in Contemporary Asia*, New Delhi: Sage.

Yu, Huang (1998) 'The Dragon Awakes: Television after Mao', paper presented at IAMCR conference, Glasgow, Scotland, July 1998.

Yu, Xu (1995) 'Dilemma in Information Management: STAR TV and Beijing's Control of Satellite Broadcasting, *Issues and Studies*, Vol. 31, No. 5, pp. ?.

Yue, Audrey and Gay Hawkins (2000) 'Going South', *New Formations*, 40, 49–63.

Zha, Jianying (1995) *China Pop: How Soap Operas, Tabloids and Bestsellers are Transforming a Culture*, New York: The New Press.

Zhang Jian (1998) *A Glance on Hong Kong's Film Productions in the 1990s* [*Jiushi niandai gangchanpian gongye yipai*], Hong Kong: Guanzhu Xiangang dianying gongye fazhen yanjiuhui.

Zhang Wei (1997) *Politics and Freedom of the Press*, Australian Centre for Independent Journalism, University of Technology, Sydney.

Zhao, Bin (1997) 'Consumerism, Confucianism, Communism: making sense of China today', *New Left Review*, 1, 222, pp. 43–59.

Zhao, Bin and Graham Murdock (1996) 'Young Pioneers: children and the making of Chinese consumerism', *Cultural Studies*, Volume 10, Issue 2.

Zhao, Xinshu and Peilu Shen (1993) 'Some reasons why the Party propaganda failed this time', in Roger V. Des Forges, Ning Luo and Yen-Bo Wu (eds) *Chinese Democracy and the Crisis of 1989: Chinese and American Reflections*, Albany, NY: SUNY Press, pp. 313–32.

Zhao, Yuezhi (1998) *Media, Market, and Democracy in China*, Urbana, Ill.: University of Illinois Press.

_____ (2000) 'From commercialisation to conglomeration: the transformation of the Chinese press within the orbit of the Party state', *Journal of Communication*, Spring, 2000, pp. 3–25.

Zhong, Danian, Guo, Zhenzhi and Wang, Jiyan (1998) *Transnational Broadcasting and National Culture* (*Dianshi kuaguo yu minzu wenhua*), Beijing: Beijing Broadcasting Institute

Zhou, Xiaoliang (1999) *Competition in the New Millennium: Searching for System Structures of Knowledge Economy*, Guangzhou: Guangdong Tourism Publisher.

Zhu Yao-Wei (1996) *The Image of China in the Contemporary Western Critical Discourse*, Taipei: Camel.

Zhu, Zhu (2000) '30 Years of increased TV access', *China Daily*, July 4.

'Zipian ren he daoyan huyu: dapo dianying longduan tizi shizai bixing'(Producers and Directors' Call: be imperative to break down the monopoly system) 27 December 2000, Http://www.filmsea.com/news/0012/00121003.htm.

Zweig, David (1992) 'Urbanizing rural China: bureaucratic authority and local autonomy', in Kenneth G. Lieberthal and David M. Lampton (eds) *Bureaucracy, Politics and Decision-Making in Post-Mao China*, Berkeley, California: University of California Press, pp. 334–63.

INDEX

Lightning Source UK Ltd.
Milton Keynes UK
UKOW031515240313

208098UK00001B/19/A